PARTNERSHIPS
FOR
PROFIT

Structuring and Managing
Strategic Alliances

JORDAN D. LEWIS

THE FREE PRESS
New York London Toronto Sydney Tokyo Singapore

The Free Press
A Division of Simon & Schuster Inc.
1230 Avenue of the Americas
New York, N.Y. 10020

Printed in the United States of America

printing number

7 8 9 10

Library of Congress Cataloging-in-Publication Data

Lewis, Jordan D.
    Partnerships for profit : structuring and managing strategic alliances / Jordan D. Lewis.
        p.   cm.
    Includes bibliographical references.
    ISBN 0-02-919050-9
    1. Joint ventures—Case studies.   2. International business enterprises—Case studies.   Cooperation.   4. Strategic planning.
I. Title.   II. Title: strategic alliances.
HD62.47.L48   1990
658¢.004—dc20   89-25633
                                                            CIP

For
LYNN

Contents

TWO
KINDS OF ALLIANCES

THREE
IMPLEMENTATION

Preface

SUDDENLY, the business world is undergoing massive, fundamental change. At the same time as global competition is raising the standards for quality, innovation, productivity, and customer value—those golden keys to success—the scope of what a firm can do alone is shrinking.

As a manager, you probably already know that quality improvements require close cooperation with suppliers, and customer value comes from close ties to users. Now, think more broadly.

In a world bursting with new technology, how much more innovative can you be if you reach out to share others' developments? Why limit productivity advances to what your firm can do alone? Why not become even more efficient, for example, by adapting others' know-how or building a larger-scale plant with a partner? More generally, why not seek excellence by focusing on those things your firm does best and work with others in areas where they excel? Can you afford to lose such opportunities?

Clearly, there is little doubt regarding the answers. In all industries, in every nation, firms have gained real power through cooperation. Around the world, the number of such efforts has risen by orders of magnitude within the past decade. We have entered the age of strategic alliances.

The sudden prominence of alliances is a dramatic change from just a few years ago. They will be far more important in the years ahead. This phenomenon raises vital questions reaching well beyond most managers' experience:

- What is driving the change? Is it here to stay?
- How should alliances affect strategic thinking?

- How can a firm benefit from alliances without being hurt?
- Is there a way to cooperate safely with a competitor?
- When should different kinds of alliances (such as risk-sharing contracts or joint ventures) be used? How should they be designed and managed?
- How can a firm work with other business and national cultures?
- What management practices does a firm need to support alliances?

To answer these questions this book builds on the experiences of some of the most successful strategic alliances and alliance practitioners in the world. It describes alliances that make diapers, cars, office copiers, jet engines, software, pharmaceuticals, trucks, alcohol, computer chips, health tests, telephone switches, and optical fiber; and others that distribute magazines, carry passengers, perform research, share technology, bottle soft drinks, lobby governments, auction vehicles, and create ads.

The illustrations include alliances of Apple Computer, Asahi Glass, Baxter Travenol, Bloomingdale's, Boeing, British Aerospace, Cadbury Schweppes, Ciba-Geigy, Coca-Cola, Corning, Digital Equipment, Dow Chemical, L. M. Ericsson, Fiat, Ford Motor, Fuji Xerox, General Electric, Glaxo, Harris, Hercules, Hitachi, IBM, Intel, Johnson & Johnson, Kawasaki Heavy Industries, Komatsu, Martin Marietta, Matsushita, Mazda, McDonald's, McKesson, Mitsubishi Heavy Industries, National Semiconductor, New York Times, Nippon Steel, Northern Telecom, Ogilvy & Mather, N.V. Philips, Pilkington, Rockwell, Rolls-Royce, Samsung, Siemens, SNECMA, Sony, Sumitomo Bank, Texas Instruments, Thorn-EMI, Toyota, and Volkswagen, plus many other Asian, European, and U.S. firms.

Successful companies that shared their experiences for this book have had few guidelines for strategic alliances. Like other accomplished pioneers, their good fortune today comes from intuition, intelligence, some luck, an early start, and a solid ability to learn from experience. That they have not translated their mastery into formal guidelines is probably because, having learned by doing, they absorbed key lessons implicitly.

Beyond that, each firm's experience is limited to alliances that have met its particular needs. Further, separate units in the same firms use alliances in different forms, for different reasons, and manage them differently. The practice of strategic alliances is thus fragmented and uncodified.

Consider that for one kind of alliance—the joint venture—there are seven distinct starting and operating conditions, and three basic ownership and governance arrangements (see Chapter 9). Each combination has unique implications for design and management.

Companies with less background in alliances thus have to experiment on their own. Unfortunately, studies of alliances cite high failure rates.[1] Even some widely acclaimed alliances, such as General Motors' and Toyota's NUMMI joint venture in California, are not the successes that have been reported, when we look at them carefully (see Chapter 4). With the rapid global growth of strategic alliances, one ought to do better.

My own thinking about strategic alliances has taken shape over the past twenty years as I have been increasingly drawn to help plan, advise on, work in, teach about, and sometimes manage alliances around the world. These experiences began in the late 1960s. By the early 1980s it was clear that a new—possibly important—trend was building.

To better understand its breadth and thrust, I assigned "cooperation in business" to a research seminar I was teaching at the University of Pennsylvania's Wharton School. We uncovered a surprisingly large number of what are now called strategic alliances. Most significantly, their number was growing rapidly from year to year. At the same time, executives I knew and visited in major firms at home and abroad also saw cooperation as becoming more important.

Yet there were no guidelines for how two or more firms—with different objectives and cultures—could work together to strengthen each, while remaining independent. Those observations, plus the documented high failure rates, led to my decision to write this book.

The core of this book is built from about three dozen case studies I wrote on a selected set of alliances. These were picked from a broad literature survey done over five years to expand the original work at Wharton. Cases were chosen with one criterion: An alliance must have produced (for a product or service) or become (for a business) an important factor in its industry.

This led to a list of about eighty alliances, which was then narrowed to include experiences broadly representative of major business dimensions: high- and low-technology, global giants and local enterprises, manufacturing and services, consumer and industrial goods, domestic and international.

Most cases were developed from on-site interviews with several people, on both sides of an alliance, plus material from internal documents that were shared with me. In total, more than a hundred executives from some forty U.S., European, and Asian firms participated, with about five hundred interview hours in all. The cases turned out to be extensive. Many run to fifty pages. Completed cases were approved by the respective firms.

As you read through the chapters you will find that many firms were willing to share their good and bad experiences. Surely this is a sign of strength.

To fill out my research, the case studies were complemented by several hundred descriptions of strategic alliances culled from the business press.

To understand what it takes to build and support effective alliances, I also spent considerable time over about two years with a wide range of mid-level and senior executives inside Corning Incorporated, Ford Motor Company, and two other major firms, which I do not identify. Corning and Ford are widely regarded as exceptionally well-managed firms, and each has been an industry leader in the use of alliances. In fact one-half of Corning's corporate earnings come from joint ventures. The unnamed firms' experiences were generally poor, and the contrasts were useful.

In the process of writing individual cases one difference between success and failure became evident. Executives with successful experiences kept redirecting our interviews to how people on both sides of their alliances had built strong relationships. For them, strategic gain was the motivation for alliances, yet strategy was an intellectual construct that worked or didn't depending on relationships.

For me, the direct evidence of close relationships was also strong. In separate interviews people on both sides of successful alliances described in the same way the issues, the arguments they had had with each other, and how they were resolved. Different firms always have different views. Good relationships make it possible to see a partner's perspective, to be sure one's own concerns are heard, and to work things out.

This crucial feature was underscored during my interviews on less successful (by their own measure) alliances. It often seemed as though people on each side were not talking about the same experiences, and by their own account didn't know each other well.

One other observation was particularly significant to me. It was clear from my research that regardless of nationality, industry, or purpose, a successful alliance requires the same basic ingredients.

An Introduction
to Strategic Alliances

A strategic alliance is a relationship between firms in which they cooperate to produce more value than a market transaction. To create that value, firms must agree on what it is, need each other to achieve it, and share any significant risks as well as the benefits. Without a shared objective, meaningful cooperation is not feasible. Without mutual need the firms may have the same objective, but each can get there alone. If they don't share the risks and benefits, they cannot expect the commitments required for cooperation.

Strategic alliances provide access to far more resources than any single firm owns or could buy. This can greatly expand its ability to create new products, reduce costs, bring in new technologies, penetrate other markets, preempt competitors, reach the scale needed to survive in world markets, and generate more cash to invest in core skills.

The way Dow Chemical and Personal Care (not the real name) introduced a radically new kind of diaper is instructive. Personal Care, a large consumer products firm, asked Dow to develop a highly absorbent polymer that would make diapers thin and dry.

To create the product, Personal Care needed Dow's technical expertise and Dow needed Personal Care's marketing strength. The firms faced major risks, which they shared. It wasn't clear that buyers would change their practices. Diapers had always been promoted as "the thicker the better." Personal Care had to make major investments in new designs, materials, facilities, and advertising. To make the new polymer, Dow had to build an expensive, reliable plant in record time. The firms' shared risks and mutual dependence fostered a high level of cooperation, which led to an important new product for each.

Shared Objectives Set the Stage

It may seem unnecessary to tell prospective partners they must first agree on what they want to achieve. The point is vital, however, because every firm has its own objectives. Some are of such long standing that they have become tacitly understood and are rarely stated. Moreover, one party will often make the assumption that another's expectations are what it would like them to be.

Azusa Tomiura, a Nippon Steel executive, tells of a machinery manufacturer that proposed a joint research effort on a novel rolling mill it had conceived. Nippon realized the mill might produce a product it was considering. Yet the machinery firm would consider the research done when a practical mill was developed, while for Nippon Steel the R&D would be complete only when its new product was realized. With different objectives, there was no hope for a successful alliance.[1]

When we fail to surface our hopes and presumptions, we set the stage for later conflict. Further, without making compromises in our separate objectives, we can't join to reach a more powerful result.

Take the experience of Fiat and Ford. These firms have become highly successful alliance practitioners, but not without some early missteps. In the mid-1980s the two spent many months planning a European joint venture that would have given them 25 percent of the market—almost twice the share of their nearest competitor. At a time when European auto firms were facing major changes, the expected efficiencies would give the firms important added strengths. Yet until the end of their discussions, each assumed the other would eventually be willing to yield control. The deal came apart when the differences finally surfaced.

Mutual Need Builds Commitment

When a relationship builds on mutual need, it helps the partners win internal support and move beyond the thicket of day-to-day problem-solving, partially conflicting interests, and contrasting cultures. It also cools arguments that one firm must dominate to succeed or could have done as well alone.

In the early 1970s General Electric and France's SNECMA, which manufactures jet engines for the Mirage fighter, formed a joint venture to build a new class of commercial aircraft engines. GE had most of the technical skills but could not afford to develop and produce the engines by itself. GE also had poor access to the growing European commercial aircraft market. SNECMA had related technical know-how, good European market contacts, and financial depth, but no commercial experience. Together, both companies had the needed technical, marketing, and financial resources neither could assemble alone.

At first there was considerable resistance. People in each firm tried to undermine the venture. SNECMA employees questioned GE's experience—it was a relative newcomer to this market. Skeptics in GE feared creating a new competitor. Senior executives in both firms had to use their authority to overcome internal resistance.

As the venture progressed, both sides came to respect each other's contribution and recognize their mutual dependence. These growing bonds supported the close cooperation needed for joint development, manufacturing, and marketing. Today the firms' teamwork is based on widespread mutual respect and a deep belief that they will need each other for a long time to come. Their joint venture, CFM International, makes the best-selling commercial jet engine in the world.

An alliance lasts as long as mutual need exists. As soon as one partner's value erodes, the other has reason to take over or to leave.

This happened in a British communications equipment joint venture between Thorn-EMI, the large electronics and entertainment firm, and Sweden's L. M. Ericsson. Thorn provided market access, and Ericsson contributed the technology. Together they won major orders over foreign competition. After the British market was opened to outsiders, the value of Thorn's marketing declined, while the venture remained dependent on Ericsson's technology. Thus even though Thorn held a majority stake, effective control shifted to Ericsson, which eventually bought Thorn's share.[2]

Continued mutual need—buttressed by each firm's efforts to keep it this way—has been a hallmark of CFM International. The original CFMI product was largely a straightforward extension of GE and SNECMA abilities. However, major technological improvements have been crucial to staying competitive in the hotly contested aircraft engine market.

Thus while GE has been the leading industry innovator, SNECMA has developed strong technologies that are now going into CFM products. In some areas, SNECMA technology has become equal to or better than GE's. Moreover, GE and SNECMA continue to need each other to win customer acceptance in different markets around the world, and to share the risks of their large investments.

Risk-Sharing Completes the Bond

If one firm has nothing to lose while its partner is highly exposed, it has no compelling reason to go the extra mile for the sake of a shared objective. With more at risk, the partner will hold back or withdraw.

This pattern has been evident in many sectors, including the American auto industry. U.S. auto makers have, until recently, used annual supply contracts that emphasized lowest cost. This produced uncertainties about future commitments that kept suppliers from making longer-term investments. The incremental, risk-averse practice severely inhibited the development of new product and process technologies by suppliers, substantially weakening the whole industry.[3]

Risk-sharing creates a powerful incentive to cooperate for mutual gain in all kinds of settings. You may not think of franchising as a form of alliance, and often it is not, because many arrangements place much of the burden on franchisees.

But consider McDonald's—the most successful restaurant chain in the world. More than most other chains, McDonald's profits depend on its franchisees' success. As in other chains, McDonald's owner-operators must buy from common suppliers for uniformity. Unlike others, McDonald's rejects the usual practice of taking a markup on supplies. If individual restaurants make money, everyone does well. The practice stimulates McDonald's to work even harder for its franchisees.[4]

We often cooperate out of mutual need. But we sometimes take the risks separately or use our economic power to force them on others. This hurts both of us when it sacrifices mutual opportunities, or if we will need each other's strengths in the future. In a successful alliance shared risks, like mutual need, foster stronger commitments.

Alliances Depend on Relationships

The risks in an alliance include how effectively firms will work together. Like a marriage, this can't be predicted with certainty at the start. Successful cooperation hinges on mutual trust and understanding, which develop only with effort, over time. When one company is engaged in a new activity with an unfamiliar firm, the quality of the relationship may be the riskiest part of their alliance.

Consider what might be needed to distribute a partner's product with your own, or to service its equipment in your territory. These activities may involve little investment risk if you are using excess capacity to perform them. Yet it is often impossible to specify everything in an agreement—particularly for a new kind of outside activity. More likely, you have to deal flexibly with unexpected events. Then, your efforts to understand and adjust to each other's particular needs may be the determinants of success.

Mutual Reliability Means Mutual Vulnerability

The interdependence of an alliance exposes firms to their partners' problems. Each firm has to think more about how its conduct affects the other.

To support just-in-time deliveries, for example, suppliers have built dedicated facilities close to Ford's auto plants. When a paint firm's operation burned down, the plant it served had to stop for five days. Since then, the companies improved their fire protection procedures, and the message of mutual dependence was reinforced.

There Are Several Kinds of Alliances

Each form of alliance is distinct in terms of the amount of commitment it represents and the degree of control it grants each partner.

In one kind of alliance—informal cooperation—firms work together without a binding agreement. Mutual commitments here are modest; control is largely in the hands of each firm acting separately. Formal contracts are used when partners want to make explicit commitments. Since significant shared risks may be involved, contractual alliances offer some opportunity for shared control.

Equity alliances—minority investments, joint ventures, and consortia—provide for common ownership, so extend mutual commitments and shared control even more. Each firm's role depends on the specific kind of equity alliance.

Finally, strategic networks are composed of any or all of the five other kinds of alliances, and thus provide varying amounts of commitment and control. Like consortia, networks may involve many firms and so have vast potential for affecting entire industries.

ONE

A NEW STRATEGIC FRAMEWORK

1

Why Alliances
Have Become So Important

Blood ties aren't that important when it's a matter of survival.

—Japanese observer commenting on Isuzu and Fuji Heavy Industries, which
broke a taboo against cooperation between companies in different groups

WHEREVER we look, cooperation is accelerating. Consider the evidence: Between 1979 and 1985 the number of alliances among American, European Community, and Japanese firms grew thirtyfold. In Eastern Europe joint venture startups have been doubling annually. In India, even while the tragic memory of Bhopal was fresh, the government was actively promoting foreign corporate links and forging stronger ties to world science.[1]

Two basic forces are behind these striking developments: the rise of technology and the globalization of markets. This new thrust affects all firms, everywhere. The consequences are enormous.

Cooperation Is Growing—and Here to Stay

Technology is relentlessly changing our world. In the process it forges new links among us, makes us more alike, and demands more of our resources to keep moving ahead.

Expanding Technological Interdependence

Technology has become so important to our lives that, for several decades, R&D growth has outpaced economic growth in the major industrial

9

nations.[2] The more we invest in R&D, the more it makes sense to look around to see if someone else might be producing knowledge we can use. This practice has been increasing around the world.

Since at least the early 1970s, R&D cooperation between organizations—businesses, universities, and government labs—has been steadily rising for major nations. This trend is shown in the following graph, which displays the fraction of the world's science and engineering articles written by researchers from more than one organization.[3] Simply put, joint publications are the fruits of joint research. Clearly, technological cooperation is already a strong and growing force.

One remarkable feature of this trend is that, except for the Soviet Union, cooperation in R&D is growing faster than investment in R&D, as shown on the facing page. An expanding share of these nations' R&D efforts is thus going into joint programs. Given the tremendous importance of technology to competitive advantage and economic growth, this is a fundamental change in global business and economics.

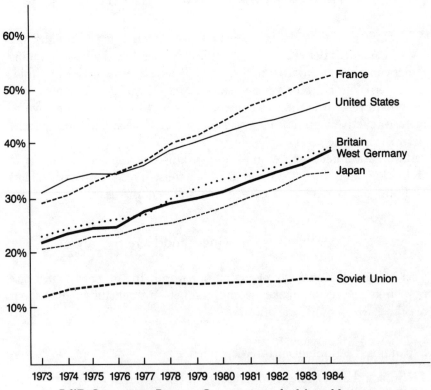

R&D Cooperation Between Organizations, for Major Nations

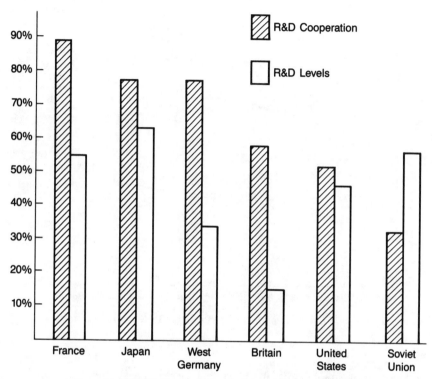

Growth of R&D Cooperation and R&D Levels, 1973–84

It is also significant that international cooperation is the fastest growing part of this thrust. This is illustrated on page 12.

The world has clearly been shifting to cooperation as a major vehicle for technical progress. Without cooperation—as the Soviets have apparently learned—technological advance becomes a less effective, almost brute-force process of spending more and more on R&D, in part to duplicate what others have already done.

World Markets Are Integrating

Growing technological interdependence is matched and reinforced by rapidly integrating markets. This raises the demand for cooperation even more.

Technology advances because new knowledge opens new paths for

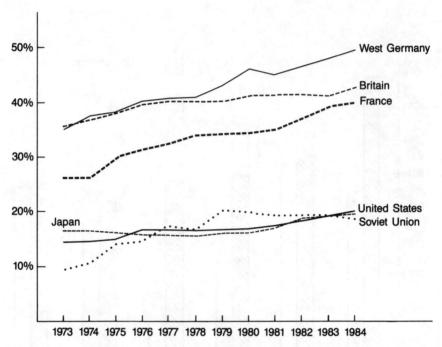

International R&D Cooperation as a Percentage of All R&D Cooperation, for Each Nation

development, and because users' needs evolve to create new requirements. These complementary forces have increased living standards around the world. And since human needs are similar, markets in different places are becoming more alike.[4]

Many consumer goods must be adapted for local tastes. It will probably always be this way. However, consumer needs and incomes are now close enough to justify a global scale in many facets of R&D, and a global or regional scale in manufacturing and distribution. For many industrial goods, which are less sensitive to cultural differences, R&D, manufacturing, marketing, and distribution are already global. Few firms can meet these challenges on their own.

The accelerating integration of world markets is evident in the way firms commercialize their technologies. Through the 1970s American firms' standard practice for introducing new products was to market them first at home and later abroad. In many consumer and industrial sectors the time lag has been reversed. Other markets have caught up or moved ahead.

Significantly, about 70 percent of U.S. manufacturing is now subject to foreign competition. And despite protectionist pressures, world trade has grown faster than national economies since the 1960s.[5]

Global market integration has been supported by giant strides in the technologies of computers, communications, and transportation.[6] The tremendous ease with which information, people, and goods move about has vastly expedited technology transfer. Newly industrialized countries have been quick to move up the learning curve. Korea, for example, has become a power in chemicals, metals, electronics, and other high-tech fields.

The world is clearly becoming a single market. In the process, the intensity of global competition is growing dramatically, raising the standards for competitive success.

Cooperation Is Changing the Business World

The powerful currents of technological interdependence and integrating global markets are catalyzing changes in national policies to promote cooperation.

Suddenly, Nations Are Changing Their Ways

In the brief decade of the 1980s:

- British economic blueprints were rewritten to give high priority to technology transfer and cooperative research.[7]
- China created its first-ever joint venture laws to bring in needed technology.
- The Soviet Union and East European nations launched sweeping policy changes to foster technological cooperation and economic integration with the rest of the world.
- The United States changed its antitrust laws to encourage shared R&D, and began more than two dozen university centers for joint research.
- Demands for more technological cooperation and a larger scale in the world market brought the European Community close to economic integration. Canada and the United States created their historic free trade agreement for the same reasons. Thailand, Vietnam, and other former adversaries in Southeast Asia launched similar moves.

The benefits of cooperation have caused nations to yield their economic independence in favor of global efforts to coordinate exchange rates, set trade and agricultural policies, adapt uniform practices for patents and trade secrets, and develop world telecommunications standards.

With their economies sadly trailing the rest of the world, less developed countries have launched an almost desperate effort to lure once-feared multinationals for jobs, investments, and technologies. While developing nations engaged in more than four hundred expropriations of foreign business assets in the 1970s, the number of such acts fell to around twenty during the 1980s.

Reflecting on the huge debts piled up by international development borrowing—with little progress to show—Francisco Swett, Ecuador's finance minister, notes "we feel it is better to have partners than creditors." [8]

The Need to Cooperate Is Joining Old Adversaries

In Japan, where everything is group-oriented, it is almost unthinkable for companies in different groups to cooperate. Yet Isuzu and Fuji Heavy Industries broke this taboo because they believed they had little choice. Both needed an American manufacturing presence to stay in business.

For similar reasons entrepreneurial software firms Microsoft and Ashton-Tate, long regarded as bastions of independence, joined forces to develop a major new product that would have been hard for either to create alone.

Every Firm Is Affected

The growing drive to cooperate is not limited to high technology or global firms. For instance, local companies without foreign opponents feel cost and quality pressures from corporate customers that compete in global markets. For them and for other firms the logic of cooperation is hard to miss.

Aetna Life and Casualty, for example, formed a joint venture with Voluntary Hospitals of America—itself an alliance of several hundred hospitals—to provide cost-limiting group health care plans neither could offer alone. As another example, hamburger chain Wendy's International and ice cream vendor Baskin-Robbins formed an alliance to explore the drawing power of their combined product lines. To do this separately, each would have had to assemble the needed expertise. [9]

2

Employing
Strategic Alliances

IBM is consciously trying to exploit new ideas and new technologies forever, wherever. The world of science and technology is a great deal larger than we can cover by ourselves. The whole race is being run faster now than it ever was.

—John Armstrong, IBM's vice president for science and technology

FOR the first ninety-eight years of its history Kubota, Japan's largest manufacturer of agricultural machinery, never made anything more sophisticated than a tractor. Then in 1988, from a gleaming new plant near Tokyo, Kubota shipped its first mini-supercomputer, one of the most advanced in the world.

The design, chips, and software were all American, resulting from alliances with Ardent Computer, MIPS Computer Systems, Synthesis Software, Exabyte, and Akashic Memories—some of the hottest startup companies in Silicon Valley. Kubota used its superb assembly know-how to combine these parts in a high-quality product.

And Kubota kept rolling. Six months after launching its first product, Kubota formed an alliance with Maxtor, another Silicon Valley firm, to make state-of-the-art high-capacity optical disk drives. Through all this, Kubota neither sought nor gained control of its partners. It kept a low profile, became an indispensable source of cash and manufacturing talent, and showed a willingness to share technological risks.[1]

This is not another tale of the Japanese exploiting American technology, because everyone gained. Kubota entered a new growth business, while its U.S. partners acquired capital and manufacturing know-how to move ahead in their markets. The point of the story is simply that

15

strategic alliances hold vast potential for reshaping firms and industries.

To appreciate fully the value of alliances it is helpful to compare them with other ways one can build strength in a firm. This understanding sets the stage for a discussion of the new strategic thinking required by alliances, and a description of how they should be included in planning.

When to Use Alliances

There are four ways a company can build strength: with internal activities, with acquisitions, through arm's-length transactions, and with strategic alliances. The best approach depends on the resources and risks involved, as well as the need for control.

Internal Activities

Obviously, a firm has full control over its internal work. This must focus on improving its core strengths—those hard-to-duplicate abilities that make it possible to produce and deliver unique value to customers. Less critical tasks can be shared with others.

In the magazine business, for instance, a publication's core strengths include its cover and contents. Publishers control these tightly. They almost always do the work inside, and shape their organizations to support needed information-gathering and creativity. Other work, such as printing and distribution, is typically done by outsiders.

Acquisitions

Acquisitions offer full control over purchased firms. But they are logical only when the value of the resources sought is a large part of the purchase. Usually, acquisitions perform well only if the buyer and acquired unit are closely related, with clear financial synergies between them.

Further, acquisitions of stronger firms perform best. However, such firms cost more and are harder to buy. At the same time, their greater strengths make these firms preferred candidates for alliances. Moreover, acquisitions often lead to executive departures. When the value of a purchased firm is in the people involved, this is a major disadvantage.[2]

Many acquisitions involve one firm's purchase of another's business unit. This tactic is not appropriate if the unit will remain substantially dependent on the original parent. Then, an alliance may be a better alternative.

Take, for example, Ford's relationship with Fiat in the U.K. truck business. When the firms first discussed a deal, they expected Fiat's IVECO truck group would purchase Ford's heavy truck unit in Britain. They concluded, however, that IVECO could not buy Ford's business without risking the loss of Ford's market image.

The IVECO name was not well known in the United Kingdom, where truck buying practices tend to be nationalistic. Also, withdrawing from heavy trucks would have cost Ford's truck dealers a large part of their revenues. This probably would have prompted their migration to Mercedes or other Ford rivals. These factors led to the firms' creation of IVECO Ford, a joint venture which combines their heavy truck strengths in Britain.

Full ownership is necessary when two firms must operate under one set of controls to meet their long-term goals. Even so, this doesn't assure the combination will work. Relatedness is still important.

As a key step to fuse computers and communications, for example, IBM made a minority investment in Rolm Corporation, and the firms pursued joint developments. But their work together was forcing Rolm to reshape its product plans substantially to meet IBM's needs. Because this compromised Rolm's ability to define its own strategic growth, IBM acquired Rolm.

However the computer firm was unfamiliar with key aspects of Rolm's business and failed to spot some critical problems. IBM also tried, without success, to mold Rolm to its style. After four frustrating years, IBM sold the unit to Siemens at a loss. IBM and Siemens then formed an alliance to build on their separate strengths.[3]

Arm's-Length Relations

Arm's-length transactions are the most common way firms get needed goods or services. Resources available this way depend on what suppliers are willing to provide. This is a function of their priorities and the risks they are willing to take on their own.

In arm's-length relations, the initial agreement governs all else that follows. With alliances, shared control offers far more flexibility.

Strategic Alliances

With strategic alliances firms can create any mix of resources that meets their separate and mutual objectives. By sharing risks with its partners, for example, Kubota gained far more resources than would have been feasible with arm's-length relations. Further, alliances make it possible to work with firms in any field. Unlike acquisitions, an alliance only has to mesh those parts of each firm's culture and functions that will work together.

Alliances thus provide unique opportunities to build strength with an exceptionally wide set of partners—including customers, suppliers, competitors, distributors, universities, and firms in other industries.

Although alliances involve shared control, they can provide more control than is possible through arm's-length transactions. In the magazine business, for instance, profits in recent years have been squeezed by competition from TV, catalog shopping, and rising paper costs. To combat this pressure, The New York Times Magazine Group (publisher of *Family Circle*, *Golf Digest*, and other titles) and Time Warner (*Time*, *Sports Illustrated*, and others) wanted to increase their sales and lower their costs.

One approach was to improve revenues from supermarkets, which are a major outlet for these publications. The publishers knew that magazine racks in the stores quickly emptied in busy checkout lanes while other racks stayed full. Yet neither publisher could justify increasing its field staff to replenish busy racks frequently. Some form of consolidation seemed necessary.

The firms chose an alliance over an arm's-length relationship with a distributor because the alliance gave them needed control. Although their activities would have been a large part of any distributor's business, they would not get enough influence on its policies and operations. One distributor, for example, did not have the labor quality needed for a high level of field service. Another could not offer priority treatment. A third would have been in competition with its own publications.

To summarize these concepts strategic alliances are compared with internal activities, acquisitions, and arm's-length transactions in the accompanying table.

Manage Key Relationships as Alliances

In marketing, best practice includes maintaining a relationship beyond the first sale. That is how you get the next sale. As an integral part of this, companies that excel at marketing treat key distributors, retailers, and final customers as partners. Each is seen as unique and valuable, with its own set of wants. Listening to their desires, finding ways to meet these and to keep satisying them for the long term, and accepting your share of the risks is what marketing is all about.

	Internal Activities	Acquisitions	Arm's-Length Transactions	Strategic Alliances
Scope	Core strengths	Closely related to core strengths	Cannot add competitive strength	Add competitive strength
		Need most of purchased firm	Limited by risks others willingly take alone	Most extensive access to outside resources
Control	Full	Full	Via initial terms	Ongoing mutual adjustments
Risks	Taken alone	Taken by buyer	Taken separately	Shared

Four Ways to Build Strength

Similarly, best practice in supplier relations includes taking a long-term view and cooperating with key vendors for mutual benefit. In Europe more than two-thirds of the most profitable firms work this way. By contrast, less than half the firms with average profits have such relations with their suppliers.

The same practice is vital around the world. A senior executive of a major American auto company compared an experience of his firm with that of a Japanese rival. Each had begun a critical effort to get its suppliers to cut costs. Yet the Americans gained only 4 percent of the reduction obtained by the Japanese.

The main reason, this executive says, was that the Japanese firm had long-term relations with its suppliers. They were willing to take more risks: The firms had helped each other in the past and knew they could count on each other again in the future.[4]

As another example of key relationships, consider business links to universities. One approach is for companies to participate in the research and share the risks. As soon as new knowledge is produced, these firms adapt it. Another tactic is to wait for results to appear in published reports. In this age of rapid technical change, the time delay can be a critical disadvantage.

Clearly, with important trade relationships and other key outside links, firms build a substantial advantage by recognizing mutual needs and sharing risks to satisfy their common objectives. By definition, these relationships are strategic alliances.

To be sure, alliances take more work than less intense relations, so it is helpful to know when such efforts are worthwhile. The criterion here is the potential value of the bond.

If close ties to others will lower a firm's risks, inhibit opponents' moves, or produce a significant competitive advantage—in terms of timing, costs, service, quality, new developments, stronger growth, better market understandings, a more responsive organization, and so on— then alliances are called for. By contrast, if close links with another firm would make little difference, then arm's-length relations are sufficient.

The Right Mix of Activities Depends on Each Market

The strengths a firm needs to win and keep customers vary from market to market. The best combination of internal activities, acquisitions, arm's-length transactions, and alliances must vary as well.

This is demonstrated by Pilkington, the world's largest glass maker. In markets where it has a strong presence, Pilkington serves local auto plants from its own facilities. In other markets Pilkington has teamed with Nippon Sheet Glass (in the United States, Mexico, South Korea, and Taiwan); and with Saint-Gobain (in France, Argentina, and Brazil). The glass maker complements these activities with selected acquisitions to add to its long-term strength. Significantly, Pilkington and Saint-Gobain are major competitors in markets where they don't cooperate.[5]

How Cooperation Affects Strategic Thinking

Strategic alliances offer more ways to build strength than any other outside activity. With these prospects available to every business, each firm's strategic thinking must adopt new concepts and leave some traditional ideas behind.

Reach a Larger Scale

With alliances, smaller firms can have the same scale as industry giants. Consider how Corning uses alliances to support world-scale R&D in optical fiber for telecommunications.

Corning is tiny in comparison with AT&T, its chief rival in this business. Yet Corning's revenue base, and thus its ability to support its critical fiber technology, vastly exceeds its direct sales to cabling firms and to others around the world. The additional revenues come from joint ventures with cable companies in major markets. These partners also provide cabling technology that adds value to Corning's product.

In some nations Corning's local partners ease access to government-controlled telecommunications groups. The combination of direct sales and alliances have helped Corning remain a leading player in the global market.

Take Advantage of Others' Technology

The pace of change in many technology-based markets is now so fast it can be more valuable to have the right technology when needed than to worry about where it comes from.

Conventional wisdom has long focused on a company's R&D as the source of its technological vitality. Secondarily, timely purchases from suppliers have also been an important way to keep up. These tactics remain critical. Today, however, useful new technologies can appear anywhere. Individual firms find it increasingly difficult to meet their technical needs alone. Waiting for a supplier's development puts you on the same footing as your competitors. Locating new technology ahead of others can make a powerful competitive difference.

Chaparral Steel of Midlothian, Texas, is illustrative. Casting a wide net for new technology has helped Chaparral become a leading low-cost producer in the industry. The firm regularly scans the world for new production know-how. When it finds opportunities, Chaparral works with others to develop new equipment. For instance, a computerized beam-rolling mill it designed with a West German firm needs only two operators, while similar mills require ten workers.

Even in a seemingly narrow field like computer chips, it has become impossible for the largest firms to do everything on their own. IBM, for example, spends more than $5 billion a year on R&D and makes most of its own chips. Yet it has turned to GE, Intel, Rockwell, Texas Instruments, and others for needed chip technologies it could not develop alone.[6]

Think in Terms of Combinations of Firms

One major consequence of alliances is that the benchmark of strategic power now includes sets of firms. It isn't enough to measure a company's strengths against individual opponents, or even to compare possible alliances with their abilities. Now, you have to consider how readily a position might be surpassed by others through alliances of their own.

Here is what can happen when firms build strength together. When IBM introduced its Micro Channel, the firm marketed this feature as a major innovation of its PS/2 computer line. IBM expected this new feature would help reassert its leadership in the personal computer industry. Yet soon after the PS/2 was introduced, several manufacturers of IBM-compatible PCs, with a combined market share larger than IBM's, formed an alliance and successfully developed an alternative to the Micro Channel to prevent IBM from dominating future designs.[7]

Another example of combined power comes from the commercial aircraft business. In 1989 a proposed Japanese–American alliance to develop a new Japanese fighter plane—the FSX—became front page news. Japan had targeted commercial aircraft as an attractive growth market, so the U.S. government tried to assure that technology flows in the deal were balanced: What the U.S. would gain would offset what would be shared. But a larger picture was missed.

Japanese firms often cooperate intensively to penetrate new markets. Time and again, this has been a key step toward a dominant position in the industry. The Japanese drive into commercial aircraft has followed the same path.

Mitsubishi Heavy Industries (MHI), Japan's lead FSX contractor, has substantial links to other firms developing advanced abilities for producing commercial aircraft. One such alliance, the Society of Japanese Aerospace Companies, is developing a high-speed commercial transport. Another alliance, Japan Aircraft Development Corporation (JADC), is working on a seventy-five-seat commercial plane and coordinates partner activities and sets priorities in that area. Besides MHI, these alliances include Kawasaki Heavy Industries (KHI), Fuji Heavy Industries (FHI), many other aerospace-related firms, and Japanese airlines.

Further, all three "heavies"—MHI, KHI, and FHI—cooperate and share experiences in other aspects of civilian aircraft development and manufacturing. In one such program the three have become major suppliers to Boeing and McDonnell Douglas. At Boeing, they insisted on being involved in all aspects of assembling a plane rather than just supplying parts. Their learning from this experience is enhanced through substantial information exchange with each other and by an arrangement that provides regular high-level meetings and intense discussions with Boeing. These contacts give the heavies a much better learning opportunity than would be possible as conventional subcontractors.

Another key MHI link outside Japan is to International Aero Engines (IAE), a jet engine venture led by Pratt & Whitney and Rolls-Royce. MHI and its Japanese partners are applying engineering understandings gained from their work with IAE to their own airframe development activities.

From the broader perspective of extensive cooperation and shared learning, treating the FSX issue as one of balanced technology flows within the deal is like predicting the result of a tug-of-war by examining what the front member of each team contributes. What really matters is how the members of each team pull together.[8]

Move Early to Win the Best Deals

Alliances involving exclusive commitments of critical abilities place these resources beyond the reach of others. This possibility gives a high priority to choosing a partner early and choosing well.

In the early 1970s SNECMA, the French jet engine maker, was seeking a partner to enter the commercial aircraft engine market, and held talks with every major firm in the business. General Electric, which also needed a partner to serve this market, had the best match of resources and a strong incentive to succeed. The engine they produced together was the first in its class to meet the new noise and pollution standards, and reached new levels of efficiency. Their improvements on the product since then have continued to leave other firms and alliances well behind.

Respond to Falling Market Entry Barriers

Strategic alliances simplify access to other markets. And by reducing entry barriers, alliances bring new competition to every sector.

In international business—from electric power equipment to light bulbs—the need to build a foreign position quickly and the availability of local expertise often make it unwise to begin with new wholly owned operations. Countless firms around the world have successfully entered foreign markets with local partners who provided critical knowledge of customer needs and government regulations, and often capital or technology.

Alliances are also breaking through entry barriers in domestic markets. An alliance between Merck and Johnson & Johnson, for example, combines Merck's preeminent research and development skills with Johnson & Johnson's outstanding consumer health care marketing strengths, to sell medicines developed by Merck. The combination allows Merck to enter the rapidly growing self-treatment market and gives Johnson & Johnson a new product line.[9]

Work with Competitors

Intense global competition is blurring the distinction between friends and enemies. To continue building strength firms have to find resources wherever they can. This means viewing competitors in a new light. From now on, competition has to be balanced with cooperation where that is in your mutual interest.

Although alliances with competitors may seem to make little sense, their value as partners can be high. Firms in the same business have the same kinds of products, purchases, marketing interests, operations, and technologies. These similarities create more opportunities for cooperation than are possible between firms in different sectors.

The strongest reason to work with a competitor is to face a common opponent:

- Major newspapers in Miami, Pittsburgh, San Francisco, and other cities compete for readers and advertisers and share facilities to lower their costs in the face of revenue losses to TV and other publications.
- Glass container makers compete with each other and sponsor joint research to improve their products in relation to cans.
- Apple Computer and Digital Equipment compete head-to-head in the office equipment market. Simultaneously, they have developed common standards to contend with IBM.
- Ford dealers in metropolitan areas sell against each other and support joint advertising to compete with other makes.
- Major pharmaceutical firms—including Hoffman-La Roche, Glaxo, Squibb, SmithKline Beecham, and Johnson & Johnson—use each other's sales forces to build market share for their products ahead of others' competing products.

Joining a rival is also sensible when companies face tough business conditions or the combined power of other alliances. For example:

- Much of the exploration and development in the North Sea oil field and other challenging locations is performed by alliances of major producers such as Exxon and Shell, who compete head-to-head in marketing.
- Coca-Cola and Cadbury Schweppes joined forces in the hotly contested U.K. soft drinks market. The savings achieved by consolidating their distribution functions, along with their newfound size, helped the firms build Europe's largest soft drinks factory and contributed to a massive marketing effort for their whole portfolio of brands.

Two years after the venture began, both firms had substantially increased their market share.

· Ford and Volkswagen merged their units in Brazil and Argentina to deal more effectively with high inflation and other economic problems.

· Hitachi and Texas Instruments cooperate in memory chip R&D because the risks of being late with the next generation exceed the risks of competing with each other, given a timely product introduction.

Rising competition leads to more duplicate efforts and more disputes regarding who has the rights to what. But litigation can be an all-or-nothing game. Deciding to share can lower both firms' risks and avoid the costs and delays of litigation. Genentech and Genetics Institute, for example, agreed to cross-license their rival versions of a drug for hemophilia. Rather than take the risk that litigation would shut one of them out of the market after both had made substantial investments, the firms decided to "compete in the marketplace instead of the courtroom," says Gabriel Schmergel, Genetics Institute president.[10]

Focus on a Few Core Strengths

Growing interdependence is forcing basic long-term changes in world business. By strengthening firms and easing market entry at home and abroad, alliances increase the level of competition. This adds new pressures for more business focus.

Mounting evidence shows that firms that focus on a few core strengths outperform others.[11] One benefit of a sharp focus is that with just a few core strengths it is easier to maintain needed investment scale in these areas. Another is that focused firms pressed by rapid change have a better chance of staying near their most important frontiers.

As the Ford Motor Company and others have learned, captive supply units not subject to their own market pressures tend to develop cost, quality, and technology gaps between their abilities and their parents' needs.

Flexibility is another benefit. New products can be introduced faster if a firm isn't bound by the capacity requirements for, and need to sequence, many different operations. Conventional wisdom holds that vertical integration eases coordination along the production chain. Yet the extra hierarchy needed impairs flexibility and innovation.

In sectors as different as U.S. auto-making, British candies, and Italian textiles, vertical depth has inhibited quick responses to competitive changes and has imposed barriers to product and process innovation.

A sharp focus sends a signal to the organization about its priorities and reduces the chance of "not-invented-here." You have to rally around the few things you can do best. Own just those resources that permit you to create distinct value. Have only enough control over the rest to meet your needs.

A business can be focused by reducing its breadth and vertical depth. This, combined with alliances for complementary resources, has succeeded in a wide variety of firms and industries. With alliances you can have the coordination benefits of vertical integration without the drawbacks.

Swedish-based communications equipment firm L. M. Ericsson, for example, sells its state-of-the-art switching technology in almost seventy countries. To win on the global stage from its small home base, Ericsson focuses its own development on its basic systems technology, where it is a leading player. Ericsson complements this core technology through alliances for components and software with U.S. firms Digital Equipment, IBM, Honeywell, and Texas Instruments; Siemens of West Germany; Seiko of Japan; Plessey and Thorn-EMI of Britain; and Matra and CGCT of France.

In the U.S. farm equipment sector, firms that survived the 1980s depression in their industry were saved partly by their willingness to abandon the popular strategy of making every model of tractor, combine, planter, and plow. Instead, they specialized in areas where they had innovative products or cost advantages, filling out their lines with products made by competitors.

Another example comes from department stores, which have been under increased competition from more focused outlets in shopping malls. The stores' wide variety of merchandise has inhibited many from displaying and selling their wares as creatively and knowledgeably as their more specialized competitors. To combat this many department stores have been cooperating with apparel firms, which design their own departments, train store employees, and even post their own people behind counters.[12]

To be sure, vertical integration has merit when key suppliers are owned or controlled by rivals. Then, favoritism toward suppliers' parents may be damaging. Yet even here, alliances can be a viable alternative to secure needed supply strength. U.S. computer firms, for instance, responded to their Japanese competitors' growing penetration of the memory chip businesses by forming Sematech and other alliances to bolster American supply capabilities.

Another argument against focus is that relying more on others makes a firm vulnerable to their dependability and quality problems. Of course, relying on one supplier may be risky—at least on an arm's-length basis. However, as every manager knows, wholly owned facilities also fail to meet schedules, and internal quality is a goal, not a certainty. Further, other competent firms have just as much incentive to perform well; as their own focus grows, the motivation to become more reliable in their core business can only increase.

Focus Helps Win Partners

In this age of alliances, having a sharp focus is a must for attracting partners. Take the example of Compaq Computer.

Compaq became a billion-dollar firm by making reliable products totally compatible with those of IBM. As part of its focus, Compaq created special software—reportedly the best in the industry—to test compatibility. Firms that had not focused as much didn't have the skills. Thus when Intel wanted to be sure its new 80386 chip would run the same programs as its other microprocessors, it formed an alliance with Compaq to do the testing.

In the process Compaq gained intimate knowledge of the chip well before its competitors. This made the decision to build a new computer around the 80386 easy. The product quickly became Compaq's best seller. "It was the biggest opportunity we've ever seen," says Compaq CEO Rod Canion.[13]

Including Alliances in Your Plans

The best way to combine internal and external resources is to compare possible alternatives at the same time. Include combinations with others that would increase revenues, lower costs, spread risks, or release internal resources for more critical activities.

Here is the way Corning does this. First, by reviewing its experience the firm has concluded it is most successful when it focuses on inorganic materials and related process technologies as prime vehicles for entering a business and gaining competitive advantage. Given this focus, Corning's need for others depends on specific applications of its technology.

Next, through ongoing discussions with others, Corning is aware of how its own strengths are relevant to their needs. Corning tries to get to know the major players—including technology developers, other potential partners, and customers—in attractive markets. Contacts are typically made by sales or marketing managers who approach another firm along the lines of, "We have this technology, your skills would add value," or "We're looking at this market, what are your requirements?"

In optical recording, for example, Corning has been developing a glass substrate with an advantage over other materials. Corning people involved in the development have visited firms performing memory R&D to understand what was going on. Then Corning has to decide whether it can be in the business on its own with products based on the glass, or whether it can do better with a partner.

3

Cooperating for Competitive Advantage

[Cooperation satisfies the] insatiable consumer appetite for more variety than any one company can handle.

—Philip E. Benton, Jr., president of Ford's automotive group

IN the 1960s Florida citrus growers were searching for ways to sell liquid juice in national markets, to compete more directly with soft drinks. The growers had successfully introduced frozen concentrate a decade earlier but needed a more extensive refrigerated distribution system to serve the wider market. Then they recognized that dairy firms' retail and home delivery networks were tailor-made for the purpose. Distribution alliances followed, and we now drink what was once an improbable product: orange juice in milk cartons.[1]

A firm's competitive strength has several parts. Alliances can contribute to each of these. The price and performance that give products unique value are one kind of strength. Others are needed as well: access to markets (such as distribution systems for orange juice) and access to resources; operations to produce the value; technology to renew products and operations; the ability to generate new growth; an organization to bring this all together; and the financial strength needed to keep it all working. The seven nonfinancial strengths are pictured on page 30.

Ways to Add Product Value

Alliances can strengthen products or services in many ways. To find opportunities, begin by asking what combinations of resources—yours

29

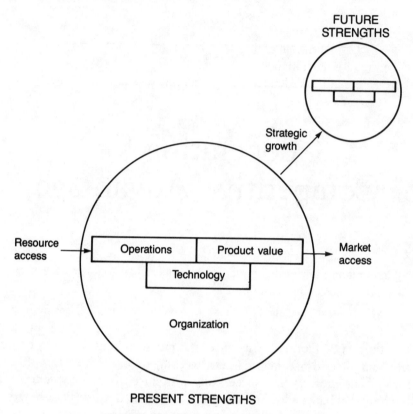

PRESENT STRENGTHS

Strengths Needed by Every Firm

and others'—might better serve customers' needs. This perspective puts you well ahead of competitors who still think in terms of what they can do alone.

Broadly speaking, the possibilities include winning with superior timing, creating new or improved performances, lowering costs and risks, providing more value-in-use for customers, building a stronger product line, offering increased compatibility with others' products, and creating an enhanced product image.

Spotting alliance opportunities is a matter of how you regard another firm. Companies that keep their distance from each other and expect only a routine transaction get just that.

Leif Soderberg, a McKinsey consultant, tells the story of two different firms that approached the same electrical components supplier. One firm saw its relationship as an arm's-length transaction, so provided detailed plans for a proprietary subassembly. The supplier responded with a bid of $75 and won with a tight 12 percent margin.

The second firm, a competitor of the first, began its relationship with an informal alliance. It described what the subassembly had to accomplish and asked the supplier to put its best people on the job. The supplier's engineers proposed changes that allowed it to use catalog parts. That cut costs to $25, giving the supplier a 40 percent margin.[2]

Winning with Superior Timing

Value quickly disappears in a fast-moving competitive environment. Then, the time needed to develop and market a product is critical. For example, in the mid-1980s Harris Corporation spotted a lucrative market for small satellite terminals. But Harris could not develop the components and distribution fast enough to take advantage of the window of opportunity it saw coming a year later. To move quickly, Harris took a license from Philips to make customer interface software, developed the terminals with Matsushita, and worked with AT&T to provide the new satellite service.

These alliances shortened Harris's normal development time by two years and saved substantial capital. Philips and Matsushita got product distribution rights in Western Europe and the Far East, thereby increasing their revenues and Harris's market reach.

Like Harris, early movers may capture an attractive position, win customer loyalty, build share, and reap the benefits of experience ahead of others, or gain leverage in defining industry standards. In fact, evidence from McKinsey suggests high-tech products that come to market six months late and on budget will earn one-third less profit over five years. By contrast, coming out on time and 50 percent over budget cuts profits just 4 percent.

Timing was also a factor in a memory chip development alliance between Hitachi and Texas Instruments. Cooperation gave the firms more options to choose from in the process of chip design, reducing the risk of delays from unforeseen obstacles along any one path. Even though the firms are competitors, the risks of being late with the next generation of chips exceeded the risks of competing with each other.

Alliances between customers and suppliers can also speed development and marketing. In addition to offering the potential for better designed and less expensive products, joint planning and early commitments compress the time both firms need to do their jobs.

Here is how this works with National Semiconductor and Xerox. National has given Xerox access to its proprietary know-how for designing and making integrated circuits. In turn, National sees Xerox's confidential sales projections and new product strategies. Xerox uses National's technology to make prototype custom chips—with features competitors cannot readily copy—for office systems under development.

National has a sole-source right to produce the chips in commercial volume. The arrangement reduces National's uncertainties about future demand, making it easier to commit capacity and schedule production for Xerox's needs. This, in turn, helps Xerox move ahead by lowering its uncertainties about an adequate supply of custom chips.[3]

Create New or Improved Performances

There are two ways to look at product development with a partner. One is to create novel performances by blending attributes from each firm.

This was how Baxter Travenol, the medical products company, solved hospitals' costly problem of having to mix unstable drugs with intravenous solutions just before use. Baxter combined what it knew about fluid stability and plastics formulation with the knowledge of drug makers Merck and SmithKline to produce stable premixed solutions.[4]

Ford has used the same tactic to improve the aerodynamic look in its cars. Over the past few years, the window area in cars has grown dramatically. This trend, plus the new aerodynamic style, required a novel approach to combining glass and body design to achieve a smooth, integrated appearance. In the past, auto makers specified windows to fit car designs. By contrast, the new look called for joining evolving window shaping possibilities with advanced body concepts at the early clay model stage of auto design.

Further, to assure final fit there must be a close long-term relationship between window supplier and car maker, beginning with design and continuing several years through engineering to final vehicle production. The firms must be confident in their mutual commitments and abilities over this period.

To build these tight links, Ford and Excel Industries, a leading window maker, created an alliance that enables their engineers to operate as a single team. Excel pays its own costs, but—assuming it meets price and quality guidelines—it has a long-term supply agreement and is assured 70 percent of Ford's business.

Joint Development for Lower Costs and Risks

A second way to consider joint product development is to share costs and risks. Depending on each firm's abilities, this may or may not lead to improved performances. But cooperation helps both firms offer products they might not chance alone. This tactic has become standard practice in the auto making, computer chip, and jet engine industries, where design and tooling costs for new products stretch even the largest budgets.

Provide More Value in Use

Other firms may be in a position to provide support for your products—during or after sales—to deliver more value to customers.

IBM, for example, has brought hundreds of computer service firms into its formal selling team. The firms teach users how to get more out of the products, thus widening their appeal.

Value-adding alliances with distributors have won customer loyalty for Lincoln Electric, the leading manufacturer of arc-welding products. When a customer asks for lower prices on Lincoln goods to meet competition, Lincoln and the distributor promise to match the price difference by finding cost savings in the customer's plant. All the customer must do is keep buying Lincoln products from the distributor. Lincoln and its partner survey the customer's facilities, recommend cost savings, and pay for any shortfall. Lincoln covers 70 percent of this.[5]

Offer a Stronger Product Line

A wider and deeper product line can reduce customers' need to shop among different suppliers, thus lowering their costs and increasing the supplier's revenues. A broad line may also appeal to a wider range of customers. And it may cut marketing, distribution, or service costs through better use of capacity in these functions, as well as from the economies of repeat business. Further, the larger a supplier's satisfied customer base, the greater its competitors' entry barriers, and the less it has to compete on price.

However, the costs of developing or producing a more complete product line can reduce these benefits. This creates opportunities for alliances—to broaden or fill gaps in a line through joint development with a partner, as discussed above, or by marketing a partner's product with your own.

Consider how Taylor Publishing of Dallas, Texas, expanded its line.

Taylor arranged to distribute titles published by Algonquin Books of Chapel Hill, North Carolina. The alliance expands the range of titles Taylor offers booksellers, extends Algonquin's market reach, and helps both firms reduce their distribution costs.

Bloomingdale's and other department stores have used a similar approach to broaden their appeal to shoppers. The stores offer beauty spas through alliances with Revlon and other cosmetics firms. Some say the treatments, ranging from facials and massages to pedicures, put customers in a mood to shop.[6]

The same strategy works in both directions when firms have complementary products and comparable marketing strengths. By linking their services, airlines such as United Airlines and British Airways, and telecommunications firms, provide end-to-end value for their customers and generate more business for themselves.

Working with outsiders can offer advantages over selling products from other units in your firm. When you go to an outside partner you are free to pick the best. Products from a sister unit may not perform as well and could drive customers away.

Compatibility Can Increase Product Appeal

In a number of markets products from different vendors have more value if they work together. In the office equipment business, for example, Digital Equipment and Unisys designed their office automation and computer products to be compatible with Northern Telecom's office telephone switches for this purpose.

Products that use the same standards have a larger potential market. Alternatively, using separate standards helps competitors differentiate their products from each other. In Europe, for instance, Digital Equipment won sales from IBM by adapting computer communications standards being promoted by major European manufacturers other than IBM.

The value of compatibility thus depends on whether a firm wants to appeal to a larger market and will compete on other grounds, or wants to differentiate more at the outset. In the latter case, the target market is smaller and potential sales are lower. Further, compatibility in a small market makes firms more vulnerable to each others' problems. Besides, having different standards requires acceptance by users. Their need for compatibility can work against this.

Philips and Sony were both hurt by such incompatibility in the early days of the VCR. Philips invented the product and made one kind. Sony developed another, and Matsushita a third. None could play the other's tapes. As Matsushita gained share on its rivals, their disadvantages was magnified by their incompatibility. Producers were reluctant to make tapes for a VCR that might not last. Consumers feared investing in equipment that couldn't play most tapes. The Philips and Sony products were eventually dropped.

Years later, when Philips was first to develop compact disc technology, it took a different tack. Philips shared the know-how with Sony in exchange for an agreement to accept its standard. Other major producers then fell into line. Competition stresses product features and price, and compatibility has spurred rapid market growth. Philips won a strong share of the world market, and the others pay Philips royalties for its technology.[7]

Clearly, it is costly to make products compatible if it means scrapping existing designs and related investments. So the best time to develop a standard is during the early design phase. However, different firms are not always in this position simultaneously. That means some firms have to make greater sacrifices than others.

Standards development is therefore easier when it applies mainly to future products based on large technological changes, for which most firms will have to make major new investments.

The merits of using a single or different standards in a market are summarized below. Note that rising global interdependence is a force in the direction of single standards.

Single Standard	Different Standards
Less differentiation	More differentiation
Larger potential market	Smaller potential market
	Possible customer resistance
Less vulnerable to one firm's problems	More vulnerable
May inhibit introduction of new technology	Fragmentation may inhibit market growth

Create Enhanced Product Images

Being in the market together gives two firms the benefits of each other's images. Cooperative advertising or sales promotion can make this explicit, while lowering each firm's cost of reaching an audience.

Saudia Airlines and Boeing have done just that, to their mutual advantage. In its advertising Saudia, a relatively small carrier, has prominently displayed its use of Boeing 747 jets. The combination helps

Saudia build an image of safe, reliable service and gives Boeing more exposure.

Ways cooperation can add product value are summarized below.

Objective	Cooperate To
Superior timing	Avoid development delays
	Create more options
	Share advanced plans
	Make earlier commitments
New performances	Combine capabilities
Lower costs and risks	Share development
More value-in-use for customers	Improve utilization
	Increase understandings
Stronger product line	Develop new products
	Market others' products
	Offer end-to-end service
Increased compatibility	Create interface standards
Enhanced product image	Joint advertising

Improved Market Access

Business competition has become a team sport. The case of Tagamet versus Zantac is a classic example. SmithKline's Tagamet was the first ulcer "wonder drug"; for several years it had the market to itself. Annual sales approached a billion dollars, generating half of SmithKline's profits. Then Britain's Glaxo created Zantac, which has similar properties.

To build Zantac sales, Glaxo teamed up with Switzerland's Hoffman-La Roche. The two assembled a marketing force of five thousand salespeople, which simply outgunned a competing squad of 1,500 SmithKline had built with Du Pont. Without much difference between the drugs, Tagamet sales fell precipitously, making SmithKline a sudden takeover target and prompting a merger with Beecham.

Another marketing alliance in the pharmaceutical business helped each partner get more out of its sales force by reallocating products to match marketing needs. In this partnership, formed by Merck and Du Pont, Merck transferred two low-volume products to Du Pont's much smaller sales group. That arrangement enabled Merck to free up more of its sales force to concentrate on other Merck products. For Du Pont's part, it got more drugs to sell that matched its capabilities.

Similar teamwork can overcome fragmented markets. Most national magazines, for example, do not have enough circulation in any one city to justify special pages or editions in each market. This inhibits their competing with other media for ads aimed at local needs—such as raincoats in Seattle or sunscreen in Phoenix.

To surmount this obstacle, *People, McCall's, Working Woman,* and *Working Mother* formed an alliance that sells advertisers a page in each publication in a given city. As an extra benefit, their combined coverage reaches a larger audience than the mass media. Further, since these magazines appeal mainly to women, the audience is more focused than those the other media can deliver.[8]

Better market coverage is just one way alliances can extend your reach. To find more possibilities, look at other firms in your market as potential members of a team. Then consider how closer ties can produce superior advertising, new distribution channels, improved channel control, and increased availability of critical resources.

Produce Better Advertising

One route to more effective advertising is increased spending. Alliances can help by raising revenues or lowering other costs so there is more to invest. Alternatively, alliances with ad agencies can align firms' interests more closely than is possible through traditional relations, producing more value for an investment.

This is what Colgate-Palmolive, the toiletries, soap, and health care firm, has done with considerable success. Colgate cannot budget as much for advertising as its larger competitors. To offset its disadvantage, Colgate consolidated its business with two agencies in place of the previous eight. It then changed its conventional agency–client relationships to alliances.

Previously, fear was often used as a motivator by making contracts vulnerable to short-term agency performance. The new arrangements focus on longer commitments, novel approaches in ads, more trust and respect between Colgate and its agencies, and streamlined approvals to avoid discouraging new ideas. The agencies run separate departments devoted to Colgate, and the people involved receive Colgate stock. One early commercial produced this way helped establish Colgate's tartar control toothpaste as the best-selling brand of its kind in the world.[9]

Open New Marketing Channels

With the right partner a firm can access segments that are hard to reach. Dairy firms' distribution of orange juice, noted earlier, is one example. Fiatallis and Hitachi provide another.

These firms created an alliance to strengthen their positions in the European construction equipment market. Before they began cooperating, Fiatallis had a strong presence in Italy but was weak in the rest of Europe. Hitachi had a solid dealer network in northern Europe but weak distribution in the south. By joining forces, the firms built a strong pan-European network. The combination, which also strengthened their product lines, has notably improved the firms' business across the continent.[10]

Gain Better Channel Control

The close links made possible by a distribution alliance offer more control over products flowing through its channels. Allied-Lyons and Suntory, for example, joined forces to improve Japanese distribution of Allied's Ballantine's scotch and other brands. Through the alliance Allied can position its brands better, and it receives part of the distribution profit as well. On its side, Suntory gained better access to North America and Europe, where Allied-Lyons has strong networks.

Herman Miller, the leading office furniture manufacturer, used a similar strategy to build exclusive relations with major dealers in key U.S. cities. In exchange for financing and marketing help, these important middlemen agreed to limit their goods to only, or almost only, Herman Miller products.[11]

These observations are summarized below.

Objective	Cooperate To
Better coverage	Join sales resources
	Combine products
More efficiency	Reallocate marketing tasks
Improved advertising	Enhance commitment, creativity
Gain new channels	Share others' channels
More channel control	Increase exclusivity

Improve Supply Links

Strong ties to suppliers can ensure access to needed resources. Of course, a long-term arm's-length contract might do this with commodities. But when your future needs will require continued developments for improved performance, cost, quality, or timing, only an alliance will ensure the strongest commitment from both firms. Given that purchases constitute about half of the average firm's sales, supply alliances present a major opportunity to build competitive advantage.

Britain's Pilkington Group uses alliances to secure strong supply relations in Japan. Pilkington provides glass for two-thirds of all Japanese-made sunglasses. To ensure solid ties to firms that cut, edge, harden, and polish the glass, Pilkington gives them needed technical and other help. It has further won their allegiance by buying and exporting sizable quantities of finished lenses from them.[12]

The following summarizes these and related points.

Objective	Cooperate To
Supply security	Strengthen supply links
	Increase exclusivity
Reduce supply costs	Gain purchasing power
	Ease ordering, delivery
	Share learning curve benefits
Shorten product cycle	Identify, reduce time drivers
Improve product quality	Reduce design, operating problems

Lower Input Costs

Through combined buying, two or more firms can gain supply or delivery scale economies to lower the costs of purchased goods. Joint purchasing may also benefit suppliers by reducing paperwork and order processing requirements and by lowering demand uncertainties. American Health-care Systems, a coalition of hospitals, uses this tactic with considerable success.

The following summarizes these points.

Objective	Cooperate To
Better market coverage	Combine sales resources
	Combine products
More marketing efficiency	Reallocate marketing tasks
Improved advertising	Enhance commitment, creativity
Open new channels	Share others' channels

Objective	Cooperate To
More channel control	Increase exclusivity
Improved supply	Strengthen supply links
Lower input costs	Gain purchasing leverage
	Ease ordering, delivery

Strengthening Operations

Boeing, pressed by capacity shortages in producing its new 747–400 jumbo jetliners, turned to rival Lockheed for a loan of six hundred workers from Lockheed's Marietta, Georgia, facility. For Boeing, which flew the workers to its Washington State plant, the move provided experienced technicians at a time when its employees were overworked, and production delays were causing problems with customers. For Lockheed, where military jobs were dwindling, the deal retained a skilled work force until new business could be developed.[13]

In addition to creating more capacity, cooperation can lower costs or risks, or improve quality, through new and improved processes or by using facilities more productively.

Create New and Improved Processes

Most likely, firms with activities similar to yours have found novel ways to make improvements. These ideas might be shared or traded for equally valuable know-how you have developed. Xerox has done this a number of times. Once, it adapted inventory control ideas from L. L. Bean, the outdoor clothing firm. Another time it swapped cost-saving plant design concepts with Kodak.

One more example: Owens-Illinois joined with West Germany's Heye Glass to blend Owens's high-productivity glass container technology with Heye's techniques for controlling forming temperatures and glass distribution. The combination greatly increased output and lowered the costs of lightweight bottles for soft drinks.[14]

When an early user of new equipment shares the risks of initial performance problems, it may also earn the right to shape the developer's thinking and adapt the latest advances before others. This can add significantly to a firm's advantage in rapidly changing fields.

A major East Coast business printer has used this strategy successfully. The firm produces high-quality full-color brochures and reports for its customers. It stays at the cutting edge in print quality by serving as a test bed for manufacturers of presses and supplies. Often, it is the first buyer or at least an early buyer of new products. Suppliers have come to rely on its expertise in understanding new applications. These dependencies have virtually institutionalized the printer's leadership advantage with customers.

Use Facilities More Productively

Cooperation makes it possible to achieve better efficiencies. Chip maker Intel, for example, gets more out of its manufacturing investment by shifting the production of mature items to partners. It then devotes the same facility to a higher-value task, while avoiding a new investment. Intel monitors its partners' quality and packages and sells the products as its own.

Some functions become more efficient with larger volumes. Cooperation can help realize these economies. One approach is to reallocate work with a partner. MAN, the West German truck maker, does this by exchanging parts with other European truck firms. MAN concentrates on making large numbers of certain components. Its partners provide a captive market for a much higher volume than MAN could use itself. In return MAN gets needed components made by them. Because each firm can focus on what it does best, this kind of alliance also offers the potential for better quality.[15]

Sharing a full-scale facility with a partner is another way to reach efficient scale. Ford and Mazda have done this with an auto assembly plant in Flat Rock, Michigan.

Cooperate to Develop Operating Standards

Having compatible operations can provide the scale needed to introduce new practices. This was the idea behind an alliance of forty-five firms, among them Westinghouse, Sears, Black & Decker, and Chemical Bank. In their alliance, the firms designed standard procedures to replace checks and invoices in trade transactions with faster and lower-cost electronic settlements.[16] The points below outline this discussion.

Objective	*Cooperate To*
Increased capacity	Share underused resources
New processes	Apply others' know-how
	Share development risks

Objective	*Cooperate To*
Improved efficiency	Shift production to others
	Share full-scale facility
New practices	Develop common standards

How to Add Technological Strength

There are two ways alliances can help put others' know-how to work. One is to apply a partner's technology directly to create new or improved products or strengthen operations, as noted earlier. The second approach improves a firm's own technical abilities.

Add Technology to Your Skill Base

Technology transfers from outside expand the variety of internal skills a firm can use, opening new avenues for its own developments. Others' technologies might be obtained by licensing or cross-licensing, or by adapting know-how to which a firm has legitimate access. R&D results from a joint venture, for example, often may be used by the parents. Sharing a technology can also be easier than inventing one's own way around someone else's patents.

The potential for technology exchange is much broader than conventional cross-licensing, which is normally used as a gap filler. In fact, trading large blocks of technology with a partner can open broad new vistas.

This was how AGA and Nippon Sanso, the Swedish and Japanese industrial gas companies, added skills in gas production and paper processing, respectively. AGA exchanged its pulp-bleaching techniques for Nippon Sanso's skills in producing and using highly purified gases. In a similar fashion, Nissan Motors traded its robot applications know-how for aerospace expertise from Martin-Marietta.[17]

Increase R&D Creativity

The benefits of technical cooperation go beyond joining different skills. R&D thrives on creativity. Yet people in R&D, like those in other fields, tend to develop their own assumptions about how to do things. Working with peers from another firm opens new perspectives.

The experience of Philips, the Dutch electronics giant, is instructive. When Philips first contemplated joint R&D projects, its managers thought cultural differences would inhibit cooperation. Yet after fifty joint projects, Philips learned just the opposite was true. "Contrary to expectations, the quality of decisions has shot up," says Robert Hamersma, manager of Philips' integrated circuits business. "Different companies and different cultures help in getting the right arguments on the table."[18]

Build Needed Scale

Developing important technologies may take a level of effort beyond one firm's abilities. With subcritical budgets, R&D productivity suffers, key avenues aren't pursued, and long-term needs may be compromised. Cooperation can make a critical difference.

In Europe, Imperial Chemical Industries and Du Pont each had 10 percent of the automotive paint business, which is highly dependent on research. To increase their R&D and compete more effectively with PPG Industries, which had about 20 percent market share, the firms combined their paint units in a joint venture.

Broad R&D cooperation across an industry can improve the industry's position relative to that of its competitors. This is the objective of International Partners in Glass Research. The alliance develops stronger and lighter bottles for European and Japanese members, whose products compete with plastic containers.[19]

Similarly, cooperation can make it possible to support long-term developments. When Corning invented coherent optical fiber in the 1960s, market opportunities seemed far off, and a business based on the fiber called for technologies Corning didn't have, such as cabling, light sources and detectors, and associated electronics. So in the early 1970s Corning formed development alliances around the world. Those efforts kept the opportunity alive and created the systems introduced when the market opened up years later. Corning capitalized on its early lead and remains a leading player in the market.

Ease Major Technology Transitions

It can be hard to develop an innovation if the activity cuts against a firm's traditions. Although changing the organization is justified when a development opens a major new business direction, this is not always warranted. Alliances offer another path.

General Motors, for example, transferred some automation developments to outside ventures in which it had invested. The move placed these projects in more entrepreneurial environments and sped development.

Technical change can force the replacement of one technology by another. Making the shift can be difficult if you have to support a present technology while mastering the new development. Again, alliances can help. When a manufacturer of metal turbine blades became convinced its blades would be replaced by ceramics with better heat, strength, and weight properties, it shifted its R&D from making cost improvements in the metal casting process to developing the next generation of materials. To ease the transition, it bought metal blades from a low-cost overseas partner.[20]

Use Market Pull to Encourage Others' Development

Technologies advance through a combination of market needs and R&D possibilities. This process is inhibited when the technical ability exists and user needs are vague. Then, an alliance of potential users can make a substantial difference. Low-pollution fuel cell technology for electric and gas utilities has kept advancing by this means despite continued uncertainties about long-term energy costs. To help clarify future demand, groups of prospective users have cooperated to define common performance specifications and to share the costs and results of demonstrations.

Different ways that alliances can add technological strength include these.

Objective	Cooperate To
Add to firm's know-how	Transfer technology
Increase R&D creativity	Explore new approaches
Perform needed R&D	Reach scale
Extend time horizons	Share costs, risks
Ease technology transitions	Shift developments
Encourage others' R&D	Create market pull

Enhancing Strategic Growth

Every firm has seen promising growth opportunities blocked by missing resources. Yet that doesn't have to happen. Strategic alliances can often provide the needed strengths.

Overcome Market Entry Barriers

Alliances can successfully penetrate markets when entry barriers are high, a condition that exists whenever a needed and hard-to-create strength—such as market understandings, local operations, or access channels—is missing. Cooperating for market entry is less costly than moving independently, and it eases departure if things don't work out.

Pave Your Growth Path

In this age of alliances it is vital to form early ties to others having skills that will be critical to your firm's future growth.

Dow Chemical identifies future needs in those core growth markets it might not be able to serve by itself. Dow then nurtures small alliances to expand its learning and to lay a foundation for future relationships with firms having technologies and other resources that may be important to its performance. Dow has done this in such fields as ceramics, advanced composites, and separation systems.

The same kind of strategy can build early ties to important future customers. For example, with more than 12 million small businesses in existence and about 1 million new starts each year, growing numbers of established firms are trying to earn future purchasing loyalties by giving a helping hand now.

Kimball Office Furniture has underwritten a series of seminars on business planning for members of the Institute of Business Designers, an organization of mostly small design firms. Similarly, insurance, tele-communications, and accounting firms run seminars for women starting businesses in the home, small businesses wanting to market abroad, and others.[21]

Join to Explore New Opportunities

Often the best course to follow in developing a new product or market is unclear, as is the extent of demand. That makes early investments risky. Yet waiting for more certainty may sacrifice a key position.

Wendy's International, the hamburger chain, and ice cream vendor Baskin-Robbins solved the riddle with an alliance to explore the drawing power of their combined product lines. All they had to do was add an ice cream counter in a few Wendy's outlets.[22]

These points are listed below.

Objective	*Cooperate To*
Overcome market entry barriers	Gain needed strengths
Pave growth path	Form early ties
Explore new opportunities	Perform joint experiments

Organizational Reinforcement

A firm's deeper strengths are in its people's shared values and collective knowledge. This is the foundation of the abilities to innovate and to improve performance continually. Alliances can add to an organization's strengths through shared learning and by helping it focus on core activities.

Learn from Others

Learning from another organization can be a powerful tool: It shows how things actually work. Ford's alliance with Mazda, for instance, has facilitated cultural changes at Ford. Driven by serious competitive problems in the early 1980s, Ford began reorienting its culture to focus more on people, customers, and quality. Ford's emerging culture recognizes, for example, that product quality can continue to improve only if procedures are in place to support it. The new culture focuses on building and reinforcing those processes needed to ensure the growth of relevant strengths in Ford's management, decision-making, and manufacturing.

Ford's close ties to Mazda have assisted these changes by creating an opportunity to learn in a mutually beneficial environment. In addition to conducting successful joint car programs and helping each other gain access to their respective home markets, the firms have shared a great deal of know-how. Part of this learning has been through the window on Japanese management that Mazda gives Ford. This has brought great value to Ford in such areas as organizational process improvement.

Ford's learning has come through the firms' ongoing informal contacts and from formal analyses. For instance, a study of Mazda's product development process showed Ford the effectiveness of multifunctional teamwork in product development. Aspects of the process were then adapted at Ford.

Focus with a Partial Spinoff

By sharing non-core activities with others, alliances can focus internal efforts on core product, technology, and other critical strengths. They can do the same for an organization by helping direct attention to essential values and practices.

One way to focus an organization is to sell units that don't meet performance targets or that require different management styles. However, forming an alliance with a spinoff can reduce such problems while providing continued access to its resources and benefits from its growth.

Dow Chemical has used alliances this way to concentrate on its core businesses. The firm's Dowell oilfield services subsidiary, for example, needed a management style that could adjust to the highly cyclical oil business. Dow found it hard to manage this unit in all but the boom phase of the cycle. Moreover, other firms, including Schlumberger, for which oilfield services is a core business, were more adept at managing such activities.

Using this reasoning, Dow moved the unit into a joint venture with Schlumberger. Dow realized the gain from selling 50 percent of Dowell and continues to participate in a growth business. In fact, Schlumberger's management input has carried the enterprise well past what Dow could have done alone. Schlumberger gained a unit that complements its basic business, plus a partner with a strong technical background to help it maintain a leadership position.

The concepts discussed here are summarized below.

Objective	Cooperate To
Learn from others	Make informal observations
	Study partner's practices
Focus organization	Perform non-core tasks
	Make partial spinoff

Building Financial Strength

We have seen how strategic alliances can improve a firm's competitive position by strengthening its products, market and resource access, operations, technical abilities, strategic growth, and organization. Directly or indirectly, these steps affect revenues, costs and risks, and the firm's capital structure—all of which are important for continued competitive strength. Alliances can also be used for financial benefit where that is the principal motivation.

Produce More Income

Dow Chemical looks for ways to get more out of its resources with applications that lie off of its core growth path. Using alliances to exploit such opportunities generates revenues without the full investments and management attention that would be needed if the firm proceeded alone.

In one case, Dow created a joint venture with Olson Farms to make egg cartons using Dow's polystyrene technology and Olson's understanding of egg packaging and marketing. Olson eventually bought out what remains a successful business and a major customer for Dow materials.

Reduce Administrative Costs

Chances are that many aspects of a firm's administrative activities are similar to those of other firms. Sharing these tasks reduces the costs for members of an alliance and helps one focus even more. Sony's U.S. headquarters in northern New Jersey and Peat Marwick, the accounting firm, have done this with a conference facility. Sony provides the audiovisual gear, and Peat Marwick contributes the space.

A similar strategy was used by seven insurers and nearly seventy businesses facing potential liabilities from the 1986 Du Pont Plaza Hotel fire in Puerto Rico. Rather than hire individual law firms to represent them, the organizations formed a coalition. They agreed to split their legal costs and to set aside arguments over who should pay how much in damages. The firms also save by sharing expert help and a central data base.

Reduce Investment Exposure

Alliances can also lower business risks by spreading investments over a wider base. Chemical maker Hercules, for instance, dominated the world polypropylene resin market, but needed to invest heavily to keep costs down. By forming a joint venture with Italy's Montedison, Hercules reduced its vulnerability in this low-margin business.[23] Ways that alliances can contribute to financial strength are summarized below.

Objective	Cooperate To
Produce more income	Add competitive strength
	Apply underused resources
Lower costs, risks	Share costs, risks
	Reduce investment exposure

Look for Wider Synergies

An opportunity to build strength with another firm may imply further mutual interests: Complementary resources often extend into areas that were not first considered. So as you contemplate forming an alliance, and invest the effort to build a relationship, think broadly.

In the rush to develop global transportation alliances by forming networks of airlines, some carriers saw these simply as coordinated linkups for end-to-end service. Others recognized more synergies that could lead to a stronger competitive position. For example, when SAS and Swissair connected their route structures, the firms also began coordinating their data telecommunications, hotels, catering, fleet planning, sales and marketing, aircraft maintenance, and staff training. Both firms recognized the wider potential to improve service and lower costs.[24]

4

Protecting
Each Firm's Interests

We complement each other well—our distribution capability and their manufacturing skill. I see no reason to invest upstream if we can find a secure source of product. This is a comfortable relationship for us.

—A senior American manager describing his
company's alliance with a Japanese partner

I will feel [bad] if after four years we do not know how to do what our partner knows how to do. We must digest their skills.

—An executive from this company's Japanese partner[1]

GENERAL Motors' widely heralded New United Motors Manufacturing (NUMMI) joint venture with Toyota is not what it has seemed to be. A close look suggests Toyota gained at GM's expense.

Toyota's objective in NUMMI was to learn how to work with American employees and suppliers. General Motors wanted to understand and adapt Toyota's skills for improved quality and lower costs. This may seem like a fair trade. But to benefit fully Toyota had to apply what it learned to one new U.S. plant. Transferring its NUMMI experience was a matter of hiring employees who met Toyota's criteria and adapting some human resource and supplier lessons from the venture. Toyota's management style was already aligned with its human resource–based production methods.

GM, by contrast, had to introduce its lessons into scores of existing plants. The numbers alone made GM's task much harder. An even greater barrier came from GM's culture. Effective worker involvement required basic changes reaching to the highest management levels. Moreover, GM faced deep-seated employee resistance bred from decades of mistrust. "You're not going to sprinkle some magic powder and fix eighty years' worth of problems," observed Johnny J. Johnson, chairman of the United Auto Workers local at a Georgia assembly plant.

Toyota gained its benefits quickly and proceeded to increase its U.S. capacity and market share. GM, on the other hand, needed many years to absorb the lessons it sought, and continued to lose market share. The balance in this alliance seems to have favored Toyota.[2]

NUMMI is broadcasting a powerful message. When two firms get together, they rarely make a perfect match. There is always some friction between objectives and some contrast in abilities. In planning an alliance, the only way to protect your interests is to form a clear picture of what it will do for each firm and to use this as a guide for partner choice and alliance design.

This analysis should be done whether or not a partner is a competitor. There is no way to know if an ally is out to disarm you. Alliances can lower market entry barriers, so any partner may become an opponent. With a good design, neither firm gains at the other's expense.

The Path to More Independence

A useful way to think about your firm is to see it as constantly building strength for more independence through a blend of internal and external activities. A firm's independence is a measure of its ability to control its destiny. Much of this comes from competitive strength, although some hinges on its financial depth and the outlook for its markets.

Mutual Dependence Can Advance Each Firm's Independence

There is no reason to cooperate unless you grow stronger from the experience. For both firms to gain, the mutual dependence created by a strategic alliance should increase each firm's independence. This may seem paradoxical: How can more dependence on another firm advance one's independence? The answer is that alliances can support the growth of separate competitive strengths and create new growth opportunities.

Consider the effect of Ford's new alliances with suppliers. Over the past few years the auto maker has greatly reduced the number of suppliers, shifted important developments to many of them, and changed from annual purchase contracts to agreements lasting the life of a part.

These steps made Ford more dependent on its remaining suppliers, while their increased share of its business raised suppliers' dependence on Ford. The moves also improved Ford's overall costs and quality, supported closer working relations and better mutual understandings, and helped the suppliers make needed long-term investments—which increase their competitive abilities. Moreover, Ford and its suppliers benefit from stronger sales. Each firm's greater dependence thus increased its independence.

Here is how France's SNECMA and General Electric gained from CFM International, their jet engine venture. CFM makes SNECMA less dependent on the French military market. The firm relies entirely on CFM for its commercial business, but with income from two different markets its independence has grown. The joint venture substantially lowered GE's investment risk for a major product. The alliance adds to the breadth and depth of GE's aircraft engine line, which is a critical strength in this business. Mutual dependence gives each firm a degree of independence neither could have realized alone.

Criteria for Independence

Independence is partly a function of a firm's ability to rely on others. GE's and SNECMA's mutual dependence, for example, has increased over the years and builds on deepening commitments. Neither firm would have relied on the other at the start as they do today.

However, even the most durable relationship cannot substitute for having a separate competence. This is essential for a firm to win customers and to bring continued value to its partners. For instance, GE and SNECMA each add considerable strength to their alliance; this is the basis of their mutual need. They use the same strengths individually for other products and markets.

Having the ability to create unique customer value is thus necessary for independence. Another requirement is to limit your dependence on others to what you can rely on. Within these guidelines you can safely make any compromises or commitments that will advance your interests.

Maintaining Core Strengths

Independence requires a set of core strengths: Hard-to-duplicate abilities that provide unique value for customers and sustain the firm. An alliance can help grow a core strength by transferring know-how or by providing resources for internal development. CFM revenues, for example, help support technical strengths in GE and SNECMA.

But alliances should not weaken a firm's core strengths or give others any control over them. Nor should an alliance reduce the difference between a firm's core strengths and those of a partner. This can happen even when core strengths are preserved, by sharing know-how that helps a partner move ahead. Another test for an alliance is whether it would divert resources from the strengths needed to serve other customers or markets.

In contemplating your core abilities, think broadly. Compromising a strength you have not considered (such as how long your organization takes to absorb new lessons) may do lasting damage. These points are summarized in the table below.

Just as a strong team needs a good offense and defense, renewing core strengths is as critical as protecting them. The question of when and how to use alliances should thus prompt another question: Where can we surpass our partner and our rivals in building new sources of competitive advantage?

A firm's core strengths depend on the nature of its business and how it competes. These strengths do not necessarily correspond to its largest investments.

Take airlines, for example. An airline's most costly asset is its fleet of aircraft. Yet there is little differentiation here; competing carriers use the same or similar planes. In fact, many airlines lease them. They also subcontract their maintenance and baggage handling, and reservations are managed by alliances with other carriers. The core of this business comes down to management know-how—including scheduling, labor relations, and service quality, plus brand image and access to gates at major airports.

How Core Strengths Can Be Compromised	
Action	*Examples*
Weakening	Reducing key operating efficiency
	Falling behind technology frontier
	Sacrificing future strategic position
Sharing control	Partner affects critical decisions
Reduced difference	Giving key know-how to others
	Granting market access to potential major competitor
Diverting resources	Weakened abilities in other markets
Narrow perspective	Overlooking organizational effects

To identify your core strengths, consider how each of the eight broad competitive strengths described in Chapter 3 (products, market and resource access, operations, technology, strategic growth, organization, finance) adds customer value. Any resource that makes a unique and significant difference is a core strength. For most firms this will include parts of some, but not all, of the eight broad strengths.

Protect Key Product Values

Part of what creates unique customer value may be in a firm's products, such as their image, performance, or price. To preserve independence, a relationship that seriously compromises this value must be avoided.

This is why firms experienced in licensing their products for sale by others are most demanding about licensees meeting rigid specifications. Inferior quality may compromise the licensor's reputation and can hurt sales. Other terms, such as royalties and fees, are less critical and may be negotiable.

In the automobile business, product image is a core strength for an established make of car. Ford almost jeopardized its popular Mustang name when it proposed using it for a car to be built by Mazda. Traditional Mustang buyers, who regard the Mustang as a uniquely American "muscle car," protested vigorously; the idea was dropped.[3]

If an alliance will serve your market, consider whether it might set unacceptable precedents. For aircraft engine makers, for instance, the combination of warranties, prices, and other sales terms is critical to a manufacturer's delivered value. Since the engines made by CFM International complement GE's commercial aircraft engine line, GE and SNECMA recognized the potential for conflict, so they established guidelines to avoid it.

Rolm's short-lived alliance with IBM illustrates what can happen if one partner makes significant product changes as part of a deal. When their alliance began, the firms expected Rolm to stay independent. Yet as they worked together, pressures grew for Rolm to change its product designs for the sake of a better fit with IBM equipment. That move cost Rolm its independence.

Secure Essential Access Strengths

Connections with important customers, distributors, or suppliers may be critical sources of revenues, advanced market knowledge, or new developments. Alliances should not compromise these links.

A group of European airlines, including Air France, Lufthansa, Iberia, and SAS, rejected American Airlines' proposal to share a version of its Sabre computer reservation system. Although the system would speed the airlines' ticketing and accounting, American was increasing its service to Europe at the time. The Europeans feared the arrangement would ease American's access to their customers.[4]

As with other strengths, the nature of a business determines whether market access is a core ability. A comparison of Corning's consumer products business with its technical materials business is illustrative. Corning's consumer goods are based on proprietary materials and designs, which are a core strength for Corning around the world. In Japan, these products are marketed by Iwaki Glass, a joint venture with Asahi Glass. Iwaki adapts Corning's wares to meet local tastes. Corning has no direct access to Japanese consumers or distribution channels. Iwaki's ties are sufficient for Corning's needs.

By contrast, direct access to Japanese display products firms is a core strength in the technical materials business. Corning must work closely with Sony, Toshiba, and others to adapt its precision glass for their applications. It must also do everything possible to be perceived by them as a Japanese firm. So Corning Japan has the lead responsibility here and works closely with these firms.

Hold On to Vital Operating Strengths

Listen to a senior American manager describe his company's alliance with a Japanese partner: "We complement each other well—our distribution capability and their manufacturing skill. I see no reason to invest upstream if we can find a secure source of product. This is a comfortable relationship for us."

Now, listen to an executive from this company's Japanese partner: "I will feel [bad] if after four years we do not know how to do what our partner knows how to do. We must digest their skills."

These statements, made to three business school researchers, Gary Hamel, Yves Doz, and C. K. Prahalad, reflect attitudes that have caused the death of the American consumer electronics industry, led to Japanese dominance of the machine tool business, and helped Koreans become the world's leading producers of microwave ovens. Such beliefs are rooted in an incomplete picture of what a firm needs to be an independent competitor: a set of strengths which, for that firm alone, can continue producing unique customer value.

Here is what has happened: Faced with tough foreign competition, many U.S. and European firms decided it was more profitable to assign their more complex and higher-value-added production tasks to Asian partners. In a typical arrangment, the Western company buys products from its partner and sells them under its own brand name, using its own distribution channels.

On the surface, these alliances make good business sense. Often they begin with the Asian partner as a low-cost product source. But as the supplier proves able to deliver good quality on time, the American or European marketing partner reduces its core manufacturing investment. Sometimes it keeps the routine assembly end of production to avoid import tariffs on finished goods. But this adds little value. By shifting core operations to others, the marketer's employees lose the opportunity to keep innovating and to learn how to improve existing products or operations.

Lacking participation in key value-adding activities, engineers and plant workers invariably lose ground, particularly in sectors where the state of the art is constantly advancing. As a company falls behind changing know-how, it gets harder and harder to catch up.

This loss of operating strength has been worsened time and again by the transfer of critical market knowledge. In a typical relationship, the marketer gives its manufacturing partner information about how to tailor products to local market preferences. Every product design delivered to the manufacturer adds to the latter's own market understandings.

As Gary Hamel and his colleagues observe, these alliances have worked like a trojan horse. The Asian partner gains manufacturing share without the simultaneous risk of building brand share. Using the marketing partner's distribution allows the supplier to focus its resources on creating clear product advantage through lower cost, good quality, and some new features.

When the marketers could neither add value to the products nor develop low-cost production abilities, the Asians set up their own distribution, offered lower prices in the same markets, and protected their positions by creating brand share. This is why RCA left the video casette recorder market while Matsushita, a former partner, built a thriving business with its Panasonic line.

One way to be secure in such alliances is to use them as short-term gap-fillers. To follow this path, limit what you source to others to a narrow range of lower-value products, and look for suppliers less likely to enter your market later on. Even if such firms are less attractive, the long-term risk of working with them can be far lower.

Companies producing significant value through operations have to build their own expertise in time to hold on. This can take substantial restructuring, cultural changes in management, and new work force relations. Unless one can hide behind protective barriers indefinitely, such changes are inevitable.

Eastman Kodak, for example, was once losing sales of its low-price microfilm equipment to Minolta and Canon. Also, Kodak feared those companies would use their low-end positions to penetrate the market further. Its first impulse was to buy a Japanese product and put the Kodak name on it.

However, the company chose instead to transform how it works. Kodak got rid of most of the red tape choking its new product development process and formed cross-functional teams of managers and assembly-line workers to design lower-cost, higher-quality, more producible products. While the process wasn't easy, the payoff was handsome. Kodak's new microfilm product met its performance objectives, needed only one-half the usual production time, and cost less than what Kodak would have paid an Asian supplier.

Another way to use this kind of supply alliance safely is to have enough hard-to-duplicate value-adding strength in design, manufacturing, or related services to keep a manufacturing partner from entering on its own. ICL, Britain's leading computer firm, has done so in an alliance with Japan's Fujitsu. The firm uses its European distribution network to market Fujitsu computers. ICL protects its market by adding value through applications design and services, which are hard for its partner to replace. Relatively small in the computer business, Fujitsu devotes its resources to battling IBM.[5]

When significant value comes from ongoing product or market research leading to unique proprietary products, and when low-cost production can be done by a labor-intensive partner, there is less risk of separate entry. That is why it has been relatively safe for clothing, sporting goods, and other firms to have their goods made in countries with low labor rates.

However, as these nations move up the learning curve and shift to more technology-intensive manufacturing, they gain opportunities to add value with improved production, higher quality, and more producible designs. The possibilities are especially good for complex products with ample room for design and production to be optimized together. Then, as the Japanese and Koreans have demonstrated, an upstream partner is positioned to compete.

Safeguard Critical Technology

Information is always shared when firms work together. Before agreeing to cooperate you have to disclose enough to judge each other's potential. Later, if you hold joint design reviews to be sure your separate developments fit, each firm will learn something about the other's skills. Further, observing a partner's mistakes may show you what not to try on your own. When the partner describes a novel approach to a problem without saying how it works, the fact of its difference gets you thinking about new concepts.

However, certain know-how is too vital to expose. Other information is shared only if doing so creates enough value. The reason for exercising such care is that patents often do not afford enough security. Having a patent is helpful only if others' use of the technology can be monitored. There may be no way to do that if examining a product won't show how key parts were made. Then, patenting may tell others what a firm would rather keep to itself. As a result, a great deal of sensitive know-how is kept secret rather than patented.

Even when many aspects of a technology are covered by enforceable patents, sharing unpatented information might help others invent their way around your claims. Whether to share a technology thus generally depends on its importance to a firm, rather than its patentability.

Guarding Core Know-How

Technology is a core strength if it provides a critical competitive advantage. At GE's aircraft engine group, this resides in the engineering skills, documents, and computer software used to design and produce the high-temperature sections of jet engines. SNECMA's core strengths include its high-pressure compressor technology.

Such know-how can be used for alliances as long as it is not disclosed. This may be done by sharing just the results of applying the technology.

CFM International builds on GE and SNECMA proprietary skills by having the relevant work done in each partner's facilities. When the firms develop a new product, they define an interface between their separate parts while keeping their core technologies to themselves. Each firm's know-how is safe, because it would be hard to reverse-engineer the completed engine modules they transfer to each other.

It isn't necessary for core technology to stay at home to be secure. Rockwell International managed to safeguard truck axle know-how it used in a European joint venture with Fiat's IVECO unit. When they planned the venture both firms knew this information could not be shared. So a Rockwell engineer was put in charge of the venture's engineering records. This way, the information could be physically located in the venture, and accessible only to Rockwell engineers.

Dow Chemical has taken on-site protection one step further. In some alliances where a jointly owned plant uses its proprietary information, Dow has a contract to operate the plant so its technology is never revealed to the partner.

Sharing Non-Core Technology

Sharing any technology where you have a lead could help an opponent catch up or move ahead. Thus whether and how to disclose it depends on the value received and on your partner.

When Dow makes technology transfer decisions, it never shares its highly differentiated "crown jewel" technologies—such as those for styrofoam and many thermoplastic products. Other technologies are shared depending on the expected risk and reward.

The larger the Dow Chemical business that uses a technology, and the more this know-how allows differentiation in the market, then the greater is Dow's risk from losing the technology, and so the more benefit Dow expects for its use in an alliance. Trust is also important. Dow must rely on its partners for safeguarding know-how shared with them.

In a chlor-alkali joint venture with Italy's Oronzio De Nora (ODN), Dow shares its technology only because the combination with ODN know-how creates high value in the marketplace, and the firms enjoy strong mutual trust. Dow also has a clear understanding of how ODN protects the information.

The same kind of thinking applies to joint R&D: The more commercial potential a firm's know-how has when used alone, the greater must be the value of combining it with a partner's to justify the risk of loss. In some cases this may limit one to product development, rather than technology development, alliances, because the former require less disclosure.

Any sharing should be confined to specific applications to avoid hurting your interests. For example, Dow and ODN both sell to the chlor-alkali industry, but their products are intended for different uses and rarely compete head-to-head. To help maintain technical differentiation in their current businesses, the firms restrict the use of each other's technologies beyond their joint venture to their internal needs.

The concepts discussed above are summarized this way.

Technology	When to Share
Core	Never disclosed
	May share application results
Important non-core	Combined value well exceeds
	separate worth
	Can trust partner to protect
	Limit scope of use to avoid harm

Obviously, technology transfer has more benefit for firms that can better use what they get. And if a partner's people speak your language but you don't speak theirs, they will learn more from meetings and visits. So consider not only what you are formally transferring, but also each firm's ability to use any information that is exposed.

Preventing Undesirable Disclosure

Under most conditions a healthy organization promotes open information flows. This must be different with proprietary know-how—both yours and what partners have entrusted to you.

To protect important information a firm has to build what some people call a "Chinese wall" around it. This entails assigning different people to separate projects, particularly when they involve competitors; granting access to sensitive information and places where it is kept on a right-to-know and need-to-know basis; restricting computer access; clearly marking confidential documents and locking them up when not in use; and destroying rather than discarding outdated materials.

Sensitive laboratories and plants should be closed to partners, and also to employees without a legitimate need to be there. People who don't have information cannot inadvertently share it.

Apple Computer, which shares secrets of advanced developments with partners, requires them to sign a pledge of secrecy. Apple's security staff enforces this pledge by making unannounced on-site visits to check for violations. Prototypes that are shared with others are marked differently in subtle ways, so a description in the press can be traced to the source of the leak. Apple partners who have compromised its secrecy have been denied access to important data and new opportunities.

A sound protection program includes periodic reminders to employees at all levels and in all functions about what is off limits to partners. Monitor what others request and receive; regular audits will make sure security is working properly. Controls may be simplified by limiting the gateways through which a partner may contact people and facilities. Fujitsu's partners all go through a single "collaboration section" to request information and assistance from different divisions. This helps the firm monitor and control access to critical skills and technologies.[6]

Such precautions do not hurt relationships. Cooperation can be close and constructive without giving others reason to believe they have free access to all of your business. It's like having a close friend without getting him involved in your family matters.

Limiting unwanted transfers ultimately depends on employee loyalty and self-discipline. In some places, people seem to be driven by vanity to share information that management regards as sensitive. This can be a particular problem for firms with substantial staff turnover, where employees' outside loyalties may be significant. Companies in this situation must work harder at building strong walls.

Preserve Growth Options

In planning an alliance, consider how it might limit your future actions. Part of this thinking should focus on protecting and reinforcing other core abilities to ensure their continued worth. Part comes from keeping critical growth paths clear by not helping a partner get in your way.

Agree to Limit Market Entry

One useful tactic, when the law permits, is to agree to limit undesired market entry by a partner, an alliance, or products of the alliance. If you can't agree, don't assume good will is enough to keep a partner from moving independently. A rational firm considers its interests first; it will break an alliance if a new opportunity merits the sacrifice.

General Electric and Rolls-Royce formed an alliance to produce a pair of each other's jet engines. Each firm also obtained access to the other's markets. The deal came apart when Rolls modified one of its engines to compete with the GE engine they shared. Past that point, further cooperation was impossible. Rolls would have had an advanced view of GE developments and would have been exposed to sensitive GE sales information. Some in GE thought Rolls was obliged not to compete, but Rolls had an unexpected sales opportunity that created a strong incentive to move on its own. Antitrust constraints had precluded a formal agreement on this.

Look for Opportunities to Build More Strength

Just because a firm is not a threat now does not mean it won't become a later problem. A firm in a closely related business that is able to build more strength than its partner—such as through internal developments or scale economies, by learning faster, or by cooperating more widely—may eventually gain the upper hand.

Look at what Korean steel firms did to their Japanese partners. The Japanese tried to stem the growth of their younger, lower-labor-cost South Korean rivals by reducing their substantial technology transfers to Korea. The Koreans undercut that tactic and went on to become a global power by finding other technology sources through a worldwide search. The time for the Japanese to impose constraints, or possibly take an equity stake to share in the growth, was years earlier, when they had a commanding lead.

Limit Time Horizons

While looking ahead, think about how technical, product, or market changes might shift your objective or alter the balance with a partner. If you anticipate such events and can't see well beyond them, or if they may work against you, limit an alliance to a finite time or event, or to the present technology generation.

For example, when Italy's SGS Microelettronica agreed to develop and globally market AT&T's bipolar circuits, the firms restricted their deal to five years. With technological advances reducing product life cycles, they knew a longer commitment might conflict with new developments.[7]

Of course, the same concepts apply in reverse. An alliance may have value only until a firm can grow needed strengths. With that possibility, it should be free to move ahead alone. There are two ways to do this. One is to avoid formal commitments that restrict future actions. The other is to gain the upper hand. This may not be a hostile act so much as it is the gradual evolution of an alliance as it becomes more dependent on one partner, which gains *de facto* control.

Maintain a Strong Organization

It can be easier to understand physical things like products than to grasp how a large collection of people with different skills, priorities, authorities, and relationships functions as a cohesive whole. Countless failed acquisitions and new strategic thrusts to which firms could not adjust point to real gaps in organizational perceptions.

Yet a strong organization is crucial to every firm's independence, and the close interfirm ties fostered by strategic alliances create more opportunities to affect its abilities than any other outside activity. Two related strengths are particularly important here: culture and the ability to learn.

Preserving Corporate Culture

A firm's most critical products, technologies, market understandings, operating abilities, and growth strategies are supported by and reflect its more deeply held values and priorities. One cannot change a firm's core strengths without changing its culture, and its culture cannot be changed without affecting its core strengths.

These connections are evident in the failed alliance between Rolm and IBM. When their alliance was formed, the merits of compromising Rolm's own product plans seemed sufficient for Kenneth Oshman, its chairman, to propose that IBM acquire Rolm. The acquisition did not work because the desired changes cut too deeply into Rolm's corporate culture. It wasn't possible to modify how Rolm worked without transforming the nature of the firm.[8]

Concerns about the same possibility get high priority at Ford and Mazda. Mazda is at the forefront of Japanese product development and production in quality and technology, on a par with its chief competitors Honda and Toyota. In many technology areas, such as four-wheel steering, Mazda is a world leader. Maintaining these strengths is critical to its competitive advantage and its value to Ford. Since the firms do a great deal of business together, and Ford is much larger, it potentially could dominate and weaken Mazda. Yet this has not been the case.

Beyond U.S.–Japanese differences, Mazda's culture is more technology-oriented while Ford's emphasizes finance. Engineers are royalty at Mazda; financial people have that status at Ford. To protect Mazda's interests, the partners created a high-level, full-time two-company team to monitor their cooperation and weigh how proposed projects might affect each firm. It has also reviewed their overall relationship to clarify understandings of cultural differences and suggest changes, especially at Ford, to improve cooperation and further safeguard Mazda's integrity.

To check if a planned change will affect your culture, ask how much adjustment would be required in internal practices. Cultural change is imposed by a significant shift in a core strength. This, in turn, leads to elemental changes in work flows, investment patterns, time horizons, and management systems. A useful but less direct signal comes when new practices are met by deep resistance—as they were at Rolm before the IBM acquisition.

Cultural change can, of course, lead to stronger performance. The danger is in adjustments that align one firm more closely with another, which may reduce its ability to serve independent needs.

When Partners Learn at Different Rates

In this age of technology, knowledge is king—not just technical knowledge about how to make things, but understandings of markets, best work force practices, basic trends, and so on. When change is rampant, as it is for more and more businesses, the ability to find and create knowledge and to translate it into new strengths is essential for lasting independence.

It is hard to miss the contrast between many Asian and Western partners in this regard. In case after case, a pronounced emphasis on learning has led to sizable Asian advantages. The pattern has been most evident in manufacturing, but it is appearing in the financial sector and other services as well.

In little more than a decade, Western firms' Korean and Japanese manufacturing partners changed from unthreatening suppliers to formidable competitors. Until recently this phenomenon was attributed to lower labor costs and higher capital investment rates. We know now that high education levels and rapid, organizationwide learning have been equally important. Further, the advantages of this talent for learning have been underscored by a striking absence of the same quality in many Western firms.

In what may be a classic example, described by Gary Hamel and his colleagues, a European firm viewed an alliance with a Japanese partner as a way to get a specific technology. The Japanese saw it as a doorway to their partner's full spectrum of skills. They met with a wide range of the European firm's marketing and product development staff, probing each contact for as much information as possible. For instance, whenever the Europeans wanted a new feature on a product supplied by its partner, the Japanese asked for detailed customer and competitor studies to support the request.

Over time, the Japanese drew a sophisticated picture of the European market to aid their own entry. The technology they got by formal agreement had a useful life of a few years. The competitive insights they gained informally will probably last far longer.

Asian–Western learning differences were summed up by a senior executive in a Japanese electronics firm. When asked about the perception that Japanese firms get more from foreign partners than vice versa, he told Gary Hamel and his associates, "Our Western partners approach us with the attitude of teachers. We are quite happy with this, because we have the attitude of students."

These Asian–Western differences are dangerous patterns, not absolutes. Many of IBM's partners, for example, have noted how fully its employees probe for wider understandings, while avoiding out-of-bounds information. Genex, the U.S. biotechnology firm, also makes an art of this. When it conducts sponsored research, Genex absorbs some of its partner's technical knowledge and market expertise. In addition, Genex sometimes gets to use a partner's manufacturing processes for the development of its own proprietary products.[9]

Imbalances due to learning differences aren't limited to East–West alliances. A large U.S. telecommunications firm faced a similar shortcoming when it invested in several product-market experiments with other companies. Even though some of the efforts exposed real opportunities, the firm was slow to absorb new experiences and so could not take advantage of them. Its partners went ahead on their own.

Protecting Your Interests

One way to balance learning in an alliance is to bar a partner's access to all people, information, and facilities beyond the scope of each agreement. Open communications on the inside is a strength; transparency to a partner is not.

Controlling a partner's access is only part of the answer, however. Companies that learn faster than others can move farther ahead even when information flows are balanced. Increasingly, learning is a core strength worthy of substantial attention. Firms that appreciate this set an objective of absorbing more know-how from each partner than the partner gains from them.

Sustain Financial Strengths

Because an independent firm must have core competitive strengths—in its products, market access, operations, or other areas—it must also have core financial strengths, the unique cash flow and capital structure needed to support and renew its competitive strengths. Holding too much cash is wasteful; too little hurts one's competitive position. Maintaining too much debt compromises new investments; too little debt may raise capital costs.

A firm's cash flow and capital structure can change if the financial performance of its alliances is substantially different from its performance alone. Corning's revenues from its optical fiber ventures, for example, have become critical to its sustained technological performance in this business.

For these reasons a growing use of alliances should be accompanied by an increasing understanding of their impact on a firm's financial strengths. Jamie Houghton, Corning's chairman, notes that although Corning sees more joint ventures in its future, it has not set a quantitative goal for them. But one constraint is that the firm's consolidated operations must continue to grow and remain important.

Plan for Unreliable Relationships

Protecting one's independence includes limiting possible damage from an undependable alliance. The first line of defense here is partner choice: Does a prospective partner have a track record of meeting its commitments? Another is anticipating its performance in a proposed alliance. This understanding comes partly from analyses and discussions before a commitment is made. An alliance that takes a firm in a new direction, or one with a partner having substantial priority conflicts, may not be dependable.

Such insights are necessary, but not sufficient—particularly if major investments are involved. Only the test of working together can build real confidence in a relationship.

Thus alliances should be constructed narrowly at first. Every project has some minimum size to be viable. The more you reach beyond this, the more there is at risk, and the more other opportunities are foreclosed. If the potential exceeds what you do at first, you can broaden the scope later. A narrow scope at the start also eases objective-setting and coordination, because it involves fewer tasks.

CFM International now produces about 20 percent of the revenues for GE's Aircraft Engine Group and more than half of SNECMA's business. This kind of mutual dependence can safely grow only over time. CFM began as a one-product venture with real questions about the depth of each partner's dedication and was surrounded by considerable market uncertainty. Larger commitments probably would have brought an early end when plans for an aircraft that was to use the product were dropped.

CFM built on its success step-by-step. People in each firm came to appreciate their mutual need and to accept their dependence at all levels. Today the firms know each other well; their bonds are far stronger than many interunit links in other corporations. Even so, they remain independent along key dimensions. Each firm makes its own investment decision when considering new developments for CFM, and each pursues other opportunities separately.

Whenever possible, back up exclusive commitments with expectations that your resources will be productively used. Dow Chemical often does this by setting minimum performance standards, such as targeting cumulative sales at a certain level in five years for its joint ventures. Otherwise Dow has an option to go nonexclusive and to seek other applications. This kind of performance expectation, rather than a minimum royalty, helps ensure the growth of the alliance.

Beware of letting an alliance subsidize other activities. RCA used earnings from sales of video cassette recorders made for it by partners to help cover its manufacturing losses on color TV sets. The arrangement slowed RCA's departure from these alliances, even as its partners undercut it in the VCR market.

Becoming dependent on a partner's resources can jeopardize a firm's position if the partner later changes course. To make a commitment more safely, agree at the outset to transfer the relevant abilities in the event a partner pulls out. Honeywell made this arrangement when it agreed to distribute L. M. Ericsson's office telephone switch in the United States. Honeywell was developing complementary products for the switch and was protected by a license to make the product if Ericsson stopped supplying it.[10]

To sustain a healthy alliance, partners' objectives, mutual needs, and risk shares must remain aligned. Should any of these weaken or evolve to favor one parent, either or both firms may be hurt. To avoid this possibility, especially for more important alliances, pay attention to how a partner's business evolves once an arrangement has begun.

The Pros and Cons of Exclusivity

Alliances may or may not involve exclusive arrangements. Clearly, one consideration reflects partner reliability. Another depends on opportunities gained and lost.

Obtaining exclusive rights to a partner's unique products, technologies, or other critical resources may give a firm an opportunity to use these for competitive advantage. In Dow's diaper alliance, for example (see Introduction), Personal Care was Dow's first customer for the new diaper material, which gave it a head start over other diaper firms. The opportunity also gave Dow a lead in the material market.

Firms often need some exclusivity to protect large investments related to a unique resource. When significant future investments will also be required, exclusivity may be continued. Distributors who invest to maintain skills related to a product bargain for an exclusive territory for this reason.

Yet there are drawbacks to such restrictions. From the resource supplier's viewpoint, exclusivity may limit revenues and deny it the volume and market experience needed to support continued development. That can hurt both firms. It is one reason Dow eventually supplied the material to other diaper makers. Further, exclusive relations are often reciprocal. The firm receiving a unique input may agree to limit its use of competing inputs, which may compromise its ability to use superior alternatives. In general, then, exclusivity is best when it helps partners invest to gain an advantage over others. Otherwise nonexclusive terms are preferable.

IBM and Texas Instruments, for example, agreed to cooperate to automate large factories. The alliance involves little new investment tied to their relationship, so it is nonexclusive. This allows the partners to jointly pursue opportunities where they offer the best combination of strengths, while giving them flexibility to seek other opportunities separately.[11]

Two-way exclusivity usually is possible only when that is in both firms' best interests. In the 1980s many commercial banks sought exclusive ties to corporate customers through "relationship banking"—offering broad product lines and building mutual rapport with customer executives. The practice withered because little in these arrangements had unique value. Companies could get the same or better deals by shopping around.

Minority investments and joint ventures may create an image of exclusivity that is not desired. In these alliances, partners have policy influence and may have access to customer data and opportunities for favored treatment. Such conditions can discourage a partner's competitiors from buying from the alliance, thereby denying it needed scale economies. If the alliance's product is unique, other customers may be willing to overlook rivalry. Otherwise the alliance needs to make an extra effort to assure prospective customers of fair treatment.

When Samsung Corning was created, it had three potential customers in Korea: Samsung, Goldstar, and Orion (later changed to Daewoo). The venture could reach desired unit costs only by selling its TV bulbs to all three firms. Corning thus spent time visiting Goldstar and Orion before the alliance was created, to learn how to win orders from them. Although Samsung Corning is managed by the Koreans, it has operated independent of Samsung in marketing. Its management constantly works on relationships with other customers and sometimes gives them better terms than Samsung receives.

Samsung probably knows the venture's unit costs, but this is not an issue because pricing is now competitive. If Samsung Corning cut its price to its parent it would have to do the same with other customers as well.

Too much dependence on one partner can limit a firm's ability to work with others. ICL's reliance on Fujitsu technology, for example, precluded alliances with other computer firms when severe competition was forcing consolidations in the industry. [12]

5

Cooperating
with a Competitor

We will continue to compete with Apple tooth and nail.

—Kenneth Olsen, chairman of Digital Equipment,
on his firm's alliance with Apple Computer[1]

IT is clearly easier to cooperate when firms' other interests are far apart. Dow Corning and Ciba Corning Diagnostics, for example, have greatly benefited from a total absence of conflict between their parents, who have been perfectly willing to share all they have relevant to these alliances.

Still, working with a competitor has tremendous potential. A firm's products, technologies, and marketing and operating resources are more similar to those of its competitors than to any other company's. Alliances with competitors can't be overlooked without sacrificing important opportunities.

Look for Clear Mutual Benefits

Rivals can weaken a firm and take away jobs. To the extent cooperation will produce greater strength, and to the extent each firm sees others as more serious threats than its partner, the easier it is to win support for an alliance and to discover a wide range of mutual opportunities, as illustrated in the figure on the next page.

To illuminate these concepts, consider Apple Computer's alliance with Digital Equipment. Although the firms are major opponents, they wanted to link some products to compete more effectively against IBM. Apple and DEC thus limited their scope to designing interface standards between certain computers. In all other areas, the firms remain steadfast competitors.

Now compare Apple and DEC with the alliance between Ford and Mazda. These firms are also competitors. Yet Mazda's major opponents are Honda, Nissan, and Toyota; Ford's are Chrysler, GM, and Toyota. A great deal of each firm's competitive energy is consequently directed toward others. This gives the partners a strong incentive to use many of their complementary abilities together; their alliance has become a powerful source of strength for each.

Mazda engineered Ford's Festiva, Tracer, and Probe cars, and has shared important quality, manufacturing, product, and process technology. Further, studies of Mazda's product development and other processes have supported the introduction of new procedures and desirable cultural changes at Ford.

The alliance also spawned a Japanese dealer network that distributes Ford-badged, Mazda-produced products sold by Ford in other parts of the Asia-Pacific region. The firms have also cooperated by using the dealerships to sell cars produced by Ford in the United States. These steps helped Ford become the largest selling foreign nameplate in Japan.

Ford generates a significant percentage of Mazda's business and has increased Mazda's North American market access and financial strength.

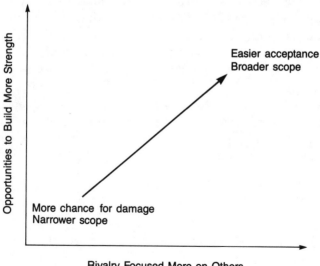

How Growth Benefits and Rivalry Affect Cooperation

Mazda has received valuable technology from Ford and also benefits from shared product development and distribution. These limit Mazda's costs and help it compete more effectively with its principal opponents in Japan. As Mazda's business with Ford has grown, its own identity has expanded in the United States, Europe, and Asia.

To be sure, Ford's minority investment, which gives it 25 percent of Mazda's profits, promotes internal acceptance. But the firms' broad involvement with each other is based on strong mutual need and competitive priorities that target others. Ford's working relations with Mazda are easier than similar relations with other auto firms, which are on a project-by-project basis. Significant mutual interests between Ford and Mazda have encouraged more buy-in, multilevel communication channels, joint planning, and rationalization in some areas.

Separate Rivalry from Cooperation

An alliance with a competitor should not be used to limit competition. This is not for antitrust reasons, but rather because mounting competition due to global integration leaves fewer places to hide. No matter who it is you work with, others are building strength to move ahead. As with other alliances, cooperation with a competitor should enhance each firm's separate abilities.

To avoid destructive conflict, limit an alliance to activities that do not affect any aspect of competition between the firms. Then potential damage can be controlled by using the concepts discussed in Chapter 4. Any joint task should be acceptable if it will strengthen both firms against others but will not significantly favor either firm in relation to the other.

This was a problem in NUMMI, the GM–Toyota alliance, where the learning Toyota sought took much less time to absorb than what GM required. Because the two are major rivals, there has been more opportunity for damage. NUMMI thus helped Toyota relative to GM.

Separation by Market

The easiest way to separate rivalry is by market segregation: Resources for cooperation can be largely devoted to a particular market, with competition relegated to other areas.

CFM International partners GE and SNECMA, for example, compete with each other in military engines but not in commercial markets.

The absence of commercial conflict has greatly eased joint planning, production, marketing, and field service. It has also helped the firms extend their relationship beyond CFM to make the new high-efficiency unducted fan engine. Although this engine competes with CFM products in some areas, working out the details was fairly easy, because GE and SNECMA had the same interests here.

Separation Within a Market

Even when firms compete in the same market, the presence of strong opponents can make cooperation worthwhile. Then competitive separation may use any tactic that focuses the alliance on the shared objective. For example, separation can be on the basis of different products or projects, or by cooperating only in a particular function or facility, or in an early phase of technical development common to both firms.

When newspapers cooperate to reduce costs by jointly operating printing plants and circulation systems, each paper keeps its independence—often with contrasting views—by having separate news and editorial staffs.[2]

International Aero Engines (IAE), a rival jet engine alliance to CFM International, was formed by Pratt & Whitney and Rolls-Royce. Unlike GE and SNECMA, these firms compete with each other in commercial markets. To avoid conflicts, IAE built its own marketing staff and other corporate functions, which CFM could delegate to GE and SNECMA. IAE costs are correspondingly higher than those at CFM. Moreover, because the scope is necessarily small in relation to CFM, flexibility and future mutual opportunities are more limited.

Clearly, the more resources there are on the cooperation side of the dividing line, the more strength firms can build together.

Here is how Ford and Mazda manage separation within their wide scope of mutual interest: First and foremost, each firm maintains its independence with its own product and market plans as well as its own capital budgets and strategic direction. Neither firm knows the other's costs. Each company tells the other only what is necessary to explore future opportunities. Further, technology exchanges are scoped to protect their separate interests. Critical items in each firm, such as Mazda's rotary engine, are off limits to the other.

To satisfy their separate objectives, Ford and Mazda also make individual decisions on joint car programs. This has more than once led to an agreement to disagree. In one case they discussed, over several months, the possibility of cooperation on a minivan, but the firms could not resolve whether it should have front- or rear-wheel drive. They finally agreed to pursue separate programs. Another time, some groups at Ford wanted to have Mazda's successful RX-7 sports car or a derivative product, but Mazda said this was out of bounds, so Ford didn't get it.

When they do cooperate on joint cars, each firm has styled its product to maintain market differentiation. Cars made at Mazda's Flat Rock, Michigan, plant, for example, share the same understructure and engine. However, Ford's version, the Probe, is a sporty hatchback, while Mazda's model, the MX-6, is a conservative sedan.

For overall balance both firms are engaged in continuing efforts at several management levels to ensure their independence and to maintain a spirit of fair treatment on both sides. Individual program approvals go to high levels in both firms. Each project must benefit both, and the constant issue of cooperation versus competition is carefully explored.

Some Conflict Can't Be Avoided

No matter how you separate competition and cooperation, there will be some conflict. When partners compete in the same market, there will be a place where rivalry appears. But then, some friction occurs in every alliance.

Ford and Mazda dealers, for instance, have expressed unhappiness about the auto makers' alliance. Concerns first surfaced among Mazda dealers, who worried about a Ford takeover. When Ford later announced plans to build trucks it would sell to Mazda, its dealers were unsettled. However, since their competition focuses mainly on others, these concerns apparently have not become major issues. Mazda has assured its dealers it will stay independent. Both firms developed information programs to help their dealers understand that the alliance is in everyone's interest.

The effects of rivalry are also felt within each firm. One result has been varying degrees of enthusiasm for the alliance at Ford.

Ford cut its staff by 25 percent in the early 1980s. Although such radical changes were due to a restructuring unrelated to Mazda, residual concerns remain. They give rise to feelings of being threatened by Mazda and cause some holding back inside Ford. Even so, concerns are far greater about cooperation with larger Japanese auto firms; opportunities with them are consequently limited.

At Mazda, people fear being dragged into doing what the more powerful Ford wants done, even if this is not in Mazda's interest.

To Keep Balanced, Maintain Separate Strengths

Competitive separation also depends on each partner's performance. Newspapers with stronger editorial abilities do better than their joint operating partners that have less strength. Similarly, some members of R&D consortia are better at absorbing the results than others. Even though research is limited to precompetitive topics, firms that are slow to transfer new developments are in effect subsidizing their competitor-partners.

6

Using Alliances
to Build Market Power

*I'd much rather stay here and build semiconductors. [But] I feel there's
no choice. The current world is not one of individual companies fighting
their battles.*

—Charles Sporck, president, National Semiconductor [1]

CHARLIE Sporck's world has changed. As president of a major U.S.
chip maker, Sporck has for thirty years symbolized the entrepreneurial virtues of his Silicon Valley environment. Yet he has been
transformed from a zealous individualist to an eager collaborator.

Charlie Sporck has a lot of company. The same forces that converted
him are pressing on every industry around the world. It isn't enough
to strengthen your firm as an individual actor. Every company is part
of a collection of firms that influence each other. Growing interdependence is giving these links new importance. Today, you have to use
alliances to reach out and shape the forces in your environment: reinforce
key partners, work within strategic networks, and use links with others
to inhibit major opponents.

Reinforcing Key Partners

Most firms accept the importance of getting close to their customers.
One benefit is stronger earnings. Alliances with customers are more

dependable than open market transactions. They lower a firm's marketing costs, help deliver unique value, and lead to more of each customer's business.

A second benefit is greater strength. Alliances with customers provide longer time horizons for a firm and its customer to plan and learn together, which increases their future value together. And by serving a customer's advancing needs, a firm is kept close to its own frontiers. However, companies depend on more than customers.

Help Your Suppliers Help You

If your firm is typical, suppliers get one-half or more of your revenues. Significantly, the R&D that goes into purchased goods contributes as much to the average firm's technological progress as its own R&D.[2] A company's products and processes thus depend critically on healthy, innovating suppliers.

Conventional wisdom holds that every firm is responsible only for its own competence. This theory asserts that if a supplier does not have the desired abilities, a customer can go somewhere else. Yet even the best suppliers may not have the scale or skills to keep up with technology or market forces, or to meet customers' changing needs. Without help, suppliers and their customers both lose.

Listen to IBM president Jack Kuehler: "There are many U.S. tool manufacturers that are very good that sometimes need a little help. We help them. In some cases they just need the financial support of a big buy. We do that. We must keep them healthy. We depend on them."

West Germany's Robert Bosch is the largest and one of the most successful automotive parts manufacturers in the world. Bosch has an explicit policy of building long-term relations with key subcontractors and giving them needed support. This help ranges from general advice on new technologies—with Bosch acting as a technical university—to cooperating in making single parts.

To assure each supplier's strength even more, Bosch limits its volume to 20 percent of each firm's total business. This allows Bosch to reduce orders without endangering its suppliers' existence, to which its own is tied. The restriction also gives Bosch the benefit of their learning in the wider marketplace.

Nippon Telephone & Telegraph provides another example. NTT is leading Japan's thrust into fiber optics. To help secure its future position,

NTT conducts joint research with dozens of firms. Its purpose is to nurture an army of suppliers of sophisticated products to complement its own abilities.[3]

Now consider the American semiconductor industry. Its supply problems suggest what can happen when vendors provide critical inputs and buyers think mainly of themselves. All chip companies depend on a little-known but crucial industry that makes wafers, equipment, and materials used to produce the final chips. In the United States, these firms have not kept up with Japanese suppliers, which have become sources of more reliable equipment and higher-quality materials.

American chip firms have thus been turning to Japanese suppliers to meet their needs. This in turn has sped the erosion of U.S. suppliers' abilities, making the Americans even more dependent on others. The prospects of continuing along this path are dismal. If foreign companies dominate the equipment and materials market, foreign chip firms are likely to have access to the latest equipment first, allowing them to make more advanced chips than their U.S. competitors. This is more than a bad dream. It is already happening in auto making and other sectors.

Several attempts are under way in the chip industry to deal with the decline of critical suppliers. One effort, Sematech, a U.S. semiconductor industry cooperative, was launched to spur advanced development by suppliers.

Treating key suppliers as partners means being concerned for their continued welfare. If suppliers' costs must decline more than they can achieve alone, help improve their productivity rather than erode their profits. If quality must advance, make sure suppliers get needed training instead of just rejecting their products. This tactic was a crucial part of the motorcycle maker Harley-Davidson's remarkable return from near death caused by competition from Honda and other imports.

If qualified suppliers must invest heavily in R&D to develop a proposal, consider using a two-step approach in which second-stage losers are paid for their R&D to avoid serious damage and encourage future proposals.

If a different supplier obtains new cost-reducing technology, don't immediately give it all your business. Unless there are other reasons to be dissatisfied, a more constructive approach is to go to present suppliers and say, "Look how XYZ cut its price. We hope you can do the same, because we would have to rethink our position if the price difference goes on for months. If you need financial help to make the new investment, let's discuss it."

To be sure, it is perfectly proper to leave a supplier if it is not giving you the best deal and not even trying to match the best deal. But remember this: Suppliers who have served you well and have kept advancing to meet your needs have demonstrated a capacity to perform and a valued commitment to your objectives. If they slip up or can't make it alone, think first about lending a hand. Their continued ability to serve you is in your best interest.

Give Your Distributors More Tools

Distributors add value to a firm's products and are a source of timely market information. Treating distributors as partners and adding to their strength will improve a firm's own position.

The auto industry, like many sectors, reaches customers through distributors. How these relations are managed has a lasting effect on buyer attitudes. Yet "We are most universally castigated and criticized for dealer service," says Ford chairman Donald Petersen. Nothing angers car buyers more than salespeople who mislead and intimidate and mechanics who seem not to care about customer problems. One bad experience with a dealer can turn away a customer—plus family and friends—for life.

To change this situation Ford initiated a multipoint program aimed at strengthening it dealers. One element is a customer survey conducted by Ford. Overall results and completed individual questionnaires are shared with dealers each month. The surveys have prompted dealers to pay more attention to customer concerns, spot issues, develop solutions, and track follow-through. Ford contributes in other ways by, for example, paying half the cost of free cars loaned to service customers.

At a more basic level, Ford is changing its relationship with dealers from being a hidebound autocrat to being a consulting partner. More decision-making has been delegated to dealers, who have also been given authority to spend up to $250 per car in goodwill money to cover problems on the spot. Before this, dealers had to go through the Ford bureaucracy for all spending authority.[4]

Help Your Competitors

Competitors force each other to keep up with change. They also share a common interest in combating substitute products. Alliances between competitors—to develop products, share capacity, support universities, and so forth—have become essential sources of strength in sectors as diverse as soft drinks, auto making, women's magazines, and semiconductors.

Strengthen Key Universities

Technological advance has made the world's universities an increasingly critical source of useful knowledge for industry. One clear measure has been the growth of business R&D sponsorship at universities. In the United States, such funding multiplied almost fivefold from 1977 to 1987; in Britain, it more than doubled from 1984 through 1989. Both growth rates were considerably faster than business's total R&D spending in these nations. Yet, as key technology sources, universities cannot always to be expected to meet industry needs on their own initiative.

That was why some three dozen U.S. firms created the Semiconductor Research Corporation. SRC's purpose is to improve the production of fundamental knowledge needed to make future generations of computer chips. SRC now sponsors more than half of all American university work on the subject. Two-thirds of the students receiving SRC support have taken jobs with member companies, thus easing the transfer of results into use.[5]

Building Strength Through Strategic Networks

The next step beyond reinforcing other firms individually is to build collective strength in a strategic network: a group of independent firms tied together through multiple links of alliances to achieve a common purpose. Important kinds of networks include vertical, or value-adding networks; technology sharing networks; development networks; and ownership networks.

Gain More Power from Your Vertical Network

Clearly, the benefits of cooperation between trading partners are substantial. A tight web of alliances between a firm and its suppliers simplifies logistics and offers longer supply production runs and larger volumes. This leads to lower costs and spurs higher quality. With just-in-time delivery and automatic order entry, inventory costs and response times are cut. Cooperation in product development adds the power of shared innovation.

Still, when interconnected firms work as a functioning group rather than sets of individual alliances, even more combined power is produced.

At Fuji-Xerox a closely woven net of suppliers—linked to Fuji and each other—has been instrumental in speeding product development. The division of labor made possible by a small number of suppliers allows each firm to acquire a high level of technological skill in its specialized area.

Although the suppliers are autonomous, they enjoy strong informal bonds and extensive communications among themselves and with Fuji. These links are instrumental to the performance of the whole network. They help each firm keep abreast of developments in the marketplace and the technical world. People cut across firm boundaries and organizational levels to work on new products or discuss ways to improve quality. The result is shorter paths for strategic information, better mutual understandings among all participants, and faster reactions to emerging needs.

The interactions support considerable collective learning. Fuji reinforces this by encouraging suppliers to experiment with a wide variety of prototypes during product development. The combination of shared learning and early experimentation maintains flexibility and speeds product development.

Close-knit vertical networks have the potential to strengthen every member firm. This advantage has been a hallmark of McKesson Corporation's remarkable success. McKesson, a major distributor of drugs, health care products, and other consumer goods, was forced to abandon its conventional wholesale business under fierce pressure from large drugstore chains. To build a sturdier enterprise, McKesson formed a network of value-adding alliances that linked manufacturers, distributors, retailers, consumers, and insurance firms. As a result, independent drugstores served by McKesson can offer their customers better prices and service, a more targeted product mix, and faster insurance payments—all of which has helped them compete with the chains.

By keeping their autonomy, the pharmacies are responsive to the needs of their local areas, which gives them another advantage over more homogeneous chains. McKesson's sales to drugstores climbed from $900 million in 1976, when the changes began, to $5 billion a decade later.

Significantly, McKesson's tight links with its partners use the latest information technology. But this is not the network's critical strength. What makes McKesson so powerful is its knowledge that each firm has a stake in the other's success.

McKesson managers see the entire network as one competitive unit. They look for opportunities beyond their own corporate boundaries, seeking ways to add value by creating new services and to use resources from one part of the network in another. Because McKesson knows its fate depends on its customers and suppliers, the company monitors competitive dynamics across the network and tries to fix problems wherever they occur.[6]

In a world of rapid change, firms that keep on top of shifting events have a tremendous advantage over competitors with limited access to strategic information.

Invariably, the best information about markets and technologies comes from people and firms that are close to breaking events, are well known to your firm, and have been found dependable. Holding trading partners at arm's length blocks this knowledge transfer, which makes a firm more vulnerable to the effects of change.

Belonging to a closely woven network opens information channels at both ends: It becomes easier to find reliable data one is looking for, and partners are more likely to understand a firm's needs and to bring it new information.

This has been a fundamental benefit for Fuji-Xerox and McKesson. Both firms are quick to learn of emerging needs or developments along their vertical chains and in the related markets where their partners work.

Building Strength with Technology Networks

It is a fact that outside sources of technical know-how—other companies, universities, and government laboratories—make an important and growing contribution to every firm's technical abilities. A network of links to key technology sources is consequently a basic dimension of business strategy.

Motorola, a leading electronics firm, has cross-licensing links with other companies throughout the world. It also participates in several U.S.-based R&D groups, including the Semiconductor Research Corporation, the Center for Integrated Systems at Stanford University, and the Microelectronics and Computer Technology Corporation. Motorola also benefits indirectly from its non-U.S. partners' participation in their government-led programs. The firm's technology network greatly increases its access to advancing know-how.

Networking is a valuable, growing way to add technical strength because it is fast and far-reaching, and can be inexpensive. Networks cover more ground than isolated one-on-one links. Because they understand each other, participants spend less effort locating desired know-how.

That was the motivation that drove Corning, Ford, Hewlett-Packard, Xerox, and others to build an informal network for sharing quality improvement ideas. Periodic discussions cover current issues and latest developments; members occasionally pair off for more intense conversations.

Creating New Value with Development Networks

When the *Providence Journal and Evening Bulletin* wanted to find ways to lower its printing costs, the newspaper formed a development network with ink and paper suppliers and other firms to experiment with new techniques.

A group of firms in Britain is using the same approach to develop advanced materials. The network, led by British Aerospace, includes Alcan International, British Petroleum, Ciba-Geigy, Courtaulds, Dunlop, ICI, and Imperial Metal Industries. Their objective is to create advanced materials with ceramics, sprayed metallurgy, and other disciplines that will be useful to the end of the century and beyond. The network's program includes joint projects between companies, university links, and multifirm interdisciplinary research.[7]

Strategic networks can be powerful tools for developing new products, processes, or technologies, because they provide the conditions for important innovation—multiple sources of different expertise flexibly connected through many links, with all members pursuing the same objective. The commercial payoff may come from continuing to work together as a vertical network, or members may go their separate ways.

The Value and Limits of Ownership Networks

Essilor, the French-based world leader in supplying glass for eyeglasses, would be an attractive takeover target by virtue of its strong long-term growth and earnings. Yet, although Essilor is publicly held, it is almost immune from predators. This spares management from having to work on takeover defenses and allows the firm to concentrate on product improvement and future growth.

Essilor's enviable position derives from the fact that about 45 percent of its ownership is held by a network of friendly shareholders, including Saint-Gobain, the leading French glass firm, and Crédit Lyonnais, the

French bank. Saint-Gobain, in turn, has only a few carefully chosen partners in its equity, and Saint-Gobain is one of their leading shareholders. Thus a major firm in an important segment of the world's fine glass industry is shielded from takeover threats and can focus more energy on building for the long-term.[8]

To be sure, cross-ownership does not always create new strength. Many firms own stock in others. Usually, these holdings are treated as pure investments.

For an ownership network to be more than the sum of its parts, network members must be willing to place their strategic need for each other above the value of their investments in each other. This requirement for clear mutual need is one condition for a network to function as an alliance. Other requirements are the presence of a strong common objective and a willingness to share risks to achieve it.

Those conditions are met by Japanese ownership networks, but their objective seems to emphasize security at the expense of competitive strength. Many larger Japanese firms belong to one of six such networks, known as *keiretsu*. These groups, including Mitsui, Mitsubishi, and Sumitomo, are neither legally defined nor formally structured. Yet each group's members are bound together through an extensive durable network of reciprocal ownerships and trading relations.

Group membership has given Japanese firms significant stability for long-term growth and has supported the moves of mature firms into higher value-added fields. These benefits have endowed a wide range of Japanese industries, from steel to semiconductors.

One source of this strength is that each firm's stockholder and management interests are more closely linked than is the case in typical Western companies. Consequently, trading partners, as stockholders, share a better-informed long-term interest in each other.[9]

However, available data suggest that Japanese firms that do not belong to *keiretsu* have had stronger growth and profits than comparable group firms.[10]

Evidently, widespread equity cross-holdings and a group's powerful central bank promote collective well-being. Yet many firms in each group are not vertically related to each other, or at least do not add critical value to other members' products. Consequently, unlike true vertical networks, there is no overall set of market signals for guidance. Shared priorities and complementary skills focused on competitive strengths are correspondingly weak.

In addition, other firms in a *keiretsu* help out in difficult times. During the mid-1970s oil shortages, for example, most Japanese oil firms provided oil to other group members at below-market prices. The groups also help individual members in lean years, both through group bank activities and by paying above-market prices for a firm's products.[11]

This behavior promotes security across a group at the expense of individual firms' performance. A Japanese R&D manager whose firm seeks technology relationships outside its group summed it up this way: Affiliates are "like brothers-in-law—people you go to when you need money or help, but not for good advice."[12]

Strategic Networks as Opponents

A network can be a rival in its own right. McKesson's vertical network, for example, competes in the retail market against wholly owned drug chains.

Networks also compete with each other. This is the basis of the construction industry in the United States and other nations, where stable networks of subcontractors—each aligned with a different general contractor—compete for business.

Competition by and between networks is fast becoming an important part of the business landscape. For two basic reasons its prominence will keep growing. First, vertical and development networks can have more competitive power than individual firms or smaller alliances. Second, Japanese companies have been winning world market battles by selectively competing through networks against stand-alone opponents.

In semiconductors, for example, Japanese firms are now the world leaders, having taken a large chunk of market share away from the Americans—including Motorola and Charles Sporck's National Semiconductor. A good part of the Japanese strength comes from successive government-initiated, industry-funded development networks that have spurred each major generation of technology from early memory chips to the latest x-ray lithography. This coordinated effort has spent more than even the largest individual U.S. or European firms can afford.[13]

The Japanese are using the same collective practices to move ahead of other competitors in commercial aircraft, superconductivity, high-definition television, and biotechnology.

When the Japanese go abroad they often take their networks with them. Mitsubishi Motors formed Diamond-Star Motors with Chrysler in Bloomington, Illinois, for example. Other companies in the Mitsubishi group came along—on their own or through alliances with U.S. firms—to supply glass, processed steel, electrical components, coil springs, and a host of other parts. Diamond-Star is also supplied by firms in Mitsubishi

Motor's vertical network, some of which built nearby plants to make lower-value-added parts. Others supply such higher-value components as engines and transmissions, as well as sophisticated capital equipment, from Japan.[14]

Western firms have met the Japanese network thrusts with a combination of import-limiting trade agreements and newly formed alliances. In the auto industry, Ford, GM, and Chrysler have begun recasting their vertical networks. In the chip business, U.S. firms created SRC and Sematech (both for R&D). An attempt to launch a chip manufacturing alliance was stillborn due to weak interest.

These partial efforts came after the Japanese network threat was dominant. It seems self-evident that Japan's competitors can't keep waiting to forge networks until after they have been attacked.

Determining a Network's Strength

There are two ways to judge a network's value. One is to assess how it contributes to individual firms' strengths. Will a proposed development network, for example, create a desired technology sooner or better than what your firm might do by other means? Another way to judge a network is by its own strengths. This perspective is necessary when a network is going to compete against other firms or networks.

Using Alliances to Inhibit Opponents

It isn't enough for a firm to be a strong competitor. Powerful customers, distributors, suppliers, or even governments may bargain away its earnings, block its actions, or strike at weak spots. Strategic alliances can provide more bargaining power or constrain a difficult opponent.

More Bargaining Power

For many firms, the playing field is far from level. Yet often others are in the same predicament and might help shift the balance. Farmers' cooperatives, for example, have long helped small producers meet the purchasing power of large buyers on more equal terms.

As another example, Voluntary Hospitals of America, an alliance of some four hundred independent hospitals, uses its combined purchasing to get better prices from suppliers.

Publishers Time Warner and the New York Times had a similar intent when they formed their magazine distribution joint venture. Before that, the firms' wholesalers and retailers controlled many terms and conditions. By combining their resources the alliance gave the publishers more bargaining power.

Inhibiting Opponents' Moves

Picture the marketplace as a forest in which companies must fend for themselves. One way to make the going easier is for some to build strength together. A different, sometimes powerful, approach is to take advantage of other firms' positions to attack selected opponents.

Attacking on a Second Front. Striking at a competitor's revenue base from an unexpected direction can destabilize its cash flow, disrupt its decision-making, and inhibit its ability to move against oneself in other areas.

That was Caterpillar's objective when it formed a heavy equipment joint venture with a Mitsubishi unit in Japan. Caterpillar faced mounting global competition from Komatsu and was strengthening its products and operations to meet the challenge. But these steps didn't go far enough. Although Japan was a small part of the world market, as a secure home base (the Mitsubishi unit had not been a serious threat) it generated 80 percent of Komatsu's total cash flow. Operationally, the Caterpillar–Mitsubishi alliance serves the Japanese market. Strategically it has been a check on Komatsu's domestic market share and cash flow.

The chip maker Intel used a similar strategy to head off Philips's entry into the U.S. semiconductor market. By licensing Siemens to compete with Philips in Europe, Intel created an aggressive competitor to draw Philips's attention away from Intel's home base.

Blocking Access to Scarce Resources. Locking up vital resources can make it hard for others to function. Procter & Gamble, for instance, tied up a Japanese supplier of the scarce polyacrylate material used in its Ultra Pampers by helping the supplier finance a plant.

Other tactics include obtaining exclusive rights to a key technology, widening a product line to fill an important distribution channel, or using bargaining power with a partner to limit its actions.

Intel forestalled Samsung Semiconductor's U.S. market penetration with just such leverage. Samsung achieved a major breakthrough when Arrow Electronics, the nation's second-largest semiconductor distributor, agreed to sell its products. Two weeks after the deal was announced, Intel, one of Arrow's major suppliers, reduced its business with Arrow. Other U.S. suppliers also protested. One month after the announcement Arrow terminated the Samsung agreement.

Raising Entry Barriers. Growth markets always attract competition. An early entrant might discourage followers by cooperating to raise early entry barriers.

Intel and Texas Instruments used this approach with application-specific computer chips, known as ASICs. When the product was first introduced, numerous startup firms entered the market along with established chip makers. To build power in this fragmented market, Intel and TI agreed to swap designs and manufacturing technologies and to act as alternate chip suppliers for each other. Their combined broad product line made it hard for small custom producers to survive in this rapidly growing market.

Forcing an Opponent to Follow Your Lead. A firm that has developed a basic technology before others might grant them rights to use the technology to help establish its own position. If the cost of shifting to subsequent developments is high, licensees have an incentive to continue with the original technology. This is how Philips set the standards for compact disc players (see Chapter 3). When licensees depend strongly on the source firm for continuing improvements, they may be forced to follow its lead. Under such conditions, granting licenses for a major advance reduces potential competition.

When General Electric licensed its advanced gas turbine know-how to foreign producers that were major potential competitors, it created a captive market for the technology in their nations. The deal also eliminated competition for the American market from these sources.[15]

Also, consider this: Licensing a significant technology to competitors helps a firm monitor their actions. The more licensees' products or investments mirror yours, the easier it is to track their moves.

TWO

KINDS OF ALLIANCES

7

Working with Informal
and Contractual Alliances

*We eventually had a contract with many details on paper. But our
alliance was really formed by the shared vision and understandings we
developed before then. The spirit was that we had two companies able
to complement each other and satisfy each other's needs. The contracts
are now years old; we haven't looked at them much.*

—Dow Chemical manager, commenting on
his firm's diaper alliance with Personal Care

ALTHOUGH many alliances involve formal agreements, a contract
isn't always necessary. Informal alliances can be a valuable way
to cooperate.

Virtually every work day people from across Corning, up to the highest
levels, are visiting with colleagues in other firms to compare notes on
new products, technologies, quality control processes, management concepts, equal opportunity programs, computer applications, and more.

In some sectors, including the U.S. steel minimill industry, there is
an extensive informal exchange of proprietary know-how between engineers in competing firms. This trading is balanced over time by tacit
agreement. It bypasses formal cross-licensing programs and involves
smaller pieces of know-how than could be handled that way.

Britain's Lucas Industries and Japan's Hitachi both make parts for
the automotive aftermarket. Neither has had a strong presence in the
other's market, and both compete with larger firms. To build strength

together, engineers from Lucas and Hitachi have met periodically to share product, market, and technical information and to plan cooperative developments.

Informal alliances are useful whenever risks are small. How far this goes depends on mutual trust.

For instance, Bill Gates and Ed Esber, the respective heads of the software houses Microsoft and Ashton-Tate, have periodically discussed the state of their industry for many years. These talks nurtured a growing friendship, even though their firms compete vigorously in several areas. Their mutual trust made it possible for the two to share highly sensitive product plans in the process of jointly developing a new generation of database software.[1]

At least once a year, executives from several major U.S. hospital groups get together for private talks about current issues. Those who attend have come to know each other well, so they feel comfortable sharing sensitive internal problems. Sessions are free of the politics and posturing that are so often a part of more visible gatherings. The resulting candor has fostered highly productive problem-solving for the participants.

Firms often work informally with their customers to develop new product applications. Corning's practice here is typical. Its decision to work with customers hinges on its trust that a customer will buy the product if Corning prices it competitively. Corning pays for the R&D to retain proprietary rights. Price, volume, and final specifications are negotiated toward the end of development.

Informal cooperation is a natural starting point for more formal arrangements. Firms have more flexibility before they commit, as well as more room to explore their relationship and resolve issues that could be troublesome later on. Then, once they are ready to make major commitments, contracts are used to formalize understandings.

When to Use Contractual Alliances

A contract is a legally recognized mutual business plan. Once performance has begun, a change is possible only if it is mutually acceptable. While they fortify promises, contracts thus restrict flexibility.[2]

One way to make an agreement more adaptable is to plan carefully for what might happen under different conditions. But there are limits to foresight. For instance, you can't be sure how a market will respond to a new product, or how an R&D project will conclude even when both firms make their best effort.

Further, drafting highly structured agreements is self-defeating. It leaves no room to negotiate adjustments in light of actual conditions. Most people object to situations—and many won't make commitments—where their performance must stick to each fine letter of a contract. Too much planning also implies a lack of trust, which can hurt relationships.

So to proceed with some activities, certain risks have to be left open. Then commitments depend on common objectives, mutual need, and risk sharing. This is the basis of contractual alliances.

Alliance Design

The concept of alliance design is to manage risks selectively. Resolve as many issues as possible before you commit. Then use a combination of risk controls, performance incentives, and risk sharing to balance your commitments.

Joint Planning Reduces Uncertainty

The first step in risk management is to choose a partner with whom you can work. Next, cooperate informally to define objectives and develop plans. This provides a clearer view of the greater risks ahead. If things don't go as you hoped, you can leave without breaking a commitment.

When Dow Chemical and Personal Care set about to shape their agreement to produce a new kind of diaper, four major issues had to be resolved. First, could Dow really develop and supply what Personal Care needed? The diaper maker would be wholly dependent on Dow during this early period, with a potential market of $3 billion. Nonperformance by Dow would have had serious consequences.

Second, the firms had to judge their speed. They knew others might be after the same objective; being first to market would create an important advantage. So timing was critical. Dow would have to scale up to a full-size plant in record time.

Customer acceptance was another issue. Dow needed to understand clearly the market risks and uncertainties. The chemical firm would be building an 80-million- to 100-million-pound-per-year production plant costing tens of millions of dollars. There was no way to convert the plant to other uses if the program failed. A fourth concern was whether Personal Care would use Dow's material.

For about a year after their first meeting, a joint Dow-Personal Care team worked informally and intensely to resolve these issues. They defined the business opportunity, conducted joint and separate market and technical research, and shared relevant confidential information. They discussed logistics, quantities, specifications, timing, and product safety. Finally they wrote a business plan.

Unlike a routine sales contract, all these issues had to be explored on both sides. Each firm would be making significant investments and taking substantial risks. The firms also separately estimated each other's costs and evaluated their respective capabilities and commitments.

Dow took the risk of forecasting its own costs. As early as possible it disclosed the prices needed to make the deal worthwhile, to avoid later unpleasant surprises. This could have been a deal-breaker. Pricing was thus negotiated, with adjustments for uncontrollables, before the deal was closed.

The partners also planned for the worst. Among other things, they agreed on what to do if Personal Care ultimately did not use the material or if Dow failed to meet its obligations. The firms also agreed to share market risks. There was no way to predict the product's acceptance, and they needed each other to advance.

The joint business plan became a formal part of the agreement. The deal was for a minimum of three years to ensure startup commitments and a minimal return on Dow's investment.

During this informal phase each firm paid for its own work. At its expense, Dow built a small-scale plant to run some tests. Most important, the firms' early cooperation built the mutual trust they needed to share the major risks ahead.

To identify the most significant risks in a proposed alliance, consider the value of the resources you will commit along with relevant uncertainties. If you can be certain investing capital, know-how, products, market access, or other assets will yield specific benefits, there is no risk. However, when uncertainty is present one is exposed to possible loss. Risk increases with the value of a commitment and with rising uncertainty, as illustrated on the following page.[3]

Two kinds of uncertainties affect an alliance: those beyond your control, such as possible changes in economic conditions, and those for which you, your partner, or both, are accountable. Common sources of uncertainty are described in the table that follows.

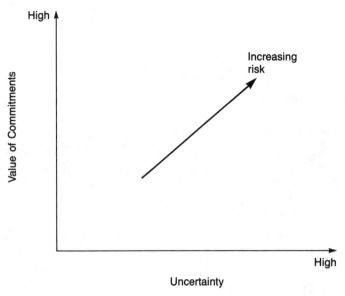

How Resource Commitments and Uncertainty Determine Risk

Risk Controls Shape Commitments

Certainty may be added to an alliance with agreed-upon rules for risks partners want resolved in advance. Most rules focus on firms' obligations to each other. Others protect them from adverse economic conditions or government decisions—such as by linking costs to a recognized price index, or ending an alliance if certain conditions become unacceptable.

Some issues, including partner abilities, latent conflicts, planning gaps, responsibilities, and relationships, can be decided only through prior analyses, discussions and experience together. Other issues are at least partly amenable to rules; breaking a rule violates an agreement.

Contract rules specify price, performance, timing, and other conditions each firm agrees to meet. These may be fixed or variable.

For instance, to ensure ongoing price and quality improvements in its supply alliances, Ford's agreements stipulate 5 percent annual productivity increases and continuing quality advances. Suppliers are also expected to stay current technically.

The rules you adapt should reflect your priorities. If you can't accept price uncertainty, and performance is fairly certain, a fixed-price agreement may be appropriate. By contrast, cost-plus contracts permit adjust-

Causes of Uncertainty in an Alliance

External Uncertainties

Economic environment	There may be shifts in public policy, industry conditions (price, technology, etc.), or in macroeconomic variables
Market responses	Customers', suppliers', or competitors' reactions are unpredictable
Partners' reactions	Other partners may be affected
Liabilities	Third parties may be harmed by one's actions
Government approvals	Authorities may not grant needed rights

Internal Uncertainties

Goals	What each firm expects the alliance to achieve, and its own role, have not been fully specified
Partner abilities	One firm may not have needed strengths
Latent conflict	Major assumptions have not surfaced, or firms may not agree on changes once the alliance is under way
Planning gaps	Important tasks have not been detailed through oversight, complexity, or the need for later decisions
Authority	It isn't clear how key decisions will be made
Relationships	Partners may not work well together
Performance	Expected results may not be achieved
Benefits	Partners have not agreed on how prices will be set, revenues allocated, developments shared
Commitments	Expected investments, duration, business volume, or future rights are unclear
Opportunism	One partner may take advantage of the other

ment to performance uncertainties when one is relatively insensitive to price.[4] Some commonly used rules are listed here.

Risk Control	Effect
Fixed price	Limits innovation
Cost-plus	Fosters innovation
Volume guarantee	Covers fixed costs
Long-term commitment	Encourages initial investment

Risk Control	Effect
Evergreen renewal	Invites ongoing innovation
Future option	Promotes near-term commitment
Contingent continuation	Controls future commitments

Defining substantial mutual commitments can encourage major investments. The shape these take reflects the investment and performance the partners want to influence. For example, volume guarantees may be included to secure a revenue base to cover ongoing fixed costs. Alternatively, committing for a specific long term without defining total volume encourages a large initial investment. Such agreements commit all or some percentage of the buyer's purchases, with actual volume subject to market uncertainties. This involves some risk sharing by the seller, as was the case with Dow's three-year agreement for the new material.

In "rolling" or "evergreen" contracts, long-term commitments are periodically extended. Renewing a multiyear agreement every year or so gives both partners continued confidence in the longer time horizon, which encourages further risky investments.

Ford's alliance with Excel Industries to make shaped car windows, for instance, includes a ten-year purchase and supply contract with a two-year evergreen clause, which becomes effective before the ten years end. This structure supports Excel's continued investments in technology for more advanced future window designs.

Contracts can also be structured to accommodate sequences of events, to match commitments with uncertain future developments. The least binding approach is known as an "agreement to agree." Both firms agree to defer formal commitments until a time when more information is available. In the meantime any reliance is based on good faith and mutual interests. Such understandings are sometimes used in informal alliances, where commitments are small and uncertainties inhibit planning beyond an early phase.

One step up from an agreement to agree is the contingency agreement, which involves binding commitments of future rights and obligations provided certain events occur. This agreement defines future benefits to the risk taker if its efforts lead to specified results. Corning used this approach when it sought overseas firms to help develop its optical fiber business. To motivate both partners, Corning granted options for technology licenses or joint ventures. Exercise of the options was contingent upon certain technical and marketing results being achieved during a five-year development agreement.

An option typically spells out enough detail to confirm a basic commitment. But significant uncertainty about future events—such as when developments will be complete or what subsequent tasks will entail—prevents full planning. Substantial trust may be needed to fill the gaps.

If plans for later tasks can be developed in detail, firms may agree to phased performance with continuation dependent on passing stated milestones. For example, Du Pont and Synergen, a biotechnology firm, agreed to develop a protein that causes new blood vessels to form. During the initial period, Du Pont agreed to study the protein and to provide research support to Synergen. If tests suggested further development, the firms agreed to invest much more in clinical trials and regulatory applications.[5]

Note how a phased contract—in which decision points are built into an accord—differs from agreeing to discuss a new agreement later, should an early phase succeed. If either firm will be seriously damaged should later phases not continue, these contingencies should be resolved in the original agreement. The prospect of renegotiations after each stage discourages longer-term risk-taking.

Performance Incentives Encourage Best Effort

For uncertainties that are under one firm's control, a combination of rewards and penalties can spur completion. Rewards promote extra effort; penalties help ensure commitments will be kept.

Merck, for example, promised a reward to Repligen, another biotechnology concern, when the two joined forces to develop and market an AIDS vaccine. In addition to payments for R&D and royalties on Merck sales, Repligen would get substantial sums if it achieved various steps in the vaccine's development.

Other kinds of awards include tying commercial benefits to performance. Being an early buyer of a new product can carry reliability risks that may outweigh early-user advantages. The purchase may be encouraged with a lower price or the right to receive product improvements before others.

Had performance incentives been used by the American nuclear power industry, it might have followed a different course. Before this, construction contractors for power plants had little reason to meet schedules or hold down costs. The risk of delays and overruns—which added years and often tripled costs—were taken almost entirely by utilities and their customers. Finally, when new plant construction had almost halted, the Bechtel Group and Philadelphia Electric chose a different path to build the Limerick 2 nuclear plant. The firms agreed that Bechtel would more than double its fee by finishing early. If the project was a month late, no payment would be made. The work was completed ahead of schedule and under budget.[6]

How to Share Risks

Partners share risks when both make investments subject to the same uncertainties. To stay balanced, each must have comparable exposure. Otherwise, whoever feels more vulnerable may hold back or withdraw.

You would not knowingly enter an alliance a partner regards as a short-term opportunity, while you depend on its long-term performance. This is why R&D alliances, unlike conventional R&D contracts, should require the performer to carry some costs and risks, and more if milestones slip. Profits are made at the end, rather than concurrent with the effort, and may be tied through a royalty to the alliance's overall performance.

Also be careful to allocate future risks so as not to divide you. This can be a critical issue with liabilities when both firms make significant contributions.

In General Electric's several jet engine co-production alliances, the finished product integrates parts made by each firm. Since these are highly interdependent, there is no easy way to assign cause when a problem occurs. For example, overheating of a part made by one firm may damage a part made by the other, and may reflect shared design shortcomings. Thus, rather than say that the party at fault will pay warranty costs, GE and a partner often agree to share expenses in the same proportion as their overall work-share agreement. This gives both firms an incentive to solve problems together rather than to blame each other.

Prices for the products of an alliance should allocate risks and benefits fairly and respond to market forces. The simplest arrangement—typical of many development alliances—is for each firm to cover its own costs, and possibly to share common costs, but to market the results separately. Then each partner sets its own prices and takes its own marketing risks.

If one firm markets for the other, as when a pharmaceutical firm sells a drug made by another company, a license fee based on retail prices gives the marketer needed flexibility and shares pricing risks. When the supplying firm will make a significant investment, as with Dow and Personal Care, partners may negotiate a transfer price reflecting the investment, production costs, different volumes, internal profit guidelines, and competitors' prices.

When both firms contribute parts of a final product or service, their pricing scheme should follow the same principles of allocating risks and benefits fairly and being responsive to market forces. An arrangement that simply adds each firm's prices works only when the market is insensitive to price. Northern Telecom and General Electric ran into this constraint in the cellular phone market, where the firms combined their respective telecommunications and radio products to build complete systems.

Their alliance worked well, earning the number-three market position, until competitors introduced rapid price cuts. These forced Northern and GE to lower their prices to stay competitive. Yet they had agreed on a price formula based on normal margins. Each partner's willingness to accept less margin depended on its costing methods and internal priorities. Price setting became cumbersome, as each deal involved a new negotiation between them. For this and other reasons, GE pulled out of the alliance and became a supplier to Northern, which assumed a larger share of the marketing risks.

An alternative approach to formula pricing, favored by General Electric in its jet engine alliances, is to allocate revenues based on each firm's percentage of the work. This approach more fully shares outside risks—including market acceptance, pricing, and liabilities. It also avoids the challenge of developing a price formula that will reflect fairly a large number of variables and conditions.[7]

Alliance Organization

Unlike arm's-length transactions, in which initial commitments govern, alliances require ongoing mutual adjustments. They also involve multiple contacts between separate hierarchies—each with its own ways of delegating, deciding, and implementing. To ensure an effective match, forming an alliance should include adjusting both organizations to the new priorities.

Know How Decisions Will Be Made and Delegate

Make all major decisions about the conduct of an alliance, including objectives, performance measures, milestones, responsibilities, resource commitments, and other key aspects of the business plan, before you commit. Also, clearly define which firm will make other decisions in the course of the work.

You may understand implicitly who has what authority for internal projects; this has to be spelled out with another firm. Agree on who has the final say for marketing, product design, sourcing, quality assurance, government approvals, and other major items.

Authority can be shared if firms must be equally involved in the same risks. Shared authority is common in joint R&D projects and when firms are marketing together. Nonetheless, sharing decisions between separate firms, especially when more than one function or management level is involved on each side, is a heavy load for a project to carry.

Here is how Ford Motor reduces this burden. During the informal, precommitment phase of a joint car program, each firm must understand and accept the final plan. Consequently, each company's normal processes bear on all major decisions about the potential program, with one difference. People appreciate that, to go forward together, their partner's needs must be satisfied as well.

Once a formal effort begins, Ford delegates many decisions to lower levels. Ford has learned that when more management levels are involved on both sides, complexity grows within Ford and in relations with its partner. Cooperation is more effective when responsibility on the Ford side is clearly defined and delegated. This reduces the need for a program to follow two different organizations' procedures. At Ford, this delegation tends to cover issues and progress decisions within the scope of agreed-upon plans. New commitments must still go to higher levels.

Having a Lead Partner Can Help

Designating a lead partner simplifies cooperation by limiting shared authority. Whenever one firm has the expertise to manage particular risks, it should make the relevant decisions.

Collaboration is easiest in Ford's alliances when one partner has full responsibility for designing, making, and delivering a vehicle. Then, comparable segments of the other firm do not have to get involved.

In the diaper alliance, Personal Care was to sell the new product. Because the firm was already proficient in the market, it had final authority on design, manufacturing, and marketing. Dow became comfortable with Personal Care's skills in these areas before formal commitments were made. On the other hand, Dow was responsible for building and operating the plant, and could make changes as long as they did not affect the final product.

Regardless of who has more economic or political power, this should not determine authority. The lead must go to whoever has the best expertise to manage the major risks. Anything else will weaken commitments.

The Soviets learned this lesson, with some embarrassment, when they launched a joint science and technology program with East European nations. The Soviets had taken much of the initiative and sought a dominant role in every project, regardless of their experience. This caused many East European officials and state enterprises to reduce their involvement or to back out of the program entirely.[8]

Define Clear Interfaces

Agreeing on who will make what decisions eases implementation by reducing the need for different groups to interact. Even clearer separation comes from sharp boundaries between activities. The more each firm can work on different tasks by itself, the less confusion is created.

Fewer interfaces are still better, if this reduces the number of units in each firm that must work together. Boundaries should be defined on the basis of performance dependencies, not just physical connections. The less sensitive one component is to another's performance, the less people on each side have to interact.

For example, General Electric's Aircraft Engines Group works out a division of labor with each partner to minimize the number of engine component interfaces. Each firm is responsible for a few major integrated units, which are then combined in a complete product. This separation has vastly simplified GE's joint programs.

Integrate Both Firms' Schedules

When cooperation involves parallel activities or must fit a tight schedule, planning should at a minimum compare the partners' normal timetables to ensure proper links between project phases and to set joint milestone reviews.

Without adjusting either firm's internal procedures, completion time will be at least as long as that of the slower partner. However, it does not have to be so. Important alliances deserve the same kinds of changes you would make for major internal programs.

To meet the critical market timing objective for the new diaper, Dow Chemical built a full-size plant in record time, in Midland, Michigan, during a typically subarctic winter. Construction was done inside a large circus tent set up for the purpose. The project became a rallying point for both teams and was completed as planned.

Beyond a certain point, however, changing internal practices is too disruptive. Then the partners have to tolerate scheduling delays, or else set up a separate facility to improve integration.

General Electric took this approach to speed the development of automation software in an alliance with Rensselaer Polytechnic Institute. GE set up a "skunk works" on the RPI campus, which eased the integration of GE engineers with RPI faculty and students, and insulated the work from other GE activities.[9]

Plan for Joint Contacts with Others

Before appearing together in public, be sure to plan how you will perform together. Every firm has its own way of analyzing customer needs, making presentations, dealing with issues, and proposing solutions. Even when one firm has the marketing lead, its partner may have to talk to customers and participate in bid development. So if both partners will interact with customers, decide how you will combine your separate styles ahead of time.

Here is what can happen when that is overlooked: Two firms in the financial services business marketed a custom-designed product to industrial clients. Although the firms could separate their developments, each was contributing major parts and had to interact with prospective customers to understand their needs and to answer questions. Yet each had a distinct way of selling. The contrasting sales methods "became a show-stopper in front of customers," reports one sales manager. When it came time to write proposals, they still had to work through their different styles, which caused serious delays in getting back to prospects. After several months with little success, both sales teams spent several days off-site to discuss their differences and to design and rehearse a single integrated approach.

Managing Contractual Alliances

Most of the work in a contractual alliance is performed separately by each firm. Combined performance thus depends on having a solid bridge between partners. This begins with mutual commitments.

Build Real Commitment

Effective commitments are developed, not mandated. Alliances can't function with top-down management by each firm. Real dedication must come from those who will be directly involved. Companies agree; people implement.

Here is how Dow and Personal Care built their alliance: At first, they simply met to discuss mutual interests. Relations were the most fragile then. Although the firms had worked together before, different people and different units had been involved.

Momentum was sustained by a champion on each side who emerged during early discussions. These individuals became committed to the concept and wanted to make it happen. They took the initiative to promote the alliance among their peers and to convince higher management of its merits.

During the period of informal cooperation, people from each firm got to know each other and became convinced their counterparts were people on whom they could rely. Mutual trust came from wide-ranging discussions of each other's needs and abilities.

"We eventually had a contract with many details on paper," one senior participant says. "But our alliance was really formed by the shared vision and understandings we developed before then. Reaching our agreement forced the discussion of hard issues, including what would happen if either of us failed to perform. The spirit was that we had two companies able to complement each other and satisfy each other's needs. The contracts are now years old; we haven't looked at them much.

"People talked about still doing business together a decade later. We both recognized we were working in an area of continued technological change, and we were committed to cooperate to keep abreast of that change. Our informal understanding was a central feature of the alliance. Building the management commitment and people commitment is what it's all about. Dow would not have proceeded without this."

Shared by top executives in both firms, this understanding became a central feature of the alliance. Toward the end of negotiations they met for two hours to discuss the principal concepts and risks involved. The deal then went to the respective boards of directors for approval.

During the years they worked together, rapport within the Dow–Personal Care team became so strong that, two years after everyone had changed positions in each firm, they got together for a dinner to reminisce.

Project Champions Are Important

At the start, when people and firms don't know each other well, a pair of champions who share a vision is the only way to plant the seeds of mutual trust and dedication. This is why the early appearance of champions in Dow and Personal Care was crucial to the launch and eventual success of their alliance. Obstacles on both sides were enormous; these people played a central role in building the collective spirit and commitments needed to overcome them.

Other firms, such as Apple Computer, have had the same experience. In fact, Apple alliances have failed when champions were not present.

As with internal entrepreneurs, alliance champions tend to be self-appointed. Dow management believes those who championed the diaper project probably would not have been chosen for lead roles. They emerged during the firms' initial discussions. More generally, Dow has found that champions can't be appointed; they have to emerge as true believers and must evolve to become natural leaders of the project.

Like internal entrepreneurs, alliance champions must be committed to project success, able to build internal support, and willing to skirt organizational bottlenecks. If an alliance involves more than one function, a champion is not likely to have full authority over everyone on his or her team. In this case, leadership skills are more important than formal position.

Championing takes more effort with alliances than with similar internal efforts. There is always some resistance to sharing an opportunity with another firm. Further, joint program management requires more coordination than comparable internal activities, because two sets of hierarchies are involved, and new understandings must be developed.

Assemble Interfirm Teams

Day-to-day work should be managed by a team in each firm responsible for meeting its commitments. Pick team members for their expertise and direct control of relevant resources, even if this involves different management levels. Having appropriate multilevel teams also reduces the need for layers of coordinating committees above them.

Interfirm contacts must be directly between people with relevant technical, market, or other information. Channeling discussions through project managers weakens mutual understandings and contributes to a feeling of isolation. Direct person-to-person links are essential for rapid communications and easy issue-spotting, and to grow real trust. Full participation also promotes internal acceptance by team members. Without this, project leaders work alone.

Initial leadership in the Dow–Personal Care alliance was by the champion on each side who kept up contacts. This changed after a few months as the work grew more complex. Contact points shifted to direct ties between technical, manufacturing, marketing, and purchasing managers from each firm. The champions became formal project leaders, but the informal structure was working well. People in each firm understood with whom they were to work. At the same time, enthusiasm for the effort spread across the two-company team.

Team continuity throughout the two-year development effort was a key factor in being able to move fast. This permanence preserved and built on people's growing mutual trust and understandings.

Communicate Often and Well

Since much of the work is done separately, it is critical for partners to keep each other informed. Interdependence thrives on growing understandings and an absence of surprises.

Dow's development of the diaper material and Personal Care's parallel development of the complete product were constantly monitored by both firms. Each was at risk and needed growing confidence in the other's progress. Performance measures included detailed understandings based on contacts so frequent that people could really see the efforts others were making to meet their commitments.

Information flowed by phone, letter, fax, and visits between corresponding technical, sales, and purchasing people. At times technical people went to each other's labs for side-by-side cooperation.

People in each firm worked hard to avoid surprising their opposites and to reinforce an attitude of open communications. For example, when Dow R&D made significant progress on a key task, Dow sales people followed up with the diaper maker's purchasing people to confirm the advance. The follow-up was made even though it was known that communications within each firm had already conveyed the results. The implicit but important message was, "We want to be doubly sure we're keeping each other informed."

Solve Problems Early

Good communications gets issues out early and helps resolve them before they grow. Careful planning makes this easier. It is simpler to raise questions in advance than to fail on a task when others were counting on you to succeed.

Much of the emphasis in formal Dow–Personal Care meetings was on future plans and activities, rather than on the past. People found that if they did a good job thinking through coming steps, they did not have a lot of unanticipated problems.

Cooperation was also smoothed by settling problems when and where they surfaced. Members of the two-firm team had an unspoken understanding that "you solve problems with your counterpart, and don't let them escalate to higher levels."

Set Up a Joint Management Process

Interfirm bridges should include ways to review progress and build understandings at a level above day-to-day activities. At Dow and Personal Care, managers of those directly involved from both sides met about every two months to review progress. That also helped them respond to questions from higher-level executives, who wanted to be kept informed.

More formal interfirm steering committees can be used to supplement internal champions and joint teams on large, complex projects, involving several units on each side. Such arrangements help build collective understandings and resolve issues when firms have not developed internal project management systems to cut across different units. However, when they perform more than a review function, steering committees tend to be bureaucratic and less entrepreneurial, and can weaken initiative in others.

Maintaining the Alliance

An alliance lasts as long as firms can serve each other's needs and are committed to doing so. The way the diaper alliance has evolved will illustrate. Some time after Personal Care introduced the new product, other diaper firms entered the market. Some became Dow customers for the material. Dow still has a long-term supply agreement with Personal Care and also conducts technical work with each customer. Dow has to keep them competitive to stay competitive itself. Its work for each firm is segregated to avoid conflict.

By serving more than one customer, Dow has built strengths it wouldn't otherwise have, which benefits everyone. To maintain links at higher levels, Dow's top managers periodically visit each customer to be sure Dow continues to meet its needs.

The practices of British clothing maker Lee Cooper, which has successfully licensed its products around the world, offer another example. A key part of Lee's strategy has been a hands-on approach to licensee relations. That helps ensure the licensees will control product quality and will respect the geographic limits of their agreements. Understanding each licensee's needs also helps Lee keep it up to date with new products and technologies as these are introduced. The mutual interest they develop gives licensees an incentive to fight counterfeits that violate Lee's patents and trademarks.[10]

Why Relationships Are So Important

The success of an alliance depends as much on mutual faith as it does on anything you can put on paper. It is hard to take risks with someone you don't trust. You can't write agreements about enthusiasm.[11]

Solid relationships are critical to every kind of contract activity where risks are shared. In large construction projects, client and prime contractor are joined from start to finish. The work is so complex, it is almost impossible to substitute a new contractor if something goes wrong. Even so, large projects most often get derailed in the client–contractor relationship, not in the maze of technical activities.

In the fast food business, franchisors and their outlets depend on each other over the long term. In more successful chains, effective coordination and problem-solving come mainly from solid relations in which franchisees are a part of the firm's decision-making structure, and communications emphasize helpful information.[12]

The greater the risk, the more important the relationship—and the higher the management levels that must be involved. This is clearly illustrated by Dow's alliance with Personal Care.

However, relationships have a role even when risks are small. If a grace period is not included in an R&D agreement, for example, people often tacitly understand that milestones may slip as a consequence of uncertainties. And in routine sales, small adjustments that vary from the detailed terms are negotiated by informal discussion for the sake of the relationship and one's reputation.

8

Using Minority
Investment Alliances

Our investment is an essential seal to the relationship. It creates a deeper mutual commitment than would be possible without it.

—Jonathan Rinehart, vice chairman of Ogilvy & Mather,
on his firm's stake in Charls E. Walker Associates

WHEN Ogilvy & Mather, the worldwide advertising and public relations group, went shopping for a Washington, D.C., lobbying firm, the best candidate was Charls E. Walker Associates, which didn't want to be acquired. But Walker recognized the possible synergies between them, so agreed to a minority investment alliance.

Now, Ogilvy offers its clients the services of a top lobbyist, and Walker draws on Ogilvy for grassroots public relations work, an increasingly important element of government affairs. The firms' volume together has grown dramatically since they formed their alliance, which blends the best of two different worlds.

Thanks to Mazda, Ford has a stronger product line, lower costs, better quality, and improved technologies, plus the best-selling foreign nameplate in Japan. And thanks to Ford, Mazda competes in global markets with strengths its executives could only dream of without their alliance. Yet these achievements would not be likely if Ford had acquired Mazda. The firms have distinctly different styles, and Mazda prizes its independence.

One popular business myth holds that total ownership is best when another firm is important to a company's future. To be sure, full control is needed when major strategic or operating changes must be made to serve a buyer's goals. Also, with an acquisition the purchaser can fully benefit from the new unit's growth and expertise. However, acquisitions of unrelated or culturally different firms have a poor track record. More often than not, hoped-for synergies are lost.

But consider this: With minority investment alliances firms can build many of the policy-level connections and operating links that make acquisitions attractive. Moreover, to the extent one firm owns another's equity, it shares in that company's growth. Further, these alliances retain the qualities acquisitions so often destroy. Strong management teams stay in place, the vitality that comes with independence is kept, and momentum is preserved.

How Minority Investments Build Commitment

In a minority investment alliance, one firm buys stock from another as part of a mutually desired strategic relationship. Buying shares in the market is outside this scope and is usually done for financial gain, which serves a different and possibly conflicting purpose.

The simplest form of minority investment is used for access to resources in exchange for capital. Amstrad, the British computer firm, did this when it bought newly issued shares of Micron Technology, the U.S. chip maker. In return for its funds, Amstrad got the right to buy up to 9 percent of Micron's scarce memory chips for the next three years.[1] But minority investment alliances have more potential than that.

Building Vested Interests

Forming close ties with customers and other firms important to one's business is an essential practice. Often, this includes visits at high management levels. Dow Chemical senior executives, for example, make regular calls on their counterparts in major customer firms.

Yet just as contracts replace informal alliances when risks are high, minority investments help build strong policy-level ties when firms have major long-term interests that can't be realized by occasional top-level contacts.

Create Long-Term Exclusivity. Policy-level connections and an ownership bridge make relationships more exclusive than with contractual alliances. Having a significant stake in a firm justifies a special bond to others with whom you do business, who might want the same kind of treatment. Further, these links signal high-level attention to your troops and open internal doors. All these factors promote a sense of common destiny, contributing to shared incentives to work on broad mutual objectives.

Ford's stakes in Mazda and in Excel Industries, the window manufacturer, represent long-term commitments that go well beyond its current activities with them. Although Ford could sell these investments if it wanted, the obligations are based on enduring mutual interest. Regarding Mazda, Ford needs a Japanese partner far into the future. Robert Reilly, Ford's executive director for strategy, points out that Mazda has become an integral part of the firm's strategic thinking. He says Ford would no more consider selling its stake in Mazda than it would think of selling any key wholly owned unit.

Ford and Excel also need a close, lasting relationship. Shaped and framed glass is becoming more critical in Ford products. The best vehicle designs come from optimizing tradeoffs between glass-forming possibilities and early vehicle concepts, with a close eye on costs. Window design must reflect the latest abilities in glass forming and must be compatible with the complex inner workings of car doors.

Ford thus wants Excel's glass-shaping know-how applied as early as possible in the design process—well before purchase commitments can be defined. Excel must stay involved through vehicle engineering to final production. Ford also needs Excel to work on advanced developments with its own R&D, with some confidence this will pay off. And as their shared understandings and involvement grow, Ford is becoming more dependent on Excel.

Clearly, Ford and Excel need mutual assurances that they will continue to benefit from their relationship and work toward a common goal. Part of this comes from a long-term evergreen purchase and supply agreement that gives Excel 70 percent of Ford's relevant business, provided it is competitive in cost and quality. Part also comes from Ford's having seats on Excel's board, which helps ensure that Excel will continue developing its window technology as a long-term strength.

Shape Peoples' Attitudes. Another reason for Ford's investment in Excel is psychological. Ford people are uncomfortable about including outsiders in the closely guarded vehicle design process. Excel's far-reaching involvement is rare for a supplier. Having equity in Excel helps make the case that Excel is more of a Ford unit and wins critical acceptance.

In addition, Bud Marx, executive director of Ford's automotive components group, notes that multiunit coordination always takes more time. Doing this with another firm requires even more effort than a comparable internal program. He observes that having a substantial share of Excel's earnings makes it easier to convince others in Ford it is worth going the extra mile to work with Excel.

From Excel's perspective, Jim Lohman, the chairman, reports that formation of the alliance gave its people a sense of security and boosted their morale and enthusiasm. Restrictions in the agreement with Ford prevent it from having any influence in running the company, so Excel people do not feel any "Ford style" pressures from above.

Similarly, a combination of minority investment and broad involvement with each other has made Ford's working relations with Mazda much easier than analogous relations with others, where Ford has no equity and less commercial impact. The alliance enjoys numerous joint activities, multilevel communication channels, joint planning and rationalization in some areas. Getting 25 percent of Mazda's profits also helps build acceptance at Ford.

Minority investments place mutual interest and relationship-building ahead of control. Some eventually lead to mergers. But this step seems most effective after firms have come to know each other well, see it as in their best interest, and understand how it will work. The emphasis on building rapport improves the chance of good working relations for the long term, regardless of ownership.

Building Lasting Strength

The long-term nature of minority investment alliances creates an incentive and an opportunity to help a partner build more durable strength. This can be done several ways. In one, the larger partner's funds are used by its ally for their mutual interest. At the time Ford bought its stake in Mazda, the Japanese firm was recovering from damage inflicted by the 1970s oil price rise. Mazda had invested heavily in its novel rotary engine, which was not energy-efficient. Ford's resources were used to restructure Mazda's balance sheet.

Similarly, Charls Walker applied some of its newfound capital to accelerate a planned expansion into environmental and other work. At Excel, part of Ford's cash was used to buy an injection molding capability to meet the new supply requirements.

Shared Activities. A second way these alliances build strength is through shared activities encouraged by the high-level bonds, such as joint design,

technology exchanges, and long-term planning. These bonds also create more latitude to experiment with different combinations of resources, as well as more room to initiate projects as need and opportunity arise, than is possible with long-term contracts alone. Excel and Ford, for example, each invests in mutually interesting activities, knowing its partner will follow through if an initiative proves fruitful.

Helping a Partner. A third way to build strength comes from knowing that it serves a firm's interest to help an important partner.

Excel's long-term strength, for example, comes from ongoing development of its ability to serve auto manufacturers' advancing needs. Ford people on Excel's board see a key part of their role as serving this objective. Excel gets substantive inputs from Ford board members, including descriptions of worldwide automotive competition and its effect on all companies. Ford's directors also advise Excel on long-term growth strategies to serve the entire market better. Moreover, they have made key introductions to Ford of Europe and Mazda in Japan.

While Bud Marx was on the board, he furnished understandings about Japanese transplants coming to the United States and the likely needs of other customers. When Dean Siddall (head of Ford's Glass Division at the time the alliance was formed) represented Ford, he contributed knowledge of glass technology. Siddall was asked by Excel to remain on the board after he retired from Ford, suggesting that the value of Ford directors has been more than just representing the auto firm.

For the same reasons, Ogilvy & Mather has been working to help Charls Walker penetrate the European market. Ogilvy's Jonathan Rinehart notes this is done primarily to help Walker grow: "I have a very strong feeling that, for the relationship to thrive, we want Charly to do well by it. We genuinely want to make sure we both profit from the relationship; we're actively desirous that this happen."

Transferring Resources and Activities. Deciding to shift critical work to others depends on one's faith in their performance. Durable high-level bonds help ensure this when the stakes are large.

Again, the experience of Ford and Excel is pertinent. Before the alliance began, Ford had built a plant in Fulton, Kentucky, to meet its requirements for shaped windows. Everything there was new: people, equipment, materials, production methods. Moreover, tooling was subject to design changes. These challenges made startup difficult.

Excel, on the other hand, had already mastered this art. It also had lower costs, high-quality output, the latest tooling and manufacturing, and the capacity to meet Ford's growing needs. Ford saw clear advantages in transferring its work to Excel. A minority investment alliance built the needed commitment.

Conditions for Minority Investments

Taking an equity position will add to an alliance only if there is underlying strategic merit to the relationship. An investment can enhance this value but cannot create it.

When AT&T bought a 23.5 percent stake in Olivetti, the two hoped to speed AT&T's penetration into European communications markets and to sell more Olivetti computers in the United States. For the long run, both firms hoped to combine their communications, computer, and software expertise in a frontal attack on IBM.

Yet the alliance was misconceived. Although AT&T had great tele-communications strengths, it had not done well in the U.S. computer market. Similarly, Olivetti is a strong office automation firm but had few skills in marketing to European communications customers. These mutual disappointments led to some well-publicized arguments, after which the alliance came to an end.[2]

Strategic Value Gets Priority

With a minority investment alliance, return on equity must take a back seat to the strategic dimension. Otherwise, financial gain will drive decisions and shift priorities from the partners' mutual interests. To meet this condition, the funds involved should be small in relation to the investor's worth, so it will be comfortable setting financial interests aside.

Ford, for instance, might at times get a higher return on the funds invested in Excel by applying them elsewhere. Yet the strategic value of their alliance plainly overwhelms such a consideration. Ford's 40 percent stake has a market value of about $30 million; Excel's window design expertise directly influences the appearance of Ford products worth billions of dollars.

The Investee Should Have a Narrow Scope

A minority investment makes sense only when the investee's business is sharply focused on products and markets with clear strategic value for its partner. The more this condition is compromised, the greater the chance that other priorities will interfere with mutual opportunities. There is little reason to formalize policy links when the investee's top management cannot give an alliance prominent attention.

Be Sure Basic Strengths Are in Place

If your firm is making the investment, limit its interest to solid, well-managed companies. Even with a voice in a partner's policies, you will have less than effective control. When this strength rule is violated, the investor must either pull out or invest more while taking control to turn things around. Acquisitions are hard enough. Saving weak companies is an even rarer art.

Making Two-Way Investments

When two firms are of comparable size, and each is focused in an area important to the other, taking reciprocal equity stakes can build the same close bonding that is possible with a one-way investment by a larger firm in a smaller partner. Cross-ownership between similar-size firms also causes less concern about dominance than is often felt in one-way deals with larger investors.

One such alliance bonds Chalone, the California winemaker, with Domaines Barons de Rothschild, the prestigious French vineyard. Initially, the two exchanged 6 percent of their equity, with a planned increase to 20 percent. To build strength together, they have exchanged personnel and technical information, and they help market each other's wines.[3]

Limits on What Can Be Done

A minority investor is not free to use its partner's resources for its own purposes. Fiduciary responsibility and corporate opportunity doctrines prevent an investor from taking advantage of its position at the expense of its partner or of other owners. Joint projects must clearly benefit the investee. Its business opportunities may not be diverted, and there may be limits on the transfer of proprietary information.[4]

Making Commitments

The objective is to create a serious commitment while maintaining the investee's strength and autonomy. Depending on the risks involved, a formal policy role may or may not be needed.

Dividends from the investment should be credited to the unit most affected by the alliance, provided this doesn't bias the unit's activities toward shorter-term or other undesirable goals. Ford's dividends from Excel, for instance, are attributed to the Glass Division. This gives the division an extra incentive to work for Excel's involvement in the design process.

As with all alliances, there should be plans for termination. To preserve the investee's interests, consider including limits on who may buy the stock. Remember this is a strategic investment that conveys a psychological commitment. A decision to sell is thus a negative signal about the alliance; it should be made for strategic, rather than financial, reasons.

Excel's chairman, Jim Lohman, observes that, from his perspective, both strategically and in terms of his firm's relationship with Ford, there is no meaningful difference between Ford's having a 20 or a 40 percent stake. However, if Ford took the initiative to reduce its share. Excel would interpret this as a decreased interest in the alliance.

Limit the Investor's Role

In Ford's alliances with Excel and Mazda, and Ogilvy's alliance with Walker, the larger firm restricted its stake to what was necessary to build effective bonds.

With Excel, Ford's rights as an investor are limited to policy measures that help sustain Excel's strength. Ford put no constraints on Excel financial matters. Also, even though it is a large stockholder, Ford has access only to publicly available data about Excel's business. There is a freer exchange of cost data on new designs than there might be with other suppliers, but Ford does not get all of Excel's data. The auto maker knows Excel's independence is part of its strength, so does not want to be involved in management.

Ford has even less policy influence at Mazda, and a limited voice in management. Similarly, Ogilvy has no control over any aspects of the Walker firm.

The power of Excel–Ford, Ford–Mazda, and Ogilvy–Walker comes from being true strategic alliances: independent firms cooperating out of mutual need, with shared risks and common objectives. Minority investments are part of the structure that makes this possible.

Now look at the alliance of publishers Time Warner and Whittle Communications. Unlike Time Warner, Whittle's growth has been heavily dependent on new publishing ideas created by its management team, led by co-founder Chris Whittle. Further, most Time Warner publications are aimed at broad audiences and carry a wide variety of advertising. By contrast, Whittle's are aimed at specific readerships and often have a single advertiser. With such differences there seems to be little chance Time Warner could run Whittle if the latter's management left. Yet Time bought a half-interest in Whittle, with an option to acquire up to 80 percent over the next five years. The danger of this incursion is that it goes beyond what is needed to build high-level bonds; it looks like an acquisition in disguise. After the alliance was formed, Mr. Whittle was reported to be considering entering politics in his home state.[5]

Choosing a Policy Role

Typically, the largest policy-level risks in a minority investment are a failure to build needed strength and a change in strategic direction away from mutual interests. Dow Chemical, for example, was squeezed out of an alliance in the photoengraving business when its partner deemphasized the area that interested Dow.

If your firm is going to be the investor, the best way to lower these risks is to choose a strong partner that wants to keep growing in a mutually agreed upon direction. Then the need for a policy role depends on three factors: your ability to add to your partner's strength at policy levels; how its policies are made; and possible management changes or events that might shift things from your initial intent. The last factor becomes more important with longer planning time frames.

To appreciate these principles, note that Ogilvy & Mather's stake in Charls Walker carries no voting rights. The firms' cooperation involves relatively short-term projects; Walker's strength hinges solely on the quality of its people—which is a clear indication of its future capabilities. Ogilvy keeps apprised of Walker's abilities through their working relationship and by paying attention to whom Walker hires and why people occasionally leave.

On the other hand, Ford's growing dependence on Excel requires that Excel continue to develop design and production capabilities to meet Ford's needs several years in the future. One reason Ford is represented on the Excel board of directors is to contribute its own understandings to these long-term strengths.

To help ensure that Excel will stay on course, the firms agreed to special voting conditions on critical issues. At least seven of Excel's eight directors (two of whom are Ford representatives) must concur on key decisions, including major acquisitions and financings, changes in business direction, and new stock issues.

Ford also agreed to vote its shares in favor of management's slate of directors. This kind of commitment gives management confidence in the relationship by making it more difficult for a third party to remove directors. On other matters Ford directors vote according to what they believe is in the best interest of all Excel shareholders.

Whether or not to assume a formal policy role also depends on the investee's style and ownership structure. Comparing Excel with Walker, Excel is far larger than the lobbying firm and is publicly held, while Walker is in private hands. Excel thus uses a more formal policy-making process, which requires a major investor to hold one or more board seats to take a role in policy-making.

Ford's minority investment in Mazda is different. Ford's influence comes primarily through the firms' needs for each other. Mazda is affiliated with the Sumitomo Bank (see Chapter 6), which plays a much larger policy role than Ford through its financial and management ties to Mazda.

The bank is represented at Ford–Mazda senior management meetings; occasionally its president visits Ford—sometimes as a courtesy, and at times to discuss business. As part of its role, the bank serves as an important communications channel on vital issues. Using an intermediary for this purpose is part of the Japanese style.

Ford occasionally uses Sumitomo Bank contacts to test positions on issues relating to Mazda, and occasionally to express its views indirectly to Mazda or to seek support on a matter about which it feels strongly. Ford also compares long-term views with the bank.

The Investee Comes First

For the sake of independence and other stockholders' rights, a minority investor in a publicly held firm cannot shift its partner's policies to serve its own interests. The people named as directors are obliged to represent all shareholders.

Ford's directors on the Excel board are at a sufficiently high level to understand the auto maker's strategic direction and long-term needs, as well as to be insulated from day-to-day working relations with Excel. Their independence is reinforced by avoiding discussions of working matters with others at Ford who are involved with Excel. To preserve Excel's independence, Ford people do not serve on any board committees.

Even so, Ford representatives on the board are present in discussions of Excel work with other auto firms. This is a board responsibility. To avoid conflicts or the appearance of conflict, they don't participate in such matters. Excel and Ford rely on peoples' integrity not to use this information improperly. Ford people have at times felt such dialogue has been close to the line. Jim Lohman expects them to leave board discussions voluntarily if their presence would compromise their impartiality.

Consider the Role of Other Major Investors

While planning an alliance, decide whether other significant investors would contribute to your purpose. Three-way relationships can be hard to manage. Different firms may have separate ideas about what is in the stockholders' best interests. For these reasons it may be necessary to negotiate others' departure and to impose limits on the sale of stock. If the investee is publicly held, you may also want to inhibit a third-party takeover.

Switzerland's Ciba-Geigy, for example, bought a stake in Spectra-Physics, a West Coast laser firm, as part of an alliance to pursue joint developments. Then another firm bought a block of Spectra shares and moved to take an active role in its business, which undermined the relationship the partners were trying to develop. Ciba's only recourse was to acquire Spectra-Physics.[6]

There are three ways to prevent such moves (none of which was available to Ciba) while preserving an investee's independence. One is to secure the desired access at the outset. This tactic is illustrated by Amstrad's alliance with Micron Technology, which gave Amstrad the right to buy memory chips in the future. Another defense is to keep enough stock in friendly hands so that an outsider cannot gain control. At Excel, for example, the combination of Ford and management ownership exceeds 50 percent, and Ford has rights to buy additional shares to match any other party's ownership percentage.

The third defense comes from an alliance's commercial value. Again, Excel is illustrative. Even if Ford and Excel management controlled less than one-half of Excel's stock, Ford provides a substantial fraction of its partner's business. If Ford were not confident a newcomer would operate Excel in a way that met its needs, Ford would have to withdraw, reducing the value of the acquisition.

How Much Equity?

In a minority investment alliance, the funds invested clearly serve a strategic purpose. While you might weigh tax and securities factors, the appropriate share of equity must reflect what is needed to get influence or strengthen the investee. Obviously, it takes more equity to have a greater psychological effect or a larger policy voice. The right amount is a matter of judgment.

Jonathan Rinehart, Ogilvy's vice chairman, did not join Ogilvy until negotiations with Walker were well under way, so he does not know why a 30 percent stake was chosen. He points out, however, that a much smaller investment, say 3 percent, would probably not be taken seriously; people would not think they could count on each other. Similarly, Ford's Bud Marx believes his firm's 40 percent stake in Excel makes a real difference. He notes that while Ford has some 10 percent investments in other firms, it has been much harder to get an internal Ford response with these.

Ford's 25 percent stake in Mazda is also a psychological number— for Americans. Among Japanese firms much smaller percentages, say about 5 percent, convey the same commitment.

Upper limits to ownership are determined by the need to preserve investee independence. They are often reflected in standstill agreements, which restrict the investor's purchase of stock and the number of board seats it may have, regardless of ownership.

One limit, for publicly held firms, maintains a healthy trading volume in the investee's stock. This was important for Excel in its negotiations with Ford. Further, securities laws in some countries, including Italy and Japan, grant automatic veto rights to investors with more than certain ownership percentages. Stay on the low side of this to support independence. Another limit stops short of giving the investor effective control. As a rule of thumb, some firms regard 30 percent of the ownership vote as an upper limit for this purpose. At best, this is a fuzzy concept.[7]

Partners in two-way minority investments often keep their respective shares small—on the order of 10 or 15 percent—to help ensure their continued independence from each other. Such investments are clearly expressions of mutual commitment rather than sources of capital.

Even with small stakes, however, cross-ownership creates a two-way bond, which is more exclusive than one-way investments. It can provide the same strong sense of dedication that is created when a larger firm buys 20 or more percent of a smaller partner.

Make It Work Like an Alliance

Remember that this is a strategic alliance; significant outside risks should be shared, and it is in the partners' mutual interest to look out for each other.

AT&T and Olivetti apparently were not aware of these principles when they formed their computer and telecommunications alliance. As part of the deal, Olivetti recorded a profit as soon as it shipped computers to AT&T, whether or not they were sold.

After more than two years of sales that fell far below expectations, AT&T slowed its orders from Olivetti and worked off the inventory it had built. This caused Olivetti's profit to plunge nearly a third, adding further strains to the alliance. At that point the firms combined their U.S. marketing abilities to sell computers, but the damage was done. Had they shared the marketing risks on a current basis, the partners would have had a stronger incentive to join forces earlier in their alliance.[8]

Follow the Principle of Shared Opportunism

It is not necessary for minority investment partners to seek a balance in their work together. Ford and Mazda, for example, draw on each other's abilities to design and produce vehicles, market Fords in Japan, and so on, without much regard for which firm is doing more or less of their total work together. Joint opportunities are driven by mutual interest and respect for the need to support each firm's independence to combine the best strengths of each.

Ogilvy & Mather and Charls Walker also see no reason for parity in the two-way flow of business between them. The firms recommend each other to their clients and engage in joint projects as opportunities arise.

This principle of shared opportunism offers considerable flexibility. It helps get the most out of both firms and eases adjustments to outside events.

When the Ford–Mazda alliance began, for example, much of the emphasis focused on supplying some of Ford's vehicle needs. By the mid-1980s the yen had strengthened so much that priorities had changed. The firms thus began working to pursue opportunities—including programs where Ford would be selling to Mazda—created by this shift.

Shared opportunism can be supported with benefits tied to each project. For a supply relationship, this involves revenue flows to the seller and needed inputs for the buyer, with appropriate risk sharing. In other alliances equitable benefits, such as balanced technology flows or other compensation, should be worked out.

Ogilvy and Walker, for instance, agreed that the business Walker generates for Ogilvy would reduce the dividends Walker pays. This is supplemented by a finder's fee, which is common in the trade. Even so, each firm's opportunity to offer its clients a wider range of related high-quality services is their most powerful reason to work together.

Be aware, however, that doing a substantial volume of business together may reinforce or compromise a smaller firm. For example, if the larger firm does not put the same emphasis on quality as its partner, or if there are differences in long-term versus short-term cost targets, then the investor's quality or cost priorities will come to dominate its partner's activities as the volume between them grows.

Conducting the Alliance

Compared with contractual alliances, minority investments can be far broader, with stronger mutual commitments. Such links must be supported by closer and higher-level management and organizational bonds and understandings.

A Need for Champions Near the Top

At the time Excel and Ford created their alliance, Ford was emerging from a history of antagonistic relations with its suppliers. While the firms saw ample need to cooperate, they carried a legacy of negative attitudes toward each other.

Fortunately, the people who negotiated the deal—Excel chairman Jim Lohman and Ford Glass Division general manager Dean Siddall— quickly developed a close friendship. This became an important part of the glue holding the firms together as they were getting reacquainted. Siddall championed the alliance within Ford, both on his own and with support from Edson Williams, then vice president of Ford's Diversified Products Organization.

"I don't think things would have gone well without the chemistry between us," Lohman says. "Dean was the only person 'working' for Excel at Ford. We had the same vision. My trust in his working to make things happen in our mutual best interest was critical to our getting going. This is not to say he didn't drive a hard bargain for Ford. In fact he did."

These events confirm common sense: Firms with larger differences between them have to invest more effort to bridge the gaps. At first, before there is any shared momentum, the only way to start building is with people who trust each other and see the same opportunity.

Ford's relationship with Mazda shows a similar pattern, but without the prior friction. Starting before this alliance began, when Donald Petersen (who later became Ford chairman) headed Ford's International Automotive Operations, he cultivated strong ties with key people in Mazda and in the Sumitomo Bank. Petersen was convinced he should be getting to know Mazda people and enjoyed doing so. He intentionally drew Harold Poling (now Ford chairman) into these relations.

Since those early days, Ford, Mazda, and the Sumitomo Bank have continued building personal relationships at top levels. Along with the firms' growing mutual needs, these ties remain an important source of strength in the alliance. Strong personal bonds have also grown between Harold Poling and Kenichi Yamamoto, Mazda's president until early 1988, and now chairman. This has continued with the new Mazda president, Norimasa Furuta.

Even when partner differences are smaller, close relationships between senior people help build mutual comfort. When the Ogilvy–Walker alliance was formed, for instance, Charly Walker and Ogilvy's Jonathan Rinehart developed a personal friendship that has become important to their firms.

Building a Shared Vision

Obviously, partners must share a clear sense of priorities. An alliance cannot function otherwise. In a contractual alliance, much of this vision is developed in the informal planning phase and reinforced by the formal agreement.

In a minority investment, especially for a large investor, the common purpose may be a small part of its total business. Further, different people from various units may work on separate projects, at different times. And there may be some organizational distance between those who forged the alliance and others who will carry it out. Then, a shared vision has to be defined and articulated.

To set a clear framework for their alliance, Ford and Mazda prepared and communicated a statement describing their common vision. It describes their goal to develop a close, effective relationship that preserves each firm's independence and improves the use of their resources.

The statement highlights their intent to pursue opportunities that strengthen each firm's competitiveness and to ensure Ford's and Mazda's profitability on joint programs consistent with each partner's contribution. It also notes their desire to improve interfirm communications and coordination to serve these purposes.

This declaration of how the firms intend to treat each other has proved highly durable. It has been confirmed periodically and used to remind people of their obligations when they have sought to shift priorities.

Needed: Continuing Senior Management Attention

While individual projects are managed by the people who normally have this responsibility, an expectation of wide, significant benefits should be supported by ongoing top-level attention. Senior management can make two essential contributions to this: visibility and reinforcement.

Here is how this works in the Ford alliances: First, each firm has a designated senior executive who has lead responsibility for an alliance. Within Ford overall responsibility for the Excel relationship is in the hands of the Glass Division general manager. He and Excel's chairman recognize each other as the appropriate contacts for top-level issues.

Second, regular high-level meetings that include reviews of joint activities remind people of the importance their firms give to the alliance. Ford's Bud Marx notes that placing joint projects on Excel board agendas helps catalyze needed actions ahead of board meetings. One significant role of Ford's representatives on the Excel board has thus been to ease multiunit coordination within Ford.

Similarly, Ford and Mazda annually hold two president-to-president meetings and two meetings of a joint senior management group. Agendas include reviews of joint programs and future program plans. Participants also discuss the business environment, economic outlook, major trends, and more. These meetings have a strong influence on individual efforts. Ford and Mazda program people iron out internal and interfirm issues ahead of time. No one wants to be regarded by senior management as a cause of problems.

Since Ford's alliance with Mazda has a far wider scope than its relation with Excel, more effort is made to reinforce this commitment. Signals from the presidents' meetings go out to employees in both firms, to reconfirm constantly the message that their alliance is important and everything should be fair between them.

To help build policy-level bonds across their cultural and geographic distance, a Ford employee serves as a resident director in Mazda and represents Ford's equity stake there. By agreement he has a voice—but no authority—within Mazda. A member of all Mazda senior management committees, he has wide access to Mazda executives and information. His role is to advise Mazda of Ford's interests, and vice versa.

These high-level practices have kept Ford and Mazda pointed toward the same shared goal and have contributed to better understandings and lowered barriers to cooperation. Mutual trust between the firms has grown significantly.

Visibility and reinforcement may be less crucial in the Ogilvy–Walker alliance. Ogilvy's organization is highly decentralized and emphasizes consensus management; Walker has a similar participative style. In addition, the firms' joint projects involve just a few people—minuscule compared to Ford-Mazda. Cooperation is thus far easier.

Yet the alliance is important to both firms, so top-level attention is still vital. Jonathan Rinehart and Charls Walker periodically sit down and discuss how well their firms are working together. This is an informal process rather than part of a formal control apparatus.

Within Ogilvy, the alliance's value is reflected in an active ongoing awareness of the quality of the relationship, at senior levels. Its status is included in Ogilvy performance reviews. To support these understandings Ogilvy has multiple information sources about the alliance. Further, its chairman occasionally contacts Walker and stops by in Washington to visit. Rinehart notes the significance of the relationship is such that any changes would be widely discussed among Ogilvy senior management.

Maintain Relationships Across the Organizations

In all alliances, trust and understanding begin with individuals. Yet, more than other alliances, relationships in minority investments must expand to embrace both firms.

Jonathan Rinehart notes that Ogilvy and Walker have gotten to know and respect each other more and more as they have worked together. Thus, when Ogilvy has brought Walker potential clients, Ogilvy has had enough confidence from its experience with Walker to know these contacts would be handled well, even when the person who became responsible for the contact was not familiar to Ogilvy. "I've come to know their music as well as the words," Rinehart says.

Such attitudes propagate more easily between small companies with participative cultures. Alliances that cut across large, multiunit firms need more structure.

Ford's various divisions, for example, are scattered worldwide and tend to operate autonomously to serve their separate markets. Mazda's operations, by contrast, are centralized and coordinated in Hiroshima. Thus as the Ford–Mazda alliance grew, coordination became an issue. Mazda complained it was hearing a variety of voices from its partner. More Ford people had contacts with Mazda, yet many of them had no experience in the Japanese culture.

For those reasons, and because of problems they had had with a joint car program, Ford and Mazda took steps to improve their mutual understandings. Each firm set up a staff function (Northern Pacific Business Development [NPBD] at Ford; International Business Development [IBD] at Mazda) as its side of a single interface where relationship issues could be discussed. Joint programs continue to be managed within relevant line structures in each firm, and program people continue to interact with each other directly.

As a complement to these links, the two staff groups, which meet monthly, have become a single forum for monitoring and reinforcing the alliance. The most intense relationships are within this context. People regard each other as members of a combined team. The significance of the alliance to Ford is illustrated by the fact that its staff unit reports to the president of Ford's automotive group.

Agendas for IBD–NPBD meetings cover individual projects, personality clashes, policy interpretation questions, identifying duplications of effort, and priority setting. Participants often go through all joint programs together to be sure both firms see things from the same perspective. There is also free time to raise other topics as needed.

In these joint meetings people spend more time discussing relations between the firms than they do on operational issues. There are very few topics that cannot be raised here.

Ford's NPBD staff gives Mazda a channel into Ford separate from individual project groups and gives Ford a unified approach to Mazda. It supports the development of a broader understanding between the firms, helps them move beyond optimizing on individual projects, and enables senior Ford management to understand the alliance direction for the longer run.

NPBD is responsible for maintaining internal understandings and increasing information flows about Mazda within Ford. The NPBD charter is to manage the relationship and point out issues that could affect it. NPBD may call meetings with Ford's president, ask questions, and help line managers get difficult issues resolved by surfacing these at appropriate times, placing them on the agendas of joint Ford–Mazda senior management meetings, and with discreet communications through its own channels.

Respect Your Partner's Independence

Like any alliance, a minority investment works best when each firm can contribute without fear of the other's unwanted actions. For a smaller investee, strong dependence on a larger firm can be a precarious position.

On the one hand, it gets valued business or resources; on the other, there is some risk of being dominated by its partner.

Maintaining a healthy separation is clearly necessary and may require specific attention. For the sake of trust, the larger firm should take the lead. Ford, for example, recognizes Mazda's concerns about dominance.

To allay these fears, Ford's NPBD staff constantly works to support Mazda's independence. People from this group go to individual Ford units, as necessary, to point out when a proposed project could hurt Mazda. Rather than judge what might be in Mazda's interest, they raise issues with Mazda early enough to understand its interests and head off harmful actions. Having direct access to Ford's automotive president backs up their views.

Further, Mazda takes considerable initiative without informing Ford. This has sometimes irritated people at Ford, but there is a broad recognition that Ford really needs Mazda to stay independent and that the freedom to move on its own is part of this.

The same concerns prevent Ogilvy & Mather, on its own, from deciding how to sort out occasional conflicts with Charls Walker Associates regarding various clients. Such conflicts appear in any large firm and must be resolved. When they arise with Walker, each firm's independence from the other requires that each must be satisfied with the resolution. At times, this has meant that some joint business cannot be pursued. But it is a minor issue in the context of the considerable benefit both firms get from their alliance.

9

Making Joint Venture Commitments

Too much stress on contingencies and on termination provisions is a stress on the wrong elements. The essence of a joint venture is mutual trust between the parents. Too much time spent worrying about failure can cause failure.

—Corning vice chairman Van Campbell

AS a separate organization owned by its parent companies, a joint venture gives the parents more opportunities to share control than other kinds of alliances. Joint ventures also have more room for friction.

Even in a single firm, people must overcome conflicting priorities to get results. A joint venture between two firms involves three organizations, which can cause still more confusion. To build a strong venture, goals, ownership, governance, benefits, and other features should be crafted to reinforce the parents' mutual commitments.

Corning uses termination provisions for just that purpose. As with all alliances, plans for joint ventures should include understandings about termination. This way, each partner can leave if it must. Yet Corning, which may be the most successful joint venturer in the world, wants termination to be difficult. Corning knows from experience that joint venture problems often stem from poor relationships. Having an easy out is a way to avoid working on these, when such efforts may produce the most value for both partners. In framing its exit provisions, Corning tries to create the attitude: "If you are unhappy, let's sit down and talk about it; don't just walk away."

Defining a Joint Venture

Firms create a joint venture to meet their separate and mutual interests. Discussions must cover everything important to each company and to the venture.

At Dow Chemical, negotiating and planning for joint ventures include "following each branch to the smallest leaf, to see where it leads," remarks one executive. Dow looks at differences in approaches to key tasks: "We do things this way, you do things that way." When significant differences appear, Dow and the other firm discuss which approach will be followed. For example, if one firm usually buys a material that will be important to the business, and the other usually makes it, they will decide which way the material will be obtained for the venture.

It isn't possible or even wise to address each contingency, but every major function, policy, and outside relationship should be discussed, as well as issues likely to affect venture performance. Be sure to include ethical, safety, and environmental standards, particularly as these exceed local mandates. Spell out basic assumptions to be sure you concur on the fundamentals. The more you probe each other's thinking, the better your chances of spotting conflicting approaches.

U.S.-based Tandy and U.K.-based Apricot Computers agreed to transform Tandy Computer Centers and Apricot franchises in Europe into a new chain of computer stores. However, their plans did not address how the marketing strategies of the two groups of outlets would be combined. When conflicts surfaced after the venture was formed, it was too late to deal with them. The venture was terminated.[1]

Much of what you agree on will be qualitative. Trying to quantify future performance in an agreement leaves no room for uncertainty. A summary of alternate scenarios, however, communicates your understanding of prospects. It is impossible to conclude how tradeoffs will be made when a venture is under way. There are too many contingencies. You have to develop enough trust and comfort with each other's approach to important issues to be willing to leave these for later decisions.

Be Specific About the Goal

The overall goal is the primary criterion for judging all other plans and activities. It is the basis for commitments and the inevitable compromises to be made with a partner and within each firm.

Whether the goal is to increase market share, become self-sustaining, get to break-even as soon as possible, or something else, you must agree on what is to be optimized for the long term and what constraints, such as minimal profitability or price levels, will be imposed. A five- or ten-year *pro forma* helps frame these understandings and reveals underlying actions and tradeoffs to be addressed. Needed compromises are made in this context as long as they don't weaken your central purpose.

There is no basis for a joint venture, for example, if one firm has a pure market share philosophy and its partner wants only to maximize return on investment. Such basic conflicts have undermined almost all of the more than one hundred joint ventures between American and Japanese auto suppliers in the United States.[2]

Each firm should develop its own understandings about a prospective venture. Substantial trust in another firm's views can only grow over time, as partners develop comfort with each other's judgment.

One European company accepted its new partner's market estimates without question in a misplaced spirit of demonstrating early trust. When the market later failed to materialize, the trusting partner still had to absorb its share of the loss.

Clarify and Resolve Separate Interests

Each company's needs should be explored at length. The greater their national, business, or other differences, the less likely it is that partners will share the same concerns. You may not agree on the best way to do things, but you must agree on what will prevail when you work together.

When Corning and Asahi Glass created Iwaki Glass in 1964, they failed to set a dividend policy. This led to a continuing debate, because Asahi looks at dividends as a percentage of par value, while Corning thinks in terms of a percentage of earnings after taxes. Iwaki thus has a larger equity base than Corning believes is needed. The venture is yielding lower dividends than Corning would have liked.

Iwaki's equity buildup also cuts its return on equity—a key performance measure for Corning. For its part, Asahi believes shifting to a higher payout would put pressures on prices and labor rates.

Another early Corning experience further illustrates what can happen when a firm doesn't communicate its needs. A chief Corning concern is to protect its proprietary technology. The firm's more commodity-oriented partners have not always had this in mind. Thus some partners have at times disclosed Corning know-how to help sell a joint venture's product by telling prospective customers, in effect, "Here is how we do it, and this is why we're the best."

Clearly, such misunderstandings have to be resolved when they arise. But they may reflect deeper conflicts between partners' basic objectives. These are best identified at the start. Disclosing proprietary information while marketing, for instance, may reflect a desire to win short-term market share at the expense of the long term, where a weakened proprietary position could hurt.

Respect Each Other's Independence

Two firms cannot have a productive joint venture if one fears a takeover by the other. Consequently, it is always a matter of good practice to preclude acquiring a partner, except on friendly terms. Further, buying stock in a partner may require opening a joint venture's books to outsiders. For best performance, preserve each firm's independence.

Be Willing to Adjust

With a goal that reaches beyond what either firm can do alone, each has to be willing to do some things differently. It isn't possible for a joint venture to combine the skills of separate firms unless both make concessions.

Here is what can happen when each firm tries to keep its own ways. Hechinger's, an East Coast marketer of home improvement products, and K-mart, the discount retailer, sought to develop a nationwide chain of do-it-yourself discount stores. Yet the companies were reluctant to give up their different styles. They could not agree on such basic issues as store layout, advertising, staffing, and merchandising. The venture ended on "philosophical" differences, significantly delaying Hechinger's entry into this promising market.[3]

Now consider the benefits of compromise. When Ford and Volkswagen joined their operations in Brazil and Argentina, the firms' shared goal was to become self-financing in this difficult market. Both made substantial adjustments for this purpose—including the way each did business, in their management styles, product development procedures, operations, quality control, and other activities.

This was a substantial undertaking. Their joint venture, named Autolatina, is the largest private employer in Latin America and the eighth-largest auto firm in the world. Autolatina has been reaching its planned milestones on schedule.

Be Sure to Recognize the Venture's Need

A joint venture needs assets, policies, and practices that enable it to compete in *its* market for resources and commercial results. Achieving this objective may require distinct financial, marketing, and other policies. For instance, human resource policies may include different salary levels, incentives, benefits, and educational requirements. Other policies may also differ from the parents', yet all must be acceptable to both.

Define Venture Boundaries

An effective scope separates parents' mutual purpose from their other interests. Define what is and is not included in the venture's markets, products, and technologies, and the field of parent commitments. Joint ventures that have unlimited freedom or leave future parent inputs vague may conflict with present or future parent interests.

Crédit Suisse First Boston (CSFB), a joint venture of Switzerland-based Crédit Suisse and First Boston, of the United States, did not have a defined scope when it was launched in the international bond market. So there was nothing to keep it from moving into investment banking and the merger and acquisition business a few years later. This put CSFB on a collision course with First Boston, causing bitter three-way battles over cost and revenue allocation, and contributing to the loss of senior First Boston people in the same business. Crédit Suisse eventually took over CSFB and First Boston; the latter's chairman and chief executive were replaced by CSFB and Crédit Suisse executives.

Similarly, when Corning and Asahi Glass created Iwaki Glass they did not require that all future specialty glass developments from the parents be committed to Iwaki. Thus in recent years, when Asahi picked fine glass as a new growth area, Corning's partner became a competitor in this market.

Use Phased Commitments

It is sometimes easier to make certain commitments after a specific milestone has been passed. This allows partners to resolve key uncertainties before getting more involved.

After nine years of a contractual marketing alliance, Astra and Merck, the Swedish and U.S. drugs companies, agreed to form a joint venture if Merck's sales of Astra's products exceeded a specific goal within the following two years. Reaching that point would justify the investments and management time required for a new company. The firms agreed on the commitments each would make and how benefits would be allocated, should that situation occur.[4]

Allocating Ownership and Governance

McDonald's is the only large restaurant chain in the world to have succeeded internationally. Part of its good fortune comes from the way McDonald's enters new countries. Knowing it has much to learn about local consumers, the chain prefers to rely on 50–50 joint ventures for this purpose. Thus, while McDonald's invests its substantial operating skills and share of capital, its local partners are involved as equals.

Jack Greenberg, McDonald's chief financial officer, reports that equality makes its partners more aggressive and innovative, and helps assure that local needs will be met. "They drive us with new ideas and stability," he says.[5]

Compared with McDonald's, many production joint ventures in the aluminum industry have unequal ownership and are managed by one partner. Yet the arrangements have not inhibited successful performance, even though some partners are also competitors.

Joint venture design clearly depends on circumstances. One important guideline is that a design should give each parent every reason to make its best effort. Another is that each firm should have the opportunity to protect its interests.

Assuring Continued Commitments

There are three ways a parent can support a venture once it is launched. The first involves capital contributions, made in proportion to each firm's ownership. The second is with goods or services needed by the venture, which it pays for if the costs are significant. Another contribution comes in the form of valued intangibles such as technology, market knowledge, or staff skills critical to the venture's core strengths.

Unlike capital, goods, and services, there is no easy way to price such intangible inputs. And with intangibles, you can't readily know if another firm has made its best effort to give support. If such inputs are essential, you want to be sure a partner is motivated to do its best.

In this case—as McDonald's illustrates—having equal stakes and governing as equals confirms both parents' continued importance to a venture and gives each the same chance to affect its performance. Most importantly, being on an equal footing gives parents the same incentive to contribute. By contrast, a minority position with a lesser governing role fosters the attitude, "They control it and get more out of it, so why should we do our best?"

To see how this works, consider Ciba Corning Diagnostics (CCD), a 50-50 venture of Ciba-Geigy and Corning. CCD is acutely dependent on continued know-how contributions from each parent. Doug Watson, president of Ciba's U.S. Pharmaceuticals unit, notes the parents' feeling of equality and their knowledge that each viewpoint will be considered foster a critical sense of shared responsibility and opportunity to contribute.

Watson observes that, while Ciba is formally committed to building links between its R&D facilities and CCD, the spirit of 50–50 gives it an incentive to forge strong bonds. He believes the same spirit might exist in a majority–minority arrangement but is much less likely.

Samsung Corning, the third-largest and most profitable TV bulb producer in the world, provides another illustration. This venture depends on Corning for its technologies; Samsung remains a crucial source of people and handles South Korean government relations. As a major industry group, Samsung hires and trains people for a central human resource pool. Individual Samsung units recruit out of the pool and also transfer people among them. Access to quality labor thus depends on being an accepted group member. The fact that Samsung Corning is a 50–50 venture and is not dominated by Corning makes a critical difference in its acceptance.

Now compare Samsung Corning with another South Korean venture, which has had endless disappointments recruiting high-quality local employees. For this venture, also with a U.S. partner, majority ownership is held by the Americans. Feeling less than equal, the local partner has offered little help in finding talented people. Consequently, performance has been weak.

Maintaining Balanced Treatment

A joint venture may become biased toward one parent at the other's expense. One way to prevent this is to require both parents' approval of major policy items. Still, these high-level controls do not avert product or operating imbalances that could harm a parent. If such imbalances seem possible, full equality in governance gives both parents the same opportunity to keep things on an even keel.

Take, for example, TDS, the magazine distribution venture of Time Warner and The New York Times Magazine Group. Because the group's magazines sell mainly as single copies, its publishers have developed close distributor relations. By contrast, most of Time Warner's magazines are sold by subscription and mailed. Single-copy sales are a small part of its volume. Before the venture was formed, Time Warner's various publishers had relatively little need to interact with distributors.

To keep its close dealer relations and to be sure it would get needed treatment by them, the magazine group insisted on a 50–50 venture. Both firms are equally represented on the management committee; decisions must be unanimous on virtually every issue. Since the group's volume would be smaller than Time Warner's, the partners have a cost-sharing arrangement based on their estimated shares of the business.

For similar reasons Autolatina, the Ford and Volkswagen venture, is also owned and governed equally. Autolatina produces Ford and Volkswagen products for its markets. Any management bias would create an opportunity to drift toward becoming the majority partner's product source by favoring that firm's product designs or delivery schedules. Equal ownership also helps Autolatina attract the best design strengths from each parent, since both have equal stakes in the venture.

When to Use a Lead Parent Arrangement

Obviously, full equality in governance takes more effort; you have to reach consensus on every issue. However, if both parents will not be making major ongoing intangible inputs, and if there is little chance of an operating imbalance, giving one parent management responsibility is appropriate. The lead should go to whichever firm has the most relevant skills and the strongest incentive to perform. The other parent gets a veto on important policy issues to protect its interests.

One aluminum smelter, for example, is owned by two firms with a 70–30 split. Each parent invested its share of the capital and takes its fraction of the output. The plant is managed by the majority owner. Occasional technical assistance is bought from the parents as needed. Although the firms are competitors, the plant's output is undifferentiated, shipment schedules are well defined, and there is no other way the plant could be used to give one parent an advantage over the other.

The same basic reasoning led Ford and Fiat's IVECO unit to use a lead parent arrangement in their British truck venture. IVECO runs the business on a day-to-day basis; the firms anticipate that someday it will become the full owner. Ford provides engines, transmissions, and some administrative services, but no intangible support that makes a major contribution to the venture's overall success. By forming the venture, Fiat and Ford ended their competition in this market, so there is no chance of imbalance.

Note that this venture is equally owned. IVECO was not well known in Britain, where truck buyers tend to be nationalistic. The partners believed a majority IVECO stake would risk the loss of Ford's market image.

Equal Governance with Unequal Ownership

Equality in governance usually requires equal ownership. Majority owners take more risks and get more benefits, so are naturally reluctant to share decision-making with minority partners. An exception to this rule is when one partner needs low visibility yet earns equality from its knowledge and experience, and shares the risks and benefits in other ways.

This can happen when a venture sells to one parent and must also seek customers among that firm's competitors. If a venture's product has unique value—for instance, if it is based on breakthrough technology—competitors that are prospective customers may be willing to overlook a parent's rivalry with them. Then equal ownership may not matter. Corning's optical fiber ventures, for example, have been able to sell the high-quality product to some, but not all, of its partners' cable-making competitors.

However, if product advantages are not unique, it may be necessary to do more to encourage others to buy from the venture. Ford Motor Credit Company and GE Capital, for example, have a joint venture that reconditions and sells used cars at auction. The venture, named GECARS, was created when Ford bought 20 percent of a GE Capital unit.

Ford took a small share to avoid discouraging other auto firms or dealers—whose participation is needed to reach scale economies—from selling through the venture. As long as GECARS's performance is equal to or better than competitive auctions, others have been willing to use it.

Parent governance in GECARS works as if it were a 50–50 venture.[6] This equality helps ensure that Ford's experience is conveyed as a full peer of GE. Ford has been in the auto resale business for many years; GE's experience is more recent. The auto maker brings substantial unique

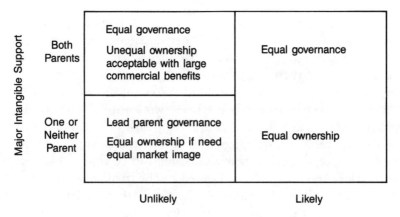

Major Intangible Support

Operating Imbalance

How Support and Balance Affect Ownership and Governance

knowledge as a customer about market behavior, dealer relations, auto reconditioning, cost controls, and pricing, which are important to the venture's success. Ford Credit provides about one-third of the venture's total volume. This gives Ford a strong incentive beyond its small stake to work to improve venture performance. It also gives GE reason to want the Ford inputs.

The figure below summarizes how different support and operating conditions favor particular combinations of ownership and governance.

Setting Ownership Percentages

A firm's stake in a joint venture depends on the value of its contribution. Valuing physical assets or a going business follows standard practice. Ownership shares are then set by the worth of each parent's investment, plus cash or other resources to get to the desired percentages.

When you are investing intangibles like technology or market access, it is hard to set an objective value. These inputs may have little worth when compared with the business that will grow from them. In this case valuation may be based on other, tangible assets. If both firms are investing only intangibles, the contributions should be taken as equal.

Committing Resources

Partners' investments in a joint venture should give it the strength to meet their objectives. This may include some part or all of the venture's product line, marketing, operations, and other abilities needed to respond to near-term forces in its market. Other resources, including those for longer-term strategic growth, may have to remain in parent firms to take advantage of their unique strengths.

Autolatina, for instance, must have a complete set of abilities to make and market its own product lines, work with thousands of local suppliers, add or drop dealers, and develop an integrated organization. The venture relies on its parents for contributions to product design. These are incorporated in its products, both to be compatible with the parents' global product lines and to reduce the tremendous design costs.

By contrast, CFM International, the GE–SNECMA jet engine venture, operates in the same markets as its parents and needs essentially the same capabilities. Virtually all its resources are contracted from the parents to take advantage of their scale economies and expertise.

The separation between resources that stay with parents and those assigned to a joint venture does not have to be at arm's length.

One joint venture, in the process industry, needed tight control of manufacturing because this represented a large fraction of its costs and strategic flexibility. Products to be made, plant loadings, timing, and other variables had to be under direct venture control. As part of this control, the partners wanted manufacturing represented on key management teams.

Yet the facilities were highly integrated into each parent's waste management, environmental controls, process research, maintenance, industrial hygiene, and safety procedures. Continuing those ties would be far easier and less expensive than establishing a new uniform set of standards and practices for the venture. To sustain those links while securing needed participation and control, ownership of the manufacturing assets was transferred to the venture. Facilities were then leased back to the parents to operate under contract. The sites are closely supervised by the venture, with the senior person at each site being a venture manufacturing employee.

Joint ventures, like all organizations, are subject to uncertainties about their future needs. To avoid having to reopen the basic negotiation, agree to provide more resources than you believe will be required. There have to be limits both parents can live with, but they must be broad enough to give the venture a good chance of success.

Dow Chemical, for example, would never enter a joint venture unless the parents committed capital well in excess of anticipated needs, subject to the venture's meeting stated milestones. If resources are needed beyond those committed and one partner can't provide them, Dow has sometimes agreed to dilute its partner's interest or to dissolve the venture and get each firm back to the starting point.

Planning Parent Benefits

Parent income from a joint venture may be any mix of royalties, technology fees, dividends, and payments for goods or services acceptable to each firm.

Since dividends are discretionary, they can be omitted when a venture is strapped for cash, which often happens in startups. For established ventures, Corning, Dow Chemical, and other experienced joint venturers set minimum dividend requirements both to encourage management discipline and to ensure parent benefits.

Usually continued modest support from both parents is not paid for. The idea here is that this is part of each firm's ongoing commitment. Yet if such inputs are clearly unequal, the venture may be expected to pay. Corning, for example, gets royalties plus its share of dividends from its fiber-optic ventures. This desire for royalties has caused some discomfort with its partners. But Corning's continued technology support reflects substantial ongoing R&D investments and has been an intense, critical contribution to improved performance in these ventures.

Management fees are generally inappropriate, except for joint ventures run by one partner without the other's involvement. A fee sets a precedent that any contributed management time must be paid for, which lowers the spirit of cooperation. Besides, a venture's own management is compensated by its parents through their share of the costs.

Shape Payments to Reinforce Commitments

The parents' split of income (or loss) should be fair over a likely range of business conditions. A different payout scheme for each parent can be divisive.

Several American–Chinese ventures have been hurt by friction due to such differences. The U.S. parents received markups on component sales to the ventures, royalties on venture unit sales, and a share of venture profits. The arrangement caused them to push for higher unit sales and lower prices to promote the sales. The combination more than offset their share of reduced earnings. The Chinese parents, in contrast, usually received no royalty payments and made no sales to the ventures. They thus wanted higher venture prices and profit margins.[7]

In another case, involving an American and a European firm, the European parent expected to be a major customer for the venture's product, so agreed to set prices it paid to ensure a healthy margin for the first three years. Meanwhile, its U.S. partner was supposed to be introducing cost-saving measures and marketing the venture's product to others. According to their plans, revenues from successful sales would lower the Europeans' unit costs. But the assured profit reduced the Americans' incentive to cut costs or to market. As might be expected, significant sales didn't develop until near the end of the three-year guarantee.

Two U.S. firms avoided this problem in a similar venture by agreeing to share startup expenses and by setting short-term earnings goals that would be unacceptable for very long. The arrangement gave both parents an incentive to work on cost reductions and encouraged the marketing partner to do its best.

Defining Transfer Prices

Airbus Industrie, the European commercial aircraft venture, has not controlled its production costs. Like CFM International, the jet engine venture, Airbus's manufacturing is done by its parents. Unlike CFM, Airbus's parents have benefited mainly from component sales to the venture and have had no incentive to lower their costs, which are passed along to the venture. This practice has contributed to losses exceeding $10 billion, requiring massive government subsidies.[8]

Most joint ventures don't have government backers with deep pockets. For this majority, prices for goods bought from parents must encourage effective parent cost control. Within this context, appropriate transfer pricing to a joint venture is guided by two parameters: whether market comparisons are possible, and the portion of a venture's total costs involved.

Using Market Comparisons. When a venture is purchasing items for which outside alternatives exist, market prices can be used as a guide. Venture and parent negotiate prices at arm's length. The venture may buy from other sources when doing so is in its best interest. Dow Chemical's joint ventures often apply this principle to material purchases.

Without a ready market substitute, a transfer price formula might still be devised by using a "market basket" of similar products for comparison. However, when a venture is buying unique or intermediate goods from a parent, it may be difficult to find comparable items or to determine their prices. Alternatives in such cases include using an accepted cost or letting transfer prices reflect actual market prices for the venture's goods.

Dealing with Large-Cost Items. Accepting a parent's costs is normal practice when they are a small fraction of a venture's total cost. This is how parent administrative services are typically priced to a venture. Sometimes a markup is included to cover marginal expenses incurred to provide the service.

When a parent's input is a large part of a venture's final costs, this arrangement breaks down. People are wary of significant costs they don't understand and can't control. One way to solve this problem is to make a detailed audit of the supplying parent's operations. However, since there are almost as many cost allocation philosophies as there are companies, you still have to agree on what costs are acceptable.

Ford and IVECO negotiators, for example, could not agree on Ford's cost allocations for engines made by Ford and sold to their British truck joint venture. The pricing issue was resolved through a compromise reached by Alex Trotman, president of Ford of Europe, and Giorgio Garuzzo, chairman of IVECO.

Cost-based pricing also inhibits a venture's own price flexibility. This can be a problem whether or not market price comparisons are possible. And, as Airbus illustrates, cost-plus pricing protects inefficient producers because there is no incentive to lower costs. Further, using markups on large-cost items can lead to parent conflicts, as demonstrated by the U.S.–China ventures.

Another way to handle large input costs is to pay the parent a discount from the venture product's market price to cover costs. Distribution

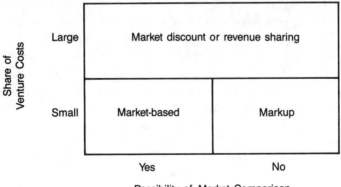

Transfer Pricing to a Joint Venture

joint ventures, for example, often give a parent sales revenues minus an agreed percentage.

In a venture that integrates substantial inputs from both parents, a form of market discounting can be used in which revenues are shared in proportion to ownership. Deductions are made to cover venture expenses. General Electric uses revenue sharing in its jet engine ventures. Arrangements are similar to GE's contractual alliances (see Chapter 7).

The figure below shows how transfer pricing methods vary with the possibility of market comparisons and with the fraction of a venture's costs involved.

Transfer pricing from a joint venture to its parents depends on whether the venture will be marketing to others. If it will, the parents must negotiate their prices on an arm's-length basis. A parent cannot appear to be getting a better deal than others, particularly if they are its competitors, or they won't buy from the venture. In other situations, pricing to a parent can be done any way that helps both parents maximize their benefits.

For joint ventures operating as cost centers, each parent covers the costs in proportion to its share of the business. Time Warner and the New York Times use this approach in their magazine distribution venture.

Allowing for Termination

At some point, even after a long and mutually productive relationship, changing circumstances may cause one parent to reevaluate its role in a venture. Whatever the reason—new priorities, a market shift, a reduction in the original risks, a change in the ownership of one firm—when it is clear parent interests are diverging, separation is as legitimate as when a firm spins off a long-held division. To avoid a dispute if the time does come, agree at the outset on how you will part.

When a joint venture is launched, building a mutual commitment requires that a future termination not damage its parents. Otherwise either firm may hold back to protect itself. This has consequences for a venture's beginning and ending phases. Once parents start transferring capabilities, there may be no way to get a return on the investment until the venture can stand on its own. If a parent will be seriously exposed until then, neither firm should have exit rights during this early period.

Ciba and Corning, for instance, agreed to have no termination provisions in Ciba Corning Diagnostics for the first few years to force them to work together.

After a venture is under way, one partner's departure should leave the other in a position to keep things going. In CFM International, GE and SNECMA agreed to concur on future customer support before either firm could withdraw. They also provided that the departing firm would give the remaining parent a complete set of drawings so it could continue on its own.

If you intend to put sensitive technology into a venture, you may want to have a say in how it will be protected should you depart. Possible alternatives include imposing restrictions on the sale of your stake and dissolution of the venture.

Although a "divorce agreement" is necessary, the process should not be simple, particularly in ventures whose strength must come from continued close cooperation. Problems in these often stem from poor relationships. Then, measures that encourage people to discuss their differences can be helpful to both sides.

Most of Corning's joint ventures, for example, involve considerable support from both parents. Corning gets the right of first refusal to its partner's shares if the latter wants to sell. Yet it avoids being precise about terms, such as specifying a valuation formula, which can make it easy for a partner to walk away.[9] The need to reach agreement on a value forces people to talk, which inhibits separation and can be best for both.

"Too much stress on contingencies and on termination provisions is a stress on the wrong elements," comments Corning's vice chairman Van Campbell. "The essence of a joint venture is mutual trust between the parents. Too much time spent worrying about failure can cause failure." When Corning chooses a partner it makes sure the firm shares these views.

10

Organizing and Operating Joint Ventures

We never fully recognized the venture's market had unique demands that required both of us to operate differently.

—Chairman of "Southern Medical," a failed joint venture

COMPARE Pekin Energy, a joint venture of Texaco and CPC International, with Ciba Corning Diagnostics, formed by Ciba-Geigy and Corning. Each venture began when one parent (Texaco and Ciba, respectively) bought a stake in a partner's unit. Both ventures are complete businesses. Both are equally owned and equally governed by their parents.

Yet there is a vast difference between them. Pekin Energy, which makes and markets ethanol from corn, has little independence. Pekin's product is a commodity; its parents manage the venture to maximize cash flow. By contrast, CCD has wide latitude to adjust its broad line of products and its marketing, operations, technology, and growth. One consequence of this difference is that CCD's parents are far more intensely involved in its governance. Parent relationships, while always important, are critical to CCD's success.

This contrast points to a basic feature of joint ventures. In some ways these alliances are comparable to wholly owned units: Joint ventures may be complete businesses, individual functions like production or marketing, or smaller parts such as a factory or research group. And like internal units, a venture's objective and strategy define much of its structure.

144

However, a joint venture involves two or more parents; so its design must also include their separate and combined performances. What this requires depends on a venture's working conditions, which can be divided into two sets.

Starting Conditions	*Operating Conditions*
Startup	Independence
Buy-in	Parent support
Merger	Integration
	Multiple parents

A joint venture's design must serve its parents' mutual goal as its top priority. Every aspect of the structure should further this purpose. As with any organization, design should emphasize easy communications, coordination, and control. Arrangements that sacrifice effectiveness for parents' separate needs or mainly respond to parent politics do not help their mutual interest.

International Aero Engines, a venture of Rolls-Royce and Pratt & Whitney, created an engineering office near Rolls's headquarters in Derby, England, and a marketing office near Pratt's home in East Hartford, Connecticut. According to Nicholas Tomassetti, IAE's president, this was a diplomatic move. But he notes that the need for close cooperation between those distant offices created "a management nightmare." The structure was changed to combine both functions at the same location.[1]

Each of the three joint venture starting conditions involves different efforts in venture development. A startup is an organization created where none existed before. With little prior momentum to build on, it is easy to set a new course.

In a buy-in, one firm acquires a stake in an existing organization. For this case, key aspects of the purchased unit must be preserved. A joint venture merger combines two established organizations, each with its own momentum. This requires a piece-by-piece assembly of a new organization from parts of the original units. Compared with other starting conditions, joint venture mergers require substantial efforts.

If one parent will have operating responsibility, its preferences must carry more weight in venture design. Even so, its partner's interests should be considered since that firm's ongoing commitment will be needed during the venture's life.

Planning Startup Joint Ventures

Startup joint ventures usually begin small. Like most new enterprises, such ventures are highly dependent on the kinds of people and skills they can attract. And like other new starts, these ventures cannot afford or draw all the talent they need.

Dow Chemical, which has launched a number of successful ventures spawned by new starts, solves this problem by loaning key people for a defined period. Dow assigns experienced top performers who can hit the ground running. Such people are often overqualified for permanent venture positions; many hold higher-level jobs in Dow. Without the opportunity to return to Dow, most could not be recruited.

Designing Buy-in Joint Ventures

With a typical buy-in, one firm acquires a stake in what was, until then, part of another company. (Unlike a minority investment, a buy-in joint venture is a separate entity under the full control of independent parents.) Less often, two firms buy a third, which they then operate as a joint venture. The same principles apply.

A buy-in is made because the investor sees significant value in another firm's unit and can add more value through its own contributions. Typically, much of the unit's original value is in its present strengths—products, technologies, operations, and so on. The creation of a buy-in must consequently preserve and build on this value. Two factors are important here: possible changes in the unit's momentum, and changes in key interfaces with others.

Continue the Original Momentum

Ciba Corning Diagnostics combines Ciba's substantial R&D skills in therapeutics (Ciba is one of the world's largest drug companies) with Corning's medical diagnostics business, which had considerable strengths of its own. When they planned CCD, Ciba and Corning agreed on a strategic direction that required adjusting the course of the former Corning business. Corning had become a fast follower in its markets by improving established tests. Ciba's knowledge of body mechanisms could make CCD a leader by developing wholly new tests. This attitude had to be infused by evolution, not revolution. It would be destructive for Ciba to come in as an outsider and suggest sudden changes.

So in designing CCD, the firms agreed on how it would evolve and chose not to assign any slots for Ciba. Ciba wanted the Corning people who had built the business to continue in their positions. Both firms believed they would be able to concur on future staffing. The partners' comfort with this crucial understanding grew from their negotiations, in which they developed substantial rapport and trust.

Thus at first, the original Corning management stayed intact. Later, when CCD was looking for a strategic planner, Corning asked Ciba to suggest someone with the needed skills who could also help build links to its partner. Both firms knew that assigning a Ciba person only because he or she was from that firm would have been dangerous. About a year later a Ciba manager became CCD's chief legal counsel when the position opened.

Pay Attention to Key Interfaces

Preserving value also requires healthy interfaces with key groups on whom a venture will rely. Either preserve current links or make changes that strengthen them.

For CCD, most key interfaces were with Corning and existing customers. Since the former Corning people kept their positions, these links were maintained. New ties were formed with Ciba to support needed technology transfers.

IVECO and Ford applied the same concept to their British truck joint venture, which included building new interfaces. IVECO Ford was created when Ford sold its Cargo product line and a related plant to a new entity owned equally with IVECO. Each firm also assigned its U.K. truck dealers to the venture.

IVECO would be the lead parent but was concerned about being effective in another culture. Differences included those between Ford's and IVECO's British and Italian staffs, respectively, and between the firms' operating styles. To support critical interfaces, key positions were assigned to people who were best equipped to manage them.

Since the operations came from Ford, the manufacturing director chosen had to be a Ford person familiar with those activities. Similarly, the top human resources executive had to be British—most venture employees were from Ford's U.K. staff. The sales director would be the lead contact with IVECO and Ford dealers in Great Britain; the parents chose a former Ford employee who was working for IVECO in the United Kingdom when the venture was formed.

IVECO Ford would report to IVECO, so the chairman had to be

from IVECO. It also got the top financial and marketing slots. IVECO was slated to run the business, and its principal objective was further penetration of the U.K. market.

Launching Joint Venture Mergers

Autolatina is a joint venture merger. It combines existing Ford and Volkswagen units in a new company, while the parents remain independent.

This kind of arrangement can come closer to being a true blend of companies' separate strengths than can conventional mergers or acquisitions, in which a firm's independence is lost. With the latter, one company usually dominates and adapts the other to its needs, often weakening the purchased unit in the process. Moreover, competition in the acquisitions market creates pressures to move quickly, to avoid losing a deal to others. This inhibits thorough planning until a transaction is closed. By then, it is often too late to draw the best from both firms.

In a joint venture merger each parent's autonomy helps it build toward a shared goal. Since the units involved are not publicly owned, there is less pressure to close. This not only allows more time to plan but offers a better chance to sort out differences before making formal commitments.

How Planning Should Work

Expect to invest more effort in designing a merger than you would with other joint ventures of comparable size. Building real synergy from a collection of disparate units takes a lot of work. Also, joint venture mergers usually combine former rivals. Unlike other alliances between competitors, which may begin gradually, mergers are all-or-nothing opportunities. Thus, while the needs to share information and to compromise are greater here, attitudes born of past friction can increase the challenge.

The story of tire maker Uniroyal Goodrich is instructive. Before this venture began, the tire businesses of Uniroyal and B. F. Goodrich were among the most profitable in the industry. Yet skills that contributed to each firm's success were not combined in assembling their venture.

For instance, there were no plans for meshing operations or accounting systems. Moreover, once the venture began, unexpected conflicts slowed interplant work flows and cost comparisons. Eighteen months after it was formed, Uniroyal Goodrich still lacked a marketing strategy and suffered huge, unexpected losses. The parents sold out to others.[2]

By comparison, look at how Autolatina was created. Ford and VW first developed a spirit of mutual commitment at the top, which then penetrated lower levels. As part of this, people from each firm paid attention to developing relationships with their counterparts as plans progressed.

Planning for Autolatina started when Ford's chairman, Donald Petersen; VW's chairman, Carl Hahn; and other top executives met over a period of several months to confirm the need for an alliance and to cement a shared commitment.

Once formal negotiations began, these early high-level bonds were reinforced by Philip Benton, president of Ford's automotive group, and Volkswagen's Dr. Günter Hartwich. Their willingness to resolve issues that might have become difficult set a constructive tone for the negotiators and for relationships among both firms' operating managers, many of whom would be moving into the venture.

Negotiations were led by Ford's Lynn Halstead (who reported to Benton) and VW's Paul Weber (who reported to Hartwich on Autolatina matters). The mutual trust and comfort Halstead and Weber developed with each other, and their positive outlook toward the venture, were clearly visible to others. This attitude encouraged easy information sharing and early joint planning, which could have been destructive if the venture didn't proceed.

Halstead and Weber were backed by an on-site negotiation task force composed of VW and Ford people from Brazil and Argentina, plus systems experts from the parents' headquarters in Dearborn and Wolfsburg. These experts helped plan the rationalization and, through their home base ties, eased acceptance by the parents.

Progress on the task force was enhanced by the participation of the CEOs of VW Brazil and Ford Brazil, along with other managers who would be continuing in the new enterprise. They had a stake in seeing things resolved constructively.

To encourage an atmosphere of mutual trust, task force members from both firms shared offices. This arrangement helped them develop mutual understandings and a sense of teamwork, and inhibited any inclination to protect confidential data. People were even exposed to each other's phone conversations since they were based in the same quarters.

The task force was led by a pair of Ford and VW managers. They began by explaining to the group why the parents were considering a joint venture, the negotiating objectives and timetable, and their desire for candor and mutual respect. They also confirmed, separately and to each other, that there would be no holding back on information sharing. The trust and openness between these leaders set the tone for cooperation.

Following a number of successful negotiating sessions, task force members celebrated their victory together with a party. By then, people from each firm had become friends.

Get the Best from Each Firm

Ford's and VW's commitments to each other created an opportunity to plan in detail, which resulted in vital benefits. First, careful planning helped people build mutual understandings about their goals, each other, and the path they would follow before the die was cast. Moreover, as Uniroyal Goodrich discovered, trying to sort things out once a merger is under way creates unnecessary confusion, a slow start, low morale, jockeying for position, uncertainty among customers and suppliers, and a greater chance that things will come unraveled.

In the Autolatina negotiations, the joint task force took a year to craft a comprehensive, mutually acceptable business plan. This evolved through twenty to thirty versions as different issues surfaced and each firm's needs became clear. The value of this effort paid off in Autolatina's smooth start, despite considerable cultural differences and a high-inflation economy.

Having detailed plans also made a tremendous difference soon after Autolatina began, when the Brazilian market unexpectedly softened. The plans made it possible to compress the rationalization timetable substantially.

As with buy-in joint ventures, a merger should preserve or strengthen important interfaces with outside groups. Planners for US Sprint, which combined the telecommunications businesses of GTE and United Telecom, seem to have overlooked this rule.

Rather than carefully phase the integration of different customer billing systems or develop a new system to replace them, Sprint tried to integrate all at once. The resulting confusion caused widespread billing mistakes, produced losses in the hundreds of millions of dollars, and angered customers at the very time Sprint hoped to build a stronger market base.[3]

For any rationalization, there is an advantage to a design that takes the best elements from each firm. Assembling parts, rather than whole systems or functions, also makes selection more objective, which avoids some of the "ours-versus-theirs" attitude more easily associated with larger units.

Here is how Autolatina's planners operated: Beginning with a common set of objectives and a list of issues to be resolved, the task force assigned a joint team for each major activity. The teams made detailed comparisons of Ford and VW in Brazil and Argentina, including organizations, systems, decision-making processes, individual functions, and parent relations.

To create an overall perspective, the negotiators set up ten-year financial models of the separate businesses and agreed how Ford and VW would perform if they continued separately. A similar model represented how Autolatina would look under different scenarios. The resulting plans came from a piece-by-piece development that drew from each firm. Plants were consolidated; product lines were rationalized to retain each firm's styling while sharing chassis, power trains, and other components; parent systems—including overall structures and decision-making processes, quality and inventory control, credit, grading and compensation, business planning, and product development—were blends. Planning for Autolatina was pushed far down in the organization to be sure each activity would work as expected.

Criteria for selecting items to be kept in operations were based on contributions to quality, cost, and productivity. This ensured the best possible combination of resources to reach the partners' goal of economic self-sufficiency. Further, using objective criteria helped win acceptance of the plan in each firm. In some instances elements from one firm or the other were kept to maintain a sense of equity.

Virtually every major Autolatina unit and procedure combines (or will when integration is complete) both parents' abilities. Some are equal blends, and some look more like Ford's or Volkswagen's, depending on the strengths each contributed.

For example, in product development, Autolatina adapted VW's engineering, testing, and specification procedures, and Ford's planning, market analysis, and product feature definition processes. Ford engineers were taught how to use the new specification method, which includes a radically different way of describing what goes into a product, and has different criteria for accepting the completion of engineering work and of various tests.

Autolatina's management system kept more elements of Ford's system of hierarchy and delegation of authority. The Ford process was germane to the need for clear control and the need to make tough decisions unique to Autolatina's market. VW's consensus process, by contrast, was more adept at making sure everyone accepted a decision. In the end elements of VW's system were integrated into the Ford system, with specific authority assigned to each position.

Autolatina was created to achieve scale economies in operations. It continues to produce and market Ford and VW products separately and maintains independent distributor networks. To avoid internal conflicts, and to treat each firm's product line fairly, a single product planning group was created to serve both lines. This group is dedicated to the success of both franchises in the market, just as Ford corporate designers are dedicated to the success of the Ford, Lincoln, and Mercury lines in the United States.

Separate Ford and VW sales organizations in Autolatina represent the needs of their respective markets to the product planning group. The sales organizations are the only units within Autolatina that are necessarily in contention with each other.

Quickly Regain Lost Momentum

In a joint venture merger, more than in other kinds of alliances, significant rationalization can hurt momentum and productivity. Ford and Volkswagen expected that to happen while Autolatina was taking shape. The business plan thus provided for disruptions that were thought to be inevitable.

To get beyond this quickly, the parents began coordinating the management of their organizations in Brazil and Argentina before a final agreement was reached. They also began committing funds and resources, amounting to tens of millions of dollars, to develop common products for the venture before it was formally launched.

Starting as soon as possible reduced confusion and saved money. Once the plans became public, there would be uncertainties among employees, suppliers, and others regarding what was going to happen. That could inhibit outside relations and constrain internal performance. Also, both firms were suffering losses; the sooner they could cut those, the better.

To reduce possible disorder, a great deal of emphasis was given to communications. As soon as they had a tentative agreement, the firms publicly outlined their plans. To build internal understandings Autolatina's senior management held several off-site meetings to explain why the venture was necessary and beneficial to both firms, to mitigate fears and uncertainties, and to begin creating a new joint identity.

Ford and VW expect it will take several years for the full rationalization and integration to be implemented; exactly how long it takes will be determined largely by product line integration and the time needed to develop new cost accounting, quality assurance, and other systems. In the interim, systems in individual plants reflect their parent origins.

Preparing for Independence

Like any organization, a joint venture needs enough flexibility to perform in its market. This independence increases with the number of activities—such as product line, pricing, marketing, operations, technologies, and strategic growth—that must be under a venture's control.

With few major variables, and in stable markets, governance emphasizes quantitative comparisons against budgets. This is typical of ventures such as CPC's and Texaco's Pekin Energy. For more independent ventures effective governance calls for solid qualitative understandings of the venture and its market, and more frequent adjustments to changing conditions. The evidence is clear that strong performance in dynamic settings demands more attention to control.[4]

Significant Independence Requires Close Parent Relations

As parent guidance becomes more important, it also grows more difficult. The richest information and best intuitive knowledge of a market or technology are found close to the action. The more the context differs from a parent's, the more the parent has to learn before it can provide constructive guidance. The larger the difference, the more one has to adjust to new ways. These factors increase the challenge for separate parents to reach the same conclusions and agree on needed actions.

Southern Medical (not the real name) was a joint venture between a medical products firm and a materials company. The two had developed a major health care advance based on a novel substance. Their breakthrough put Southern on a fast track in a field new to each parent. It soon had 50 percent of a growing world market.

Southern Medical prospered until its original products began to mature. This called for significant improvements and a new product line. Yet no new developments were under way. Even after the need was clear, three critical years passed without action.

Before that, both parents frequently disagreed about controls and product development. Each looked at the business from its own perspective. The medical parent was used to fast product and market change, while the materials firm was in the slowly evolving bulk commodities business.

Those conflicts were brushed aside in the time of rapid expansion based on the original products. When the need for new growth made it crucial for the parents to resolve their differences, there was no basis of mutual trust or understanding. Each firm saw the other's proposals as irrelevant to the venture's needs or as a way to dominate.

Relationships, which always had an air of distant cordiality, became confrontational. Although their styles were quite different, the parents never recognized the venture's market had unique demands and never even acknowledged their different cultures might cause disagreement on new product strategies. During the long hiatus, several competitors stepped into the breach. Southern Medical never recovered.

Unlike Southern Medical, CCD has greatly benefited from strong efforts on the part of Ciba-Geigy and Corning to build close understandings, a willingness to surface and resolve strategic and cultural issues, and growing mutual trust. As a result, control of CCD has evolved from a sorting out of differences, some of which were substantial, to a joint search for best answers.

CCD is setting its own strategic course. This is defined primarily by what is best for CCD in its market, and only secondarily by how well the course fits Ciba or Corning interests. CCD moves independently in directions important to its growth if it can build sufficient strength there. The parents use the best combination of opportunities and synergies to support this.

It was expected that, as CCD evolved, Corning's role could diminish. CCD might then become wholly owned by Ciba. Even before CCD was launched, the partners openly discussed that possibility. Ciba and Corning recognized that building a successful business would profit both of them; CCD had to be run in its own best interests.

Staffing for Independence

In any joint venture people must place loyalty to its goals and strategies above loyalty to either parent. A venture with significant independence should formalize this separation by developing its own staff.

At the start of Genencor, the industrial enzymes venture formed by Corning and Genentech, people were allowed to keep their jobs with the parents while on assignment to the venture. Rivalries developed between the New York and California staffs, who dubbed each other "Genencor East" and "Genencor West." Two years after it began, Genencor still hadn't developed a product or strategy. The situation changed after Genencor employees were required to resign from the parents. Their careers then hinged on the venture's success.

Today Corning people who transfer to a venture end their Corning employment. The firm makes a formal statement to each person that his or her loyalty will be to the venture. All signals are to come from the venture board. People are told, "We don't expect you to play Corning's hand," says Corning's vice chairman Van Campbell.

Corning and its partners integrate their benefits programs in domestic joint ventures, all of which are independent. Van Campbell notes that this is hard but worthwhile: "The mental set we want people to have is that you no longer work for Corning. You work for the venture." Corning people assigned to overseas ventures usually go for a short term and are expected to return home. While there, their allegiance is expected to be to the ventures.

Unlike Corning's situation, CFM International, the GE–SNECMA jet engine venture, has virtually no independence. CFM is an interface mechanism between GE and SNECMA and works in the same environment as its parents with essentially the same variables. CFM staff members are thus on loan from the parents and retain their separate benefits. Still, people assigned to CFM are expected to serve its priorities first.

Location Also Matters

Independence is also affected by a venture's location. Of course other factors, such as costs and access to customers and resources can also be important. But physically separating a venture from its parents helps it develop a unique identity.

CCD, for example, is away from its parents. For the same reason, European Vinyls Corporation (EVC), a venture of British-based ICI and Italy's EniChem, is headquartered in Brussels. EVC operates facilities across Europe; Brussels is neutral ground for both parents.[5]

Providing Parent Support

A joint venture should have the authority to decide what inputs best meet its objectives. Otherwise it cannot serve its parents' mutual interest and may benefit one parent at the other's expense.

The value of this rule is illustrated by Dow Chemical's early experience with a joint venture overseas. After lower costs became available from others, Dow's foreign partner continued to be a captive source of raw materials. The volume this provided helped Dow's partner sustain high capacity use. But the uneconomical dependence hurt the venture's profits and sped its demise.

Dow has changed its practices since then. Now its joint ventures are planned and run so that decisions about partner contributions are made by venture management, with board approval on major items. Dow's joint ventures may find their own technology, often have the right of first refusal to fund parent R&D within their scope, and get title to the results of sponsored work. The freedom to build their own strengths has been basic to the success of these ventures.

The Venture Should Control Coordination

Be sure to assign control over parent support to the venture. This gives management the authority and accountability needed to reach its goals.

Saab Fairchild International (SFI) illustrates what can happen when that isn't done. SFI was created to develop and market a small commercial airliner. Although the plane received high passenger acceptance, SFI was disbanded following unexpected losses due largely to poor coordination.

Believing its production capacity exceeded Saab's, Fairchild lowered its manufacturing rate to be compatible. At the same time, Saab quietly geared up to match Fairchild's higher capacity. The resulting mismatch threw off delivery schedules, causing skepticism and lost orders among prospective buyers.[6]

CFM International manages parent support differently. CFM is totally dependent on its parents for all its activities. The venture buys all hardware, assembly, testing, and product support from GE and SNECMA. Marketing is also contracted to the parents. The CFM staff consists of fifty people; in the parent companies thousands of employees work on CFM projects. About one hundred people from each firm and every discipline interact regularly.

All CFM program decisions are made by its executive office. Each parent is free to make decisions and changes in its parts of the program, provided these do not affect its obligations to CFM, the other parent's activities, or product technical requirements. Any proposed changes must be submitted to the other partner to be sure they don't affect its work. All changes must go through CFM to be certain each parent is aware of the other's activities.

CFM may also question any decision either parent makes about its work, on the premise that such decisions are not purely internal to either firm. CFM has the authority to reverse parent actions if it does not accept their effect on the program or customers.

Some Support Should Be Free

A joint venture should not be expected to pay for all the support received from its parents. Other benefits can be more important. Corning, for example, provides its joint ventures with free staff support in areas like engineering, finance, legal, accounting, treasury, purchasing, and marketing research. Having people who can be called on for consultation has proved to be an important source of bonding. Corning people build key relationships at operating levels and are a vital part of its institutional memory regarding ventures.

Corning doesn't charge for support services with modest costs because it wants the joint ventures to use its expertise, and doesn't want them to decide not to use it on the basis of cost. This support is not stipulated in Corning's agreements. Corning does charge direct costs for major new projects or expansions.

Substantial Support Requires Close Parent Relations

Significant parent support depends on mutual trust. Parents may agree, for example, to transfer all relevant technology to a venture. While know-how covered by patents can be monitored, there is no way except trust to be sure all appropriate information is shared.

Further, there is no practical way to monitor work inside a parent's organization. You have to rely on mutual trust to be sure things are done right. Trust also promotes flexibility.

For example, the CFM partners' agreement calls for unanimity on all major actions, including individual sales, before they are closed. Yet some sales are made by GE or SNECMA and then confirmed after the fact. Richard Shaffer, director of airline sales, observes: "We know each other so well each partner can take some risks and be assured the other will go along."

Integrating a Joint Venture

As with significant independence and parent support, more integration takes more effort, trust, and understanding.

Integration Requires Good Parent Relationships

When US Sprint was formed, the parents' telecommunications networks and billing systems were radically different. Integrating them was an enormous challenge. Moreover, the market was in rapid flux, requiring quick development and implementation of a coherent business plan. Yet the venture began with the parents wrangling over which firm would have control and suffered continued feuds over the direction of the business.

The discord at higher Sprint management levels inhibited integration in the ranks. Conflicts between marketing and operations led to product offerings, including toll-free 800 numbers, WATS lines, and the highly promoted FON credit card, which Sprint couldn't support.

Clashes between the conservative style of former GTE employees and the free-wheeling ways of people from United Telecom led to conflicting programs. A series of three CEOs in two and a half years underscored the turmoil. Finally, United bought GTE's stake. "When you have a two-headed horse you often want to go in separate directions," William T. Esry, United's CEO, observes.[7]

Contrast this experience with Autolatina, which is larger than US Sprint and more complex. Like Sprint, Autolatina required an extensive integration of people, products, and operations in a challenging environment. However, Autolatina was more demanding. To combine two massive organizations, the parents worked through Argentine, Brazilian, German, American, Ford, and Volkswagen cultures. Like Sprint, Autolatina is governed equally by its parents. Yet Autolatina's integration has progressed as planned, and this joint venture has been meeting its objectives.

Hallmarks of Autolatina's success include strong high-level bonds between Ford and VW, an intensive planning effort that probed the details of integration in great depth, and the appointment to the venture of senior people with outstanding relationship skills. Further, the Autolatina board has been a decisive force in encouraging integration through its own consensus style and its focus on integration issues within the organization.

Eliminate Barriers Between People

Effective integration removes obstacles between people. Again, Autolatina is illustrative. Since Autolatina required substantial integration, it was important to break through cultural patterns by avoiding having "VW" or "Ford" units—except in marketing, where product line separation was essential. Human resource plans thus involved two kinds of integration, which were introduced when Autolatina began.

One kind was vertical: The second person in a function was generally from a different parent than the top person, and so on down the line. This arrangement was occasionally moderated by the availability of talent, the demands of geographic location, and the desire to emphasize Ford or VW strengths in particular areas. The other integration was across the organization: There is an approximate 67–33 VW/Ford allocation of slots in every office and unit, reflecting the 40 percent and 20 percent VW and Ford market shares.

When people will be together for a long time, persistent differences in how they are treated can inhibit integration. CPC managers who moved to Pekin Energy, for example, are paid more than Texaco people in comparable positions. This has caused some problems in Pekin.

Integration can sometimes be bolstered by dual-slot staffing. This has the most value as a temporary measure to develop new understandings. In the original CFM International structure, each functional director had a deputy from the other parent. The arrangement was awkward because of cultural differences and some vagueness about who had what authority. But it proved to be quite helpful in integrating the parents' work. CFM evolved away from this as mutual understandings grew.

Multiple-Parent Ventures

In the early 1970s, the New York Times Magazine Group participated in a distribution joint venture with a number of other publishers. However, with several owners it was hard to decide on direction and get needed responses from the venture. Eventually, it failed.

Airbus Industrie, the European aircraft manufacturer, owes its tremendous commercial success to a pair of strong engineering and marketing executives who spent a decade welding together the four parents' contributions. However, tension between the several different factions on Airbus's board long inhibited the financial reforms needed to stem its multibillion-dollar losses.[8]

Corning has also been involved in joint ventures with more than two active parents. It, too, has found these a greater challenge to govern. Corning has learned that, as hard as it is to build trust and resolve issues between two firms, it is far more demanding with three.

One Corning venture is in the optical fiber business, like several others. Despite this similarity, having three parents has made quite a difference. "It has been like a three-ring circus," reports a Corning executive.

Joint ventures with significant independence, support, or integration and more than two active parents are by nature hard to run. Such ventures typically require parent equality in governance. Yet it is far more difficult to keep things balanced and fair when three or more parents are all trying, in concert, to guide an independent venture, or to adjust changing support activities, or to manage the integration of several cultures.

For these reasons, multiparent joint ventures work best when only one or two parents are active in governance.* Other parents may enjoy the benefits of co-ownership but should not play a central role.

One common form of this kind of joint venture is a facility with several owners, managed by one of them. A high-technology communications cable across the Atlantic Ocean, for example, is owned by a joint venture of twenty-nine European and North American telephone companies. The cable was installed by AT&T, one of the owners, which also operates it.[9]

Consider Corning's participation in Genencor, the industrial enzymes venture it launched with Genentech. At a time when Genencor needed additional parent capital, Corning's optical fiber joint ventures were also growing and had similar needs. Corning did not have the funds to serve both, so brought in Kodak and Staley as new parents while it became a passive investor. Since then, Genentech has also taken a more passive role, while Kodak and Staley have become quite active.

Each parent has one person on Genencor's executive committee. With several firms involved, it has been difficult to make all the relationships work. Even so, reaching a consensus is not as arduous as it would be if Genencor were in the same business as any of its parents. "If Genencor starts moving into one partner's backyard there could be problems," says a Corning executive.

---

* Consortia, which are many-parent joint ventures, follow the same principles. They seem to work best when they pursue activities involving at most modest support and incremental change, from each member's perspective.

11

Governing Joint Ventures

Keep in mind that you and your partner must live together. While you certainly have to be as tough as possible about protecting your own interest, you also have to understand your partner's interests. Otherwise the joint venture will be damaged.

—Giorgio Garuzzo, chief executive, IVECO Fiat SpA

ONE presumed truth about joint ventures is that decisions take longer with two parents. However, it doesn't have to be that way. With effective governance, decision-making can be faster than it is in either parent.

Ciba Corning Diagnostics, for example, is responsible only to its board. It has no reason to get embroiled in the morass of Ciba and Corning paperwork and committees. To be sure, CCD didn't start like this. At first, Ciba board members were inclined to take decisions back to Ciba. After much board discussion about this, Ciba people agreed that if the board could fund a decision, it should make it.

Board members have since confirmed to each other how much easier it is to make decisions on their own than to get the usual approvals in each firm. A golden rule emerged: "If you want to clear a decision at home that is okay—but do it before the next board meeting."

Decision-making is, of course, slowed by the need for consensus. But as CCD illustrates, giving a board full authority over a venture avoids each parent's internal bureaucracy.

More significantly, parent delegation to a venture board is needed for effective performance. To serve its parents' objective, a joint venture must work as a single organization with clear and consistent signals coming from the top. This is possible only if the board itself functions as a coherent team. Without authority to govern, board members have little reason to build together. They are simply conduits to their employers.

Building an Effective Board

At the start of a joint venture, its board of directors is a crucial link that converts understandings developed in negotiations into a functioning enterprise. Later on, as the venture's highest policy-making body, the board continues to be the place where parents' knowledge of each other and their venture grows. It is where decisions and compromises are made in response to parent and venture needs.

Board members are responsible for asserting and protecting their own companies' interests, meeting their partner's needs, sustaining the atmosphere of trust and common purpose on which a venture depends, and exercising effective control.

The Board Must Control

Look at Warner Amex, the cable TV joint venture. Initially, the parents, American Express and Warner Communications, gave management vast autonomy. In its zeal to win urban franchises, Warner Amex greatly overestimated demand and underestimated costs. In an early year it lost $150 million before taxes. When things turned sour, each parent imposed its own rules.

Drew Lewis, who was then brought in as CEO, found "a company out of control. You had two firms with diverse views on almost everything that came up, and we had people all over us from both trying to call every shot."[1]

Except for major changes or new commitments, which may go as far as each parent's board, a joint venture board should decide all policy questions. Among these are large investments, loans, commitments to parents or others, asset sales, plans and budgets, dividends, and changes in scope, product line, financial structure or direction.

When parents are equally involved in governance, the board must exercise operating control, either directly or through an executive committee. The alternative, as Warner Amex's parents learned, is vague or inconsistent supervision and poor performance.

Even when one parent accepts operating control, both usually have future commitments to a venture and may be affected by its actions. They consequently have to agree on major policy items.

British-based truck maker IVECO Ford is operated by Fiat's IVECO unit. Ford and IVECO agreed to share profits and losses equally with no limit and to maintain the initial equity level on the same basis. In addition to these future commitments, changes in the joint venture could affect other Ford or IVECO activities, so the parents share important decisions.

To secure a board's governance, directors from each parent must control all policy links between the venture and their firms. Parent staff work may be done between board meetings to support decisions—but under the authority of each firm's board members. This arrangement may require internal parent changes.

When Autolatina was formed, for example, direct policy ties between Ford corporate staff in Michigan and Ford's operations in Brazil and Argentina were ended. These links are now made only through Ford board members. Technical support relationships were not changed. These do not affect Autolatina policy and must be as direct as possible to be effective.

Joint Venture Boards Are Different

There is a sharp contrast between boards of joint ventures and those of other companies. Unlike the directors of most publicly held firms, many of whom are present only as individuals, people on joint venture boards both represent and encourage their firms' commitments. To keep a joint venture on course, resolve differences, and maintain balance, board members need more information about the business and each parent's needs. They must also be more active than directors of comparable public firms.

Most joint ventures have just two owners. Boards of publicly held firms often represent a diverse and even transient ownership.

In joint ventures, top managers participate in board meetings but usually do not vote. At other kinds of firms management frequently dominates the boards. In those boardrooms, dissent is stifled by an etiquette that leads directors to vote for a CEO's proposals even when they disagree.[2] On a venture board, differences on issues in which both parents have a say must be surfaced and resolved before things can proceed.

Parent managers who serve on joint venture boards often have no earlier board experience. Yet being a manager is quite different from serving as a board member. Managers have far more opportunity to interact with and guide the work of their subordinates. A board of several people is too unwieldy for this. It has to expect management to propose plans and make modifications in response to board concerns. The board, in turn, must reach a consensus to give management clear guidelines.

In the early days of CCD, Ciba people, who had no prior joint venture board experience, went beyond expressing their views to voicing their individual desires about what CCD management should be doing. The prevailing attitude was that when management brought the board a proposal, the board's job was to develop alternatives before reaching a conclusion. The resulting confusion significantly inhibited CCD progress until this was resolved.

The Board Needs Balanced Expertise

Be sure to give a board the full set of expertise needed to provide sound guidance. Dow Chemical tries to anticipate the types of issues a joint venture will face and the magnitude of the decisions to be made. It then selects people who are more than capable of handling these. Dow also knows in advance whom its partners will put on a board and tries to ensure compatibility.

Board members must be able to deliver their organization's support and feel personally responsible for doing so. Ciba helped ensure that its R&D know-how would flow to CCD by winning its R&D chief's acceptance before the venture was approved and by giving him a board seat. Despite internal Ciba concerns that his schedule would not permit board membership, his participation was seen as vital. Ciba made a conscious effort to get him on the board to cement his contribution. Corning placed its R&D chief on the board for the same reason.

Having a senior corporate executive on a board signals a venture's importance to your partner and to your own troops. For example, Dr. Gaudenz Staehelin, a member of Ciba's corporate executive committee, initially served on the CCD board to show Corning how important the venture was to Ciba. His presence also helped marshal support at Ciba. When CCD began, it was relatively small in the context of the giant drug and chemical firm, but the parents had great expectations.

Similarly, Corning's chairman, Jamie Houghton, sat on the board to indicate CCD's importance to Corning. CCD was formed when Ciba bought a half interest in a Corning business, so Houghton's presence was also intended to let Corning's former employees know they were not being cast adrift.

In filling board positions, it may be necessary to have people from different management levels. Managers who are far above the relevant activities have neither the knowledge nor the direct influence to contribute. Those who are too low don't have enough authority. Directorships should thus be assigned by needed position. The right people are often found at different levels.

Corning's joint venture boards, for example, have people from as many as three management levels. The board of IVECO Ford includes the chief operating officer of Ford of Europe, which distributes IVECO Ford trucks there, plus operating people in positions to help. Ford's U.K. treasurer, rather than its chief financial officer, has a seat because raising cash in the United Kingdom is necessary, and that is his normal role.

For similar reasons, a board chairman should not necessarily be the highest parent delegate. This position ought to go to the senior person who is close enough to understand the venture. For example, when Houghton and Staehelin were on the CCD board, Corning's Marty Gibson, group president for health products, was the first chairman. He was followed by Doug Watson, president of Ciba's U.S. pharmaceutical division.

With different management levels on a board, things work best if parent hierarchy is kept out of board relationships. Each person is there to contribute as a director. The venture loses if directors are inhibited by internal politics. Of course, people tend to defer to the highest-ranking executive in a meeting. This person contributes to a board's effectiveness by avoiding a dominant role and letting the venture chairman run things.

Except in East Asia (where cultural forces more closely align managers' interests with those of their firms) joint venture employees usually do not get board seats. This helps to separate management from parent controls, giving a venture a clearer sense of its own identity. It also avoids the difficult task of building a consensus among three, rather than two, sets of interests. However, a venture's senior management should attend board meetings to understand the board's thinking.[3]

Filling Management Positions

A joint venture's top executives should initially come from its parents. This helps transfer parent skills and moves early understandings about the venture into practice. Select the best candidate for the job, regardless of such other factors as which parent brings the most business or the largest value-added technology.

US Sprint's experience highlights what can happen when this rule is violated. Sprint began with GTE dominating senior levels, apparently because it was larger and brought more business to the deal than United Telecom, Sprint's other parent. Yet GTE control of the units it contributed to Sprint had been weak. Also, most top managers from GTE had far less long-distance experience than people from United. Besides, much of GTE's outmoded network had to be replaced with the type of advanced system United had already installed. The bias toward GTE management seems to have been a major factor behind Sprint's early problems.[4]

Choosing the Chief Executive

A joint venture's top executive reports to the board on policy matters and to the lead parent, if there is one, on operating items. The CEO takes the initiative on new issues, steers proposals through the board, looks out for parent interests, and keeps board members informed between meetings.

Although a lead parent normally appoints the CEO, he or she must have the confidence of both parents to be effective. There should be a mechanism for removing the CEO for good reason at either parent's initiative.

To build on parents' initial enthusiasm, a joint venture should get off to a fast start. The first CEO should thus have in-depth knowledge of the business, plus skills to build the new team and support links to the parents, if these are important.

In a venture between Dow Chemical and Italy's Oronzio de Nora (ODN), ODN wanted the CEO position, and it made sense for the Italian firm to have it. ODN had been in a closely related business for many years and had developed relevant business skills and market knowledge. Dow had experience in the technology and its use, but not in the markets. The venture also represents a larger piece of ODN's total business than it does of Dow's. Dow expects to gain this experience over time. The next CEO may not be from ODN. The decision will be made through bargaining and candidate evaluation.

The chief executive typically has less control over a venture's senior staff than in a wholly owned unit, especially during the early years, when relationships are new. If there is to be significant staffing from each parent, the CEO must be accepted as a leader beyond the limits of formal authority.

To the extent a venture differs from its parents, its leadership must promote the new style. Corning's U.S. optical fiber joint venture with Siemens, for example, operates in a highly competitive market. It needs more independence than some of Corning's other fiber ventures, which market more heavily to government telecommunications agencies with which Corning's partners have close ties. To build the needed style, Corning has given this venture entrepreneurial CEOs.

Choosing Other Senior Managers

Control of a joint venture can be enhanced by filling some management positions with parent employees. This aspect of control is implicit. The objective is not to place your people in a venture and discreetly influence them. Rather, the values, experience, and judgment of tenured employees have been shaped in your organization. Assigning people to a venture helps transfer expertise, ensures things will run as expected, and promotes the venture's understanding of its parents.

Going beyond these tacit links damages consensus governance. Each parent should inform its people that their allegiance must be to the venture. Since the employees assigned to a venture are there to serve its purpose, their performance must be evaluated by venture management. If parents will be reimbursed for their salary and benefits, these must be tied to evaluations in the venture.

Once under way, all management slots are filled by a venture's CEO, except for positions designated for either parent. The people named to senior positions must meet the venture's starting and operating conditions (see Chapter 9). CFM International, for example, must continue to draw on GE and SNECMA people to manage parent support. Knowledge of the inner workings of each firm is essential for these jobs. Equally governed joint venture mergers should have some parity at the top to foster a sense of organizational equality.

Reserving positions for either parent beyond what is absolutely necessary limits a venture's performance and inhibits integration. The most essential positions are, almost by definition, the hardest to fill. Designating these for one parent or the other restricts the already small talent pool upon which a venture can draw.

To launch Autolatina, the chief executive slot was designated for VW and the chief operating officer for Ford. These positions reflect the skills each parent brought to the venture and the fact that VW invested a much larger fraction of its total business than did Ford. Ford took the senior financial position, while VW filled the top manufacturing, supply, and product development slots. These assignments helped draw on parent strengths during the startup phase. Subsequently, managers were chosen because they were the best qualified, regardless of which parent they were from. Selection criteria included interpersonal and technical job skills.

For any kind of joint venture, equal staffing of key positions is not the same as equal control—as CCD illustrates. In addition, mutual interests and high staff morale are best served by finding the most appropriate person for each slot. Consider that CFM International gets two-thirds of its people from GE. Because it is smaller than GE and has a different marketing background, SNECMA has fewer people with relevant experience.

Information for Venture Control

As with other organizations, joint venture governance builds on information from periodic reports, meetings, and informal contacts between management and board.

Some care is needed to avoid overloading a venture. Each parent typically has its own information needs. These can include separate strategic reports and operating summaries to fit each firm's control system, along with information to match different fiscal periods, accounting and financial practices, and tax and customs requirements.

Consequently, joint ventures may be asked to produce more information for their parents than similar wholly owned corporate units. This can be a heavy burden. Extra staff time is needed, and management has to divert attention from venture business to regularly review and approve two sets of documents.

Reducing separate reporting requirements can make things less burdensome. In most organizations, some information is required because it might be needed but is actually rarely necessary. This is the best kind of data to avoid. Strong venture CEOs help ward off some formalities by pointing out how double paperwork deflects time and effort from more pressing activities.

Extra reporting demands have been an ongoing issue in Corning's joint ventures. To reduce these, Corning often recasts the numbers it gets from a venture to fit its own needs rather than ask for separate reports.

Usually, the largest information needs occur during a venture's early years. This is a time of intense cooperation as initial plans are translated into actions. Much of the information needed then is qualitative or for comfort, as partners get to know each other and shape their venture. This kind of data flows most easily in face-to-face interactions between board members and venture management. It is better to have more frequent board meetings than to keep your distance and ask for lengthy reports.

If one parent has accepted operating control, the other should be able to reduce its reporting requirements. IVECO and Ford negotiators, for example, developed an absolute minimum reporting system to avoid a double load on their venture. Ford agreed to seek information only to meet statutory and basic budget needs. IVECO came close to the same position. However, since it would be operating the venture, IVECO's information needs were stressed. Even so, IVECO Ford has much less formal reporting than either parent normally requires for its own operations.

Governing Lead Parent Joint Ventures

It can be easier to operate a joint venture with one parent in charge than with equal governance. With a lead parent you don't have to reach a consensus on every question and can avoid some cultural confusion. Having a lead parent makes sense if there is little chance of operating imbalance and both parents do not provide critical intangible support (see Chapter 9).

Assigning Authority

In a lead parent arrangement, one firm runs the venture as an internal division. Key executives owe their allegiance to that parent. Operating controls are designed to meet its needs.

When one firm agrees to operate a joint venture, its partner gets the right to veto decisions affecting its commitments and venture policies. Nevertheless, on issues where the lead firm has final authority, keeping good relations requires that it hear its partner's views.

IVECO Ford is managed on a day-to-day basis as if it were an IVECO company. The venture's employees even participate in IVECO management meetings. The board, which meets three time a year, does not formally review operations, with the exception of items provided for in the shareholders' agreement. Informally, however, Ford gets all the operating information it wants.

To protect Ford's interests, the shareholders' agreement requires unanimity on major issues like substantial commitments, withdrawing from the market, and changes in products or employment practices that could affect Ford's U.K. activities. There is also a set of items, including the annual profit and capital investment budgets, operating plan, and borrowing program, which must get majority board approval. Since IVECO has the majority it may pass these.

However, the requirement for board approval gives Ford a chance to present its views before action is taken. Ford would be paying one-half of any loss if IVECO Ford were not run well; it wants to be heard on such items at the board level. There is also a class of topics requiring board review, but not approval, before management acts.

The IVECO Ford board must reach a consensus on all items requiring unanimity. IVECO generally listens to Ford concerns on other matters and has made changes in response. But it was given the lead because it is in the best position to make operating decisions.

Parent Relations Are Important

When one parent has the lead, good relations are still needed to ensure cooperation and to ease reaching a consensus when that is necessary. A lead parent should thus keep its partner well informed and give it a chance to be heard. Because surprises may cause mistrust, issues should not be raised in board meetings without prior discussion. Formal votes are then taken to confirm understandings developed between meetings.

IVECO Ford gets engines and transmissions from Ford and depends on Ford for administrative services; the parents share profits and losses and maintain the initial equity level equally. Close parent relations are thus essential for continued cooperation.

At IVECO Ford all board agenda items are discussed ahead of time to prevent surprises or embarrassments. At least one issue raised this way has caused some discomfort in Ford. The question was resolved before a board meeting.

Well ahead of each meeting IVECO Ford sends each parent information on all items that will go to the board. Ford's representatives then have internal briefings before board meetings. Even though Ford may be outvoted on many items, it expresses its views on all matters in board meetings. Ford's candor is due to the positive and constructive relation-

ship between the firms and with their venture. All items requiring unanimity have received it.

To maintain good relationships, venture management would never
ask the board to approve something contrary to Ford general interests
regarding unions, vendors, dealers, or anything else. Management thus
checks informally with Ford on significant items before going to the
board, to determine whether an action might compromise Ford. Although
this takes more time for some decisions, the delays are not significant.
Part of the reason is that Ford responds promptly.

Because of potential Ford impacts, discussions between IVECO Ford
management and management within IVECO must be handled more
carefully than they would if the venture were wholly owned. For example,
IVECO Ford is independent in its own labor relations but must be
careful not to upset Ford labor relations policies in the United Kingdom.
Aside from such intended constraints, IVECO Ford may take an operationally different path from Ford.

Top-level contacts are maintained by IVECO's chairman, Giorgio
Garuzzo, and Alex Trotman, president of Ford of Europe. As chairman
and vice chairman of the board, the two meet periodically or talk on
the phone to review various issues, including senior management items.
A key objective in these meetings has been to make sure the firms
understand each other on matters that would not be going to the board.

At one time IVECO wanted to change the venture's commercial
relations with dealers from the prior Ford system to the IVECO system.
IVECO, as the operating partner, had the right to do this. But Garuzzo
was certain there would be internal resistance from IVECO Ford commercial people, because the change meant a major adjustment for them.
He thus explained to Trotman why it was in the venture's best interest,
and did so as early as possible, before Trotman might get distorted
information from others.

Regardless of which parent has the right to fill a position, or whether
people are nominated by management, Ford and IVECO share views
on all candidates. Neither parent wants to have a person in a senior
position who is not acceptable to the other.

Management reports are complemented by frequent dotted-line contacts between joint venture staff and relevant functions in IVECO,
and by ongoing interactions among Ford, IVECO, and IVECO Ford
staff regarding all matters of interest to Ford, even if it does not approve
the relevant decisions.

These interactions deal with day-to-day operating relations between

Ford and the venture, keep Ford informed on the venture's status, keep IVECO apprised of Ford concerns on all matters, and help prevent minor issues from escalating to major problems. Discussions are open, and Ford's views are always heard. Regular staff contacts, for example, have been instrumental in resolving several minor issues that were expected to arise in a venture of this complexity.

Garuzzo observes there are probably channels of information to Ford that he doesn't even know exist. This is perfectly all right with him, because keeping Ford comfortable and fully informed is crucial to maintaining an effective relationship.

Overall there is a strong, healthy relationship with a steady two-way flow of information. Ford can learn almost anything it wants about the venture. The quality of the three-way parent-venture relationship comes down basically to people. Senior Ford and IVECO corporate staff, for example, have developed close personal working relations. They trust each other implicitly and are open with each other on all matters.

Since IVECO has operating responsibility, there is no opportunity for these parent-venture contacts to bypass the board with messages that conflict with what management gets from the board. The situation is different when both parents share authority for operations. Then, one has to be more careful about even the appearance of conflict.

The close trusting relations between high levels at Ford and IVECO set the pattern for everyone else. These bonds have been a cornerstone of IVECO Ford's growth in market share, which has been well beyond the parents' initial plans.

By contrast to IVECO Ford, relationships between directors of Crédit Suisse First Boston (CSFB), the Swiss-led investment banking firm, were so bad in its beginning years that the joint venture almost came apart. It was hard to get people from each parent even to play tennis or golf together. In its first three years CSFB went through four chief executives.

Improvements came after a 1981 meeting, when a yacht carrying Peter Buchanan, First Boston president and chief executive, and Ranier Gut, Crédit Suisse chairman, got lost near the Bahamas. "It took a lot of cooperation to get back to land," Gut recalls. "It sort of broke the ice between us." CSFB became a major force in its industry, until other parent problems cut it short.[5]

12

Governing 50–50 Joint Ventures

We regarded this as good textbook stuff: Joint Ventures 101. We felt it couldn't work in practice.

—Ciba-Geigy Pharmaceuticals president Doug Watson, on Corning's desire to form a 50–50 venture with Ciba

SOME people believe a true 50–50 joint venture is an invitation for trouble. They observe that a failure to agree on any item can cause a destructive deadlock, that the only thing equality assures is the right to fight. According to this logic, every venture must have an unambiguous way to resolve conflicts, such as 51–49 ownership with one parent able to cast a deciding vote.

Yet some of the most successful joint ventures have equal governance: CFM International, which makes the best-selling commercial aircraft engine in the world; Autolatina, now the world's eighth-largest auto firm; Corning's optical fiber ventures, which have made it a world leader in the industry; Samsung Corning, the world's third-largest and most profitable TV bulb producer; and Ciba Corning Diagnostics, now a major medical diagnostics firm. Notably, each of these bridges significant cultural differences.

A 50–50 joint venture creates a spirit of true partnership. It gives both firms the opportunity to affect all decisions equally. It presses parents to overcome any problems by working together. However, equal ownership and equal rights do not make them act as equals; 50–50 is not so much a magic number as it is an attitude about cooperation.

Look at it this way: Sharing full control of a joint venture is like

173

rowing a boat with a friend. You make progress only if you cooperate and adjust together to the shifting currents.

When Equality Is a Source of Strength

When conditions call for parent equality, it is a must. To see this, imagine being a manager in a parent firm providing critical know-how to a joint venture, yet having no voice in how it is used. How hard will you work for this venture? Or imagine that venture operating imbalances may damage your interests, and you can't make changes. How long should your firm stay involved?

Equality Helps Surface Difficult Issues

Having an equal voice in all matters assures that a decision cannot be made against your will. This lowers the risk of raising difficult issues. Most significantly, being on an equal footing gives both parents the same incentive to contribute and the same chance to affect venture performance. Then, true equality adds considerable strength to a joint venture.[1]

Listen to an American executive describe his firm's joint venture with a European company, in which the Europeans had the deciding vote: "This fact was always there behind issues and conversations. You always knew if it came to a showdown you would lose. Needless to say, we did not feel we could invest our best effort on this."

Ciba Corning Diagnostics is another story. In the final weeks of negotiations, Corning and Ciba-Geigy had a long debate about the merits of a 50–50 deal. Ciba viewed 50–50 as a guarantee for a stalemate, so wanted one firm to have clear authority. Corning responded that it must be 50–50 or nothing. In Corning's view equality creates an atmosphere that encourages cooperation; if intelligent business people cannot agree on where they are going, then a joint venture dies regardless of ownership.

"We regarded this as good textbook stuff: Joint Ventures 101," says Ciba Pharmaceuticals president Doug Watson. "We felt it couldn't work in practice." Corning's chairman, Jamie Houghton, then met with Ciba-Geigy's chairman, Louis von Planta, and was able to ease von Planta's concerns about full equality.

In CCD's early days, cultural differences and inexperience led to critical problems. When management proposed a small acquisition, and another time when it wanted to expand a laboratory, the approval process it used caused Ciba serious discomfort. "Management was underwhelming the CCD board, and the board was confusing management," reports Marty Gibson, Corning's group president for health products. CCD management was also having trouble working for a board. This was a new experience for management and board members. Management was expecting the board to take more initiative, and the board was still learning to function as a board.

To solve the puzzle Dr. Gaudenz Staehelin, Ciba's top representative, asked for a meeting to discuss board–management relations. Staehelin flew from Basel to New York for the meeting, where he was joined by Ciba's Doug Watson, Corning's Marty Gibson, and the CCD president, Bill Zadel. It could have been a dangerous meeting. Things were not going well. Two Ciba directors were present, and only one from Corning.

During their day-long meeting, Ciba learned that Corning has an informal decision-making process. By the time papers come along, a conclusion has already been reached. Corning learned that Ciba has a formal style in which documentation is the key.

The joint venture was created when Ciba bought a half interest in a Corning business, so everyone in management was from Corning. When they sought approvals, they kept doing things the informal Corning way and assumed a spoken Ciba "okay" was enough. However, Ciba people believed nothing was serious until formal papers were circulated. Thus when management thought it had an approval, Ciba directors felt nothing had been proposed.

To avoid similar problems in the future the representatives agreed to use a more formal process. They also clarified board and management roles.

Looking back, Ciba's Doug Watson notes that through this crisis the spirit of equality encouraged the partners to stay the course, so today they are seeing the fruits of their strategy. He believes equality made it much easier for Ciba to call the New York meeting and for the firms to reach a consensus than if Ciba held, for instance, 49 percent of CCD.

Equality Eases Change and Innovation

Being equal facilitates difficult changes that might otherwise be impossible. Both firms know that neither can take advantage of new events at its partner's expense.

At CFM International, for example, proposals for major product innovations like engine downsizing for the Boeing 737 have led to real differences of opinion within and between GE and SNECMA. Major change raises such issues in every firm. Resolving them is often hard. The challenge is greater when two firms are involved. The CFM partners' equality and mutual respect helped them work through their conflicts.

Building a High-Performance Board

Unlike lead parent arrangements, where operating decisions don't get to the board, parents of 50–50 joint ventures must agree on all significant issues. This puts a premium on mutual understandings. You choose a partner out of need; you have to respect its people's views and respond to their interests. It isn't possible for every decision to go your way, and it doesn't even make sense.

Careful advance preparation before board meetings can be valuable. Corning board members, for instance, often engage in constructive debates before attending meetings. The process helps them spot key issues that otherwise might not surface until later, and better prepares them for discussions with Corning's partners.

The debates also cultivate internal relations in support of a venture. "Trying things out at home is like having a friendly sparring partner," says Dick Dulude, Corning's group president responsible for its optical fiber ventures.

Conducting Board Meetings

Productive venture boards have a distinct style. There is a fundamental need to avoid polarization that goes well beyond other kinds of boards. Voting on 50–50 boards should reflect consensus decisions, regardless of how many seats each parent has. One firm's enthusiasm is easily weakened by another's unwillingness to compromise.

Know your strengths and needs, sharpen your views, and be ready to articulate your thinking. And be as responsive to your opposites as you would have them be to you.

"We go through a give-and-take, being very conscious of the need to have our partner see things working out," says Bob Keil, Dow Chemical's executive vice president.

A fundamental criterion for board conduct is to view matters from the perspective of what is best for the venture. Corning, for example, tells those assigned to venture boards to make decisions in the best interest of the venture and to represent both owners with equal concern.

Board meetings should be a forum for open exchange. There is a real benefit in hearing differences of opinion from people on each side; it creates a healthy environment for growing mutual understandings. The more that people share their views, the more a venture can draw on their expertise; the more people feel they belong to a single team, the less risk there is of polarization. This style on a board also sets an important pattern for venture management, notes Dick Dulude: "We are all in this together."

On the CCD board, Ciba people at first developed a uniform position on issues before board meetings, which did not please Corning. Corning said they were ten directors of the venture, and not one Ciba-Geigy vote and one Corning vote. Now both sets of directors accept and encourage open discussions, with individual differences of opinion.

Over time, people on a high-performance board recognize where each person and company has particular strengths, and give more weight to these views. Corning now accepts Ciba's growing role in CCD technology strategy; Ciba has accepted Corning's views on U.S. human resource practices, since CCD is based in the United States. Such understandings are implicit. To maintain equality each parent may veto any item.

When to Vote

Voting on a 50–50 board should happen only to ratify a consensus that has already been reached. Polarized positions are best resolved outside formal meetings. It is awkward and can damage relations to discuss highly sensitive topics with several people present.

Thus much of a board's work in formal meetings is to discuss issues and explore options. Items that can have a large effect on the venture or on either parent may be included, but if there are significant differences you should agree to resolve them by the next meeting. This gives people from each firm a chance to review the question among themselves, explore alternatives with their counterparts in private, and reach an acceptable agreement. Subsequent voting is then *pro forma* and visibly demonstrates agreement on a difficult issue, which reinforces the board process.

Practices to Improve Venture Performance

A 50–50 board must provide clear and consistent signals to management. Consensus decision-making and taking care of each other's needs are essential here. Other important practices hinge on a venture's starting and operating conditions and on the need to build a strong organization.

Autolatina, for example, is pursuing a massive integration of two multibillion-dollar enterprises. Rationalizing factories and other physical assets is the easy part. The real challenge is in moving from different parent styles to one new culture. The board thus pays considerable attention to the progress of integration.

Autolatina board members look for differences of opinion in management, which surface through one-on-one discussions, executive committee meetings, and board presentations by managers championing their projects. These multiple contacts expand opportunities to hear views on how the organization is working and produce better project and operations information. The board has moved topics to later meetings when it has felt there was not enough acceptance within management.

Another illustration of how a board keys on a venture's circumstances comes from CCD. CCD was to be governed equally, but it was a buy-in. Corning had a head start since it ran the business before CCD was formed. Thus while Ciba people were learning how to function on a venture board and were developing their knowledge of the business, Corning people could easily have positioned themselves as the experts. Instead, Corning took a low profile and encouraged Ciba to ask questions and get involved. This posture helped Ciba get up to speed quickly.

Work on Becoming a Team

A high-performance board is an effective team. People understand their roles, depend on each other, and move forward as a unit. As with any excellent team, it is important to work together to develop this quality.

Today, the CCD board formally critiques itself and how it handles issues. Board members discuss how well they reach consensus, whether the board gave management clear signals, and if clarification is needed. "We are trying to avoid the sense that one parent wants one thing, and the other parent wants something else," says a Ciba representative. "We are trying to give life to the idea that management reports to the board. Thus the board has to function as a team."

Equality makes it both easier and harder to raise issues. Neither firm feels wholly responsible for the venture; there is a natural tendency in both firms to say, "It's working okay." To counter this, Doug Watson, as CCD chairman, routinely probes in board meetings and asks for comments on how well specific synergies are really working.

Corning and Ciba representatives try to have a dinner together before each board meeting. They talk about issues, discuss how well their relationship is working, and express any concerns. Candor is a hallmark of these conversations. Frank and comfortable discussions ease misgivings. For instance, an occasional lack of consensus among Ciba executive committee members has been a topic of discussion.

One time Corning asked, "Why did you guys meet separately last night? Why is that important? What is going on?" Ciba pointed out that its people are geographically dispersed and don't see each other between meetings, while Corning people are in constant touch.

Relationships are now so close that an outside observer at a board meeting could not distinguish the parent company of any member.

"We feel good about each other as people," says Doug Watson. "We openly and easily tease each other about our differences—which is a sign of our mutual respect and comfort with the differences." Corning people have quipped, "If we could ever get one opinion out of Ciba-Geigy it would be a miracle."

Expect to Invest a Substantial Effort

Since all aspects of control are shared, people who serve on a 50–50 board have to invest as much time as they would on comparable internal efforts.

Some planners at Ford expected that with two parents, Autolatina would save senior executives' time. However, both Ford and VW have to do the homework needed to stay on top of things, just as they would for wholly owned internal units.

Without defined parent roles there is a greater chance that, over time, small adjustments will set increasing precedents for one parent to take a stronger role. That may be driven by outside events, such as market or technology changes favoring one parent. If these reduce its partner's value to the venture, a shift in control may be inevitable.

Imbalance may also result if a parent carries more weight in board discussions through persistence or with superior information. The other partner can avoid such imbalances by responding in kind.

One active American joint venturer found its position in a 50–50 deal being eroded by an aggressive partner, which hoped to shape the venture's dividend payouts and strategic growth to its needs by pressing harder to set precedents on related issues. This was a gradual process that evolved over time.

The American firm, which had been changing directors every year or so as people moved to other positions, at first didn't see the pattern. When it did, it began naming senior people to the board who were likely to be in their jobs for some years, and gave them more time and staff support to be better informed in board meetings. Following those changes, the venture took a more neutral course.

Restrict Informal Contacts

With a lead parent joint venture, such as IVECO Ford, management owes its allegiance to the parent that is in charge of operations. Contacts with the other parent serve to keep it informed; relevant information may flow through many channels. The situation has to be different with 50–50 joint ventures, in which, by design, each parent has an equal right to influence operations. Unrestricted contacts create opportunities for either parent to impose its wishes out of view of the other.

It is essential that all significant parent influence on a 50–50 venture be visible. Avoid any attempt to convey hidden signals. Otherwise trust and open communications—the core of consensus governance—are violated. It is not appropriate for a board member or other parent executive to have private contact—for any reason—with former employees in the venture. Even when the motive is pure, perceptions can be damaging. Policy-level parent–venture contacts should be through the board and with the knowledge of the CEO.

Ongoing parent–staff contacts at operating levels are a valuable complement to higher-level relations. They should be conducted in full view of venture management.

How an Executive Committee Improves Performance

It is almost impossible for a group of eight or ten busy people meeting three or four times a year to keep up with the many policy and operating issues of a complex joint venture in a dynamic environment, to develop mutual understandings, and to reach a consensus on every item.

When one parent has the lead, much of the monitoring, advising, and routine approvals is done by that parent's own management. Also, lead parent ventures are usually in fairly stable contexts and have fewer major policy issues. Parent staff may still be involved when there is equal governance, but here everything flows through the directors, and there is more to work on.

Having a small executive committee can speed decision-making, greatly ease cooperation, and assure better control. It is a comfortable place for candid discussions of partner relations, management performance, and parent interests beyond the venture.[2]

Decision-Making Is Faster

As with any organization, authority for a joint venture's day-to-day operations is delegated to its management. Still, as with other organizations, assorted matters must be approved above the CEO's level. Waiting for a board meeting or calling every director doesn't make sense. Delegating some authority to an executive committee gets quicker action.

CFM International, for example, needs fast approvals of prices, concession levels, sales agents, changes in warranties, and other important terms and conditions for individual sales. To support such actions, the CFM board created an advisory committee and authorized the president to act with committee approval of such items. Over the years, shorter competitive response times have caused the board to delegate more authority to the executive office.

Cooperation Is Closer

The active give-and-take needed to explore major issues and reach consensus is much easier with a few people in an informal setting. Autolatina's parents, for example, refer to their executive committee meetings as "shirtsleeves meetings."

An executive committee is a surrogate for the board and not a substitute for management. It reviews recommendations developed by management, which is expected to take the initiative on all matters. The committee makes recommendations to the board on management proposals.

Committee members share with management the responsibility of selling other directors on individual items. Members are more involved and better informed than other directors. Their collective support is essential to the board's reaching a consensus. They may report to the board on the status of unresolved issues, but the board cannot be expected to settle them. The committee should reach a consensus before forwarding a proposal to the board.

One cause of the early confusion in Ciba Corning Diagnostics was an executive committee of six, which was unwieldy and not working well. After the New York meeting, the committee was replaced by a group of four people charged with reviewing all major issues before they go to the board. The new executive committee is the focus of partner relations. Real in-depth grappling over issues goes on here and in the board's technology committee. CCD's board takes its role seriously. Reaching a consensus on the board is never automatic and is not always easy, but the board is not expected to invest the time that committee members must.

The CCD executive committee works with management to bring parents' collective wisdom into the venture. This creates an environment of experience and counsel similar to what a business unit CEO gets in a wholly owned corporate framework, without the attendant bureaucracy. The executive committee gets more involved than the board and asks more questions. As CCD's management team has developed, the committee has evolved from dealing with a mix of operational and strategic issues to focus more on longer-term strategic matters.

At times the executive committee visits only with the CCD president, Bill Zadel, to review people issues, compensation, and any discomfort among participants. Regular meetings involve the full management team. Because they work more together, the committee tends to identify more with management than does the board. The board meets three times a year, the executive committee twice as often. At times board technology committee members are invited into the discussions.

Filling the Control Gap

An executive committee is better positioned than a board to control a joint venture. Periodic operating reviews should thus be conducted by the executive committee. This is where parents' basic supervision of a venture happens. The board gets the results of these reviews with less detail.

With shared governance a fast-moving venture may get less operating control than a similar lead parent arrangement or wholly owned unit, for two reasons. First, individual directors may know less about an independent venture's business than a corporate hierarchy does about an internal unit. Second, to avoid imposing a monumental burden on management, each parent does not get as much formal reporting as it normally requires. The combination of less background knowledge and reduced reporting creates opportunities for gaps in control.

These factors make 50–50 ventures more dependent on the people closest to them. To be effective, executive committee members should invest the time to understand a venture in depth. This includes working within their own organizations as needed to fill the gap.

Who Should Serve

The executive committee is where partners must really come together. Committee members must share the same goal, stay in touch, raise issues early, build mutual understandings, and generally keep calamity at bay.

Such small, familiar gatherings are essential. One Corning joint venture failed when different people came in on the other side who didn't understand what was going on and didn't share the vision. Having higher-level contacts in a partner's firm does not avoid such problems. Needed understandings and relationships have to be between those who are seriously involved.

An executive committee has to be small, influential, coherent, and well-informed. It works best with two or four members, typically including the chairman and vice chairman, and possibly one board member from each parent chosen to advise on the most important issues. Good interpersonal skills are crucial. Members must be open and honest with each other to make the relationship work.

The Critical Job of Lead Representatives

Having a lead person from each firm can vastly improve the dialog and parent support. These must be senior people, usually the venture's chairman and vice chairman, with in-depth knowledge of the venture and diplomatic skills to work across the inevitable culture gap. They should also be in a position to build consensus and get things done in their own firms.

Each parent's lead representative is the person held accountable for a venture's performance, from that parent's perspective. Corning measures its lead people by the achievement of key objectives, such as return on equity. With Samsung Corning, for instance, these have included successfully fighting off Korean pressures to go public and reaching agreement with Samsung on an overall strategy to both firms' mutual satisfaction.

Like Having a Foreign Minister or Secretary of State

For a high-performance board it is essential to have one person from each firm who can tactfully summarize its views on difficult matters in board meetings, sense when board discussions should be tabled, stay on top of issues between meetings, work to get them resolved, and present its vote when a consensus has been reached. Board members do not all have the same status within their firm. Most are too busy to keep up to date between meetings, and some lack the tact to work with others under occasionally trying circumstances.

Corning designates more senior executives as its lead individuals.

They are given time to invest in understanding the ventures and to develop relationships.

The lead person operates like a nation's foreign minister or secretary of state. He or she pushes and probes on an issue at home and with his or her counterpart, proposes tentative solutions, and generally maintains trusting relationships. Without a person in this role on each side, important things may not get done.

In a European financial services joint venture, for example, one partner's board chairman served as the venture chairman and was his firm's lead representative. Too busy to stay on top of issues, he assigned a senior staff manager to take that role. The manager knew the venture well but carried little weight in his firm. Important matters, including a key new investment, could not be resolved. When other issues began to slip, the chairman made more of his own time available for the job.

Discussions between partners go a lot better if they confer at the beginning on who has the lead for each firm. Relationships do evolve without this understanding, but not always clearly. Roles must also be discussed when new people become involved. A replacement for the person with the lead may not take that role.

Ciba-Geigy does not have a lead representative in CCD. That may be because three are from Switzerland and two from a U.S. subsidiary, and there is little contact among them between board meetings. Not having a Ciba spokesperson has made it harder to get things done between meetings. Marty Gibson, Corning's lead person, has had to call all five Ciba directors on important issues. Doug Watson sees the lack of a lead person as a weakness on Ciba's part.

Having Champions Can Make a Difference

It takes an extra spark of energy to conquer the uncertainties that often come with 50–50 joint ventures. Partners depend more on each other in these alliances, and the markets or technologies may be new. To build momentum and keep a balance, you need a strong champion on each side. The lead person is in the best position to play this role.

CFM International would not have been formed and could not have survived without forceful sponsorship by Gerhard Neumann, group executive of GE's aircraft engines unit, and René Ravaud, president of SNECMA. Although the firms had solid market and economic reasons to cooperate, many people in GE were reluctant. Some were openly hostile. Neumann had to push long and hard to make the deal. Ravaud's role was equally vital. "Ravaud could get things done in the French government and in SNECMA," Neumann says. "It was the strength of his personality and leadership that got things going." Ravaud had to retire or fire SNECMA people who opposed the alliance.

After CFM began, unexpected market changes disrupted the original plans, causing months of heated debate within GE and SNECMA about continuation. Steadfast championing by Neumann and Ravaud saved the venture from termination.

Two champions were also vital to Corning's optical fiber business. After Corning invented the fiber, Chuck Lucy, who became project manager, saw a bright opportunity. Others were critical of his vision. Commercial prospects seemed far off, and AT&T, which had a monopoly in the U.S. market, was developing its own fiber. Lucy was told to find outside help. In two years he traveled extensively to Europe and Japan, looking for partners to help develop systems based on the fiber. This was breaking new ground. Corning had little relevant overseas experience.[3]

Lucy eventually reached five-year development agreements, including options for technology licenses or to form joint ventures, with a firm in each major market. Yet among Corning's partners all but Siemens saw the arrangement as an option on an uncertain future. Berndt Zeitler, head of Siemens's cable division, shared Lucy's vision. He successfully championed starting a joint venture at once. Zeitler's commitment gave the project needed credibility at a critical time.

About two years after the fiber alliances started, picturephone development was curtailed, killing the one known market. To go after the voice communications market Lucy totally revised the business plan and had to cut costs a hundredfold. Most of Corning's partners lost their enthusiasm, but Lucy persuaded them to keep going. Dick Dulude, the Corning group president, recalls that in a wilderness of doubters, Lucy remained the real believer. He delivered when needed by bootlegging and cutting corners in Corning. By the time the development phase was over, costs were low enough to be credible, and the U.S. market had been deregulated.

The Chief Executive's Role

The top executive of an equally governed joint venture has more autonomy than CEOs in similar parent units or in lead parent ventures. There are three reasons for this. First, within a corporation, priorities can be changed to suit parent interests. This can't happen in a joint venture unless both parents concur. Second, any shifts in a venture must be driven by the CEO. Only he or she is in a position to marshal the forces behind a new thrust. Third, an executive committee cannot easily provide the close supervision internal parent units get.

This independence of the CEO creates room to play one partner off against the other, to win even more autonomy. That happens, for example, when a CEO claims to one partner that the other is being unreasonable about investment, reporting, or personnel policies to the detriment of the venture, hoping such policies will be relaxed.

The same leeway gives a CEO room to win authority at the board's expense. For instance, management polarized the board in one Corning joint venture. To bring the parties together management was told it could not get needed contributions if each parent was going its own way.

As in wholly owned contexts, the CEO's objectives, priorities, and performance measures should be well defined. But it takes more effort to apply these controls in a joint venture. Factors that determine market position, for example, may be out of the CEO's control. A manager's boss in a wholly owned unit is more likely to know this than executive committee members, who may be exposed to different conditions in their other work.

To compensate for such gaps, executive committee members—particularly lead representatives—have to invest more time in understanding the venture. As a complement, incentives and compensation should be used to align the CEO's interest with venture goals and objectives.

Corning has found it quite important to give joint venture CEOs incentive compensation packages tied to venture objectives. Venture management gets equity in Corning's independent startups. Risk-takers who will give up their job security are needed here and must be rewarded accordingly.

Because neither parent has control, roles aren't as clear as with internal units. Consequently, issues may slip by unnoticed or not get needed attention. A venture CEO thus has to be more action-oriented. Soon after CCD began, for example, Bill Zadel, its president, realized that authority and personality problems were impairing technology transfer from Ciba to the venture. Zadel thus raised the issue with Ciba's pharmaceutical research head, who is a CCD board member. The two formed a technology committee of Ciba and Corning people, which developed and launched a more effective program.

Three Ways to Build Relationships

A 50–50 joint venture involves three separate organizations, with no one in full control. These circumstances make relationships among all three essential bonds in the alliance.

There Must Be Strong Bonds Between Lead Representatives

When partners share major risks, things don't go far without people from each firm who trust each other implicitly, are driven by the same vision, and are emotionally committed to make it real.

The difficult early years of CFM International are illustrative. Gerhard Neumann and René Ravaud were totally dependent on each other; for the venture to proceed each had to deliver his firm against heavy resistance. Each had to trust the other's ability to do this.

Their willingness to take this risk was backed by a growing friendship that started even before talks about a joint venture began. Neumann and Ravaud first met at the 1971 Paris Air Show and became fast friends. "When we looked each other in the eye we knew we were at the same frequency," Neuman recalls. "We only spent 15 minutes together, but our chemistry immediately clicked." Looking back on CFM, he observes: "In the final analysis no matter what you guarantee, it's the personal relationships that make things work."

Similarly, Corning's Chuck Lucy and Siemens's Berndt Zeitler became and remain good friends. People Lucy dealt with in other firms were less enthusiastic. Zeitler had a different attitude. Lucy believes the strong bond between them was a big part of their mutual desire to proceed.

When two firms take risks together, disagreements are inevitable. Private arguments can then be a great help in clarifying issues and growing a new perspective. Only a trusting relationship can withstand the stress of an intense debate.

During the critical early years of their alliance, Lucy and Zeitler argued tremendously. Their debates expanded to include others and made it possible to sort out the critical issues. Corning's Dick Dulude notes that Zeitler and Lucy are strongminded people. They could argue only because they had a relationship which became "a friendship for life."

Such comfort was missing in Southern Medical, the joint venture with the breakthrough health product described in Chapter 10. The lead executives knew there were serious contrasts between their firms, yet discussions were strained whenever they addressed the question in private. Neither felt comfortable with the other. There were differences in their personal styles, and each mistrusted the other's motives. After a few awkward meetings the issue was put aside and Southern Medical slowly withered.

Parent-to-Parent Relations Are Also Needed

With a well-designed joint venture it is unlikely there will be fundamental disagreements where neither firm can change its stand. Most often, polarization comes from awkwardness in the consensus process, weak high-level support, or the failure of partners to see the importance of meeting each other's needs.

When discussions are marked by candor, you may at times learn a particular outcome would be far more important to your partner than to you. Then it pays to be genuinely concerned that the other firm sees things working out for its interests. Meeting such needs is vital. It strengthens a relationship and gives a venture needed flexibility.

In CCD, for example, Corning has been willing to concede on points about which Ciba felt strongly. This has included short- versus long-term investment strategies, as well as questions of strategic direction for individual projects. Ciba regards Corning's attitude as a key element of their relationship.

As another example, Dow Chemical worked with Corning to resolve Dow Corning's position in South Africa independent of Dow's own position, because this was more important to Corning.

Bob Keil, Dow Chemical's executive vice president, notes that Dow often uses the language, "If that's more critical to you, go ahead. If we had to do it, we'd rather not." In this way Dow lets a partner know their positions differ but that Dow is willing to yield on an issue significant to the partner and noncritical to Dow for the sake of their relationship. This builds psychological and diplomatic credit for other issues that could be important to Dow.

Support for a joint venture ultimately depends on backing at high parent levels. Corning's chairman, Jamie Houghton, visits the top executive of every joint venture partner once a year. These are not protocol meetings; they review performance, search for issues others have not surfaced, and make sure these get needed attention. The mutual understandings and bonding at this level set an important tone of cooperation for Corning's ventures.

Houghton notes that it is good for "the child" to see the parents talking. Executives who report to him feel these meetings send a clear message about cooperation and help get things done.

The Child Should Earn Its Parents' Trust

A joint venture CEO wins parents' trust by taking a "what's best for the joint venture" attitude. He or she builds mutual comfort by nurturing one-on-one rapport with directors from each parent to be responsive to their concerns. Knowing who is interested in what, and bringing issues to their attention, is a key part of the job. People invest more energy when someone is looking out for their needs.

Before CCD board meetings, president Bill Zadel calls individual board members he knows would be concerned about a topic. This is done not just for the sake of lobbying people, but more importantly for building relationships. Spotting issues for others on the board is a way of saying, "I care about your concerns."

Staying Equal in Foreign Markets

Sharing governance in a country where your firm has little experience compared with a local partner can put you at a disadvantage. When problems arise, you may be slow to respond or may be overly dependent on the partner to explain issues and propose solutions. Once your firm's know-how is delivered, its strength erodes as power shifts to the local firm. The net effect is having a lead partner when you don't want one.

This sequence of events happened to a Dow Chemical venture in India. Dow's partner was a strong local company. At the time the market was not attractive enough for Dow to pay the attention needed for a balanced power structure. That gave Dow's partner effective control. The firm redirected the business to areas of greater interest to it than to Dow. Dow eventually pulled out.

Even when a foreign venture depends on a firm's continued know-how inputs, distance and cultural differences may operate to weaken its position. Often, evolution toward the local parent is not a calculated strategy to win control but a result of three circumstances: responsibility for providing management, local issues, and a locally inexperienced distant parent.

It makes sense for a local partner to supply most or all of management in a country where you have little background. You may have the right to approve executive appointments, yet without a local office staffed by senior local nationals, it can be hard to evaluate candidates in another culture. Skills you would discount at home may be critical there.

Further, a local parent always has vital concerns about its own labor, customer, supplier, distributor, and government relations. Every firm is inclined to act on its own behalf, without being fully aware of how this might affect its partner. With other priorities beyond the venture, its own people on the scene, and a remote partner, there is ample opportunity for local bias. Although the local partner may not have more authority, it will tend to regard the venture as an internal unit and encourage management to favor its position, even at the venture's expense.

When your firm is the distant parent, it serves your mutual interests to offset these forces. "What we're constantly trying to do is create a balance against nature," says Corning's vice chairman Van Campbell.

Providing Your Own Expertise

One way to create more balance is to make sure an executive committee member has the time to learn about a venture and the local scene. He or she should be sufficiently informed to raise issues and spot events that might favor your partner. Another step is having a manager in the venture from your firm. A full-time person will have less difficulty learning about local practices.

However, it can be hard to find someone who will be sensitive and effective in the other culture. It is also more difficult to get people to relocate. In addition, there may be a greater need for people in positions lacking full exposure to local issues. Corning's foreign optical fiber ventures, for example, depend on technology managers who are on loan to assure that effective know-how flows from Corning.

Building Close Venture Relations

Obviously, the greatest sensitivities about a joint venture are in the venture. Hence, the more its management is aware of and identifies with your needs, the more you can be confident that local bias will be reduced.

Corning has a strong implicit policy of developing close relations with joint venture chief executives from partner firms. This improves working relations, maintains the spirit of balanced interests, and helps overcome cultural differences by fostering increased communications and understandings.

Corning's Chuck Lucy, for instance, has spent most of his time as lead representative to its optical fiber ventures in building credibility for fairness and openness with their management and showing that their interest is Corning's interest. Venture managers know this and value it. For example, when a venture wants to develop new products or spend more for capacity insurance, and Lucy agrees, he works hard for approvals in Corning.

Chuck Lucy describes his bonds with venture CEOs as more important than ties to his counterparts in partner firms. Management turnover there has sometimes made it difficult to treat executive committee or board relations as the cement that holds things together.

Corning also nurtures relations with venture executives by including them in its management and technology reviews and honoring them when they leave. When venture CEOs from overseas retire, Corning recognizes each with a photo album and other memorable gifts at a retirement party at its corporate headquarters. Guests include Corning employees with whom the CEO has worked through the years.

"We try to make them feel as though they're Corning employees," Van Campbell says. Such measures, and the friendships and personal obligations they nourish, encourage people from partner firms to look out for Corning's interests.

Close relations at operating levels can also help keep things balanced. Corning's ongoing staff support to Samsung Corning, for example, helps reinforce a feeling of dependence.

Corning builds additional comfort with overseas management by avoiding steps others often take. It will not ask for the accounting slot, for example. Corning believes that insisting on control of this slot says to a partner, in effect, "We don't trust you." If a partner's accounting system is not highly developed, Corning may initially assign someone to train its partner to take over. This is only a temporary move. Corning would rather conduct an annual agreed-to audit. Other firms reserve the right to keep track of the books, and their partners resent this.

Relations Between Top Executives Are More Important Here

Good relationships between senior parent managers are always needed in alliances. These bonds deserve more attention in foreign 50–50 joint ventures, where there is likely to be more uncertainty about the alliance.

Some of the steps Corning chairman Amory Houghton, followed by his brother, Jamie Houghton, have taken to develop Corning's relationship with Samsung, are indicative. One time, when Samsung chairman B. C. Lee was given an honorary doctorate at Boston College, Amory Houghton was asked to be the speaker. In his comments, Houghton was highly complimentary of Samsung and its impact on Korea. He described how Lee created and built Samsung, and compared it favorably with IBM, AT&T, and other major American firms combined.

The Houghtons have also nurtured the Samsung relationship through meetings with B. C. Lee and with Korean government officials—which led to the government's extolling Corning as good for Korea. It probably also reinforced B. C. Lee's good attitude toward Corning.

They have also gone out of their way to respect important events. For example, after Jamie Houghton had become Corning chairman, B. C. Lee passed away. To show his respect, Houghton canceled a packed U.S. travel schedule, returned to Corning, flew to Korea for the funeral, and then went on to Paris for a meeting that had been previously scheduled for the following day. Another time, Jamie Houghton was at the groundbreaking for a new Samsung Corning plant in Korea, and promised to return for the opening fifteen months later, which he did.

The message sinks in that Corning really cares. Its practices were summed up by H. C. Shin, president of Samsung Aerospace and past president of Samsung Corning: "Korea and the United States have significant differences in their ways of thinking and their ways of doing business. This requires both parents to make an extra effort. It is critical that each parent trust, support, and most importantly respect the other side." Corning seems to understand this intuitively.

13

Alliances with Universities

We spend 3 percent of our total research budget on university collaboration. This generates about 15 percent of our genuine discovery activities.

—Howard A. Schneiderman, Monsanto's senior vice president for R&D

IN 1982, after Monsanto committed more than $50 million to sponsor biotechnology research at Washington University in St. Louis, alarms rang on campuses around the world. The deal was widely seen as a major breach of academic freedom and a threat to the progress of basic research. Since then, business sponsorship of university research has accelerated worldwide. The potential conflicts are still there, but the possible benefits for academics and businesses are tremendous.

American universities perform about 60 percent of all U.S. basic research, and a much smaller but still significant amount of applied research. The percentages are comparable in other nations. In the not-too-distant past, there was ample time for the results of this work to trickle slowly into use. Today the time between the creation of new knowledge and its practical application is shrinking rapidly. Universities are consequently playing an increasingly direct role in shaping the ideas industry turns into new goods.

University links can be valuable regardless of company size. Bell Laboratories, for instance, has more than eight hundred science Ph.D.s. Yet president Ian Ross regards universities as the main source of the Labs' R&D knowledge. About 5 percent of the Labs' nine hundred research projects are joint efforts with academics.[1] But great size is not a requirement for university collaboration. Much of the recent growth in business–university relations is coming from ties to small- and medium-size firms.

Connecting with Universities

Universities have a scale and scope that exceed the R&D resources of the largest corporations. In the United States about $10 billion goes into university R&D annually. Most of this is government funds, and little is classified. The results are openly available.

The arrangements a firm can make to tap this wealth are limited only by its knowledge of the opportunities and a definition of mutual interests. Prospects run the gamut from practical problem-solving to long-term basic research.

Recruiting is a critical side benefit to college ties. For any firm the quality of its own R&D depends on the quality of the people doing the work. Universities provide a crucial input, because new graduates have been exposed to the latest frontiers. Familiarity developed through close contacts makes it easier to recruit promising candidates. In fact, some university research centers discourage student recruitment by and faculty consulting with firms that are not center members.[2]

Business–university activities may be organized several ways: university group research, outside group sponsorship, individual projects, individual faculty contacts, and shared facilities.

University Group Research: A Window on Progress

More than fifty university–industry research and engineering centers operate in the United States, in fields as diverse as materials handling, iron and steelmaking, advanced manufacturing, glass research, and non-destructive testing. While most began with government funding, a few are self-supporting. Some centers offer only group programs. Others accept individual firm sponsorship as well.

Group programs typically give corporate sponsors a window on emerging developments. Members attend seminars, receive research newsletters, may be able to place their scientists at the centers, and may get nonexclusive licenses to center developments. Depending on the center and level of sponsorship, members may sit on joint company–faculty committees that help define agendas. Sponsorship fees often vary with firm size.[3]

Research centers operate on fixed budgets with limited staff. Sponsor benefits depend on the skills and aggressiveness of those involved, as well as the interests of other sponsors. These factors can limit research to incremental progress.

Outside Group Sponsorship Provides More Flexibility

A more aggressive approach is to form an independent group to sponsor work at selected universities. Like university-based groups, this offers the power of multiple sponsorship yet has more flexibility to select individual projects.

For example, the Edison Polymer Innovation Corporation is a not-for-profit organization with seventy-six member firms, created to sponsor materials research at Ohio universities. Each member has made three-year sponsorship commitments that range from less than $2,000 to more than $50,000 a year, depending on its size. The State of Ohio has also contributed funds in the hope that resulting new products will keep jobs in the state.[4]

Single-Firm Projects Offer More Focus

Sponsoring an individual research effort grants a voice in the agenda that isn't possible with group programs. In general, the scope, duration, and structure of a project depend only on mutual interests. Depending on a firm's needs and a university's policies, the firm may also get exclusive patent rights and the right to review research articles to excise proprietary data before publication. Individual projects are conducted at established centers or with a particular professor chosen for his or her expertise.

Most such projects are fairly small, short-term arrangements made to pursue a specific development. The Belgian firm UCB used this approach with Belgium's Inter-University Micro-Electronics Center to develop a new chemical that increases the capacity of integrated circuits. Similarly Norelco, the consumer products firm, sponsored the design of a new coffee maker at Rensselaer Polytechnic Institute.

At Washington University, Monsanto set up a fund to reach out to the entire faculty for the same research goal. This helped the firm connect with work being pursued across a number of disciplines in different parts of the university. Monsanto has also found that competition for funds encourages breakthrough opportunities. Although Monsanto spends 3 percent of its total research budget on university collaboration, this generates about 15 percent of its genuine discovery activities.

Some universities are willing to set up dedicated groups, similar to multifirm groups, to focus on an individual sponsor's particular needs. This can be a constructive way to foster interdisciplinary cooperation and to channel researchers' work along specific lines of interest to the sponsor. Having a separate organizational unit also helps integrate university and sponsor work and speeds technology transfer.

Rolls Royce took this approach to accelerate its search for ways to use ceramics in place of metal in aircraft engines. Working with Warwick University, the firm created a Rolls-Royce Ceramic Development Unit on campus. Before that, Rolls had maintained links with several universities and had belonged to a separate ceramics research group.[5]

Faculty Contacts Link Firms to Specific Expertise

Sponsored research isn't the only way to build on university expertise. You may prefer to keep sensitive research in-house, or may need specific technical inputs from individual faculty. IBM, for example, has a visiting technical staff arrangement which brings professors to company laboratories while the professors are on sabbatical.

"The consultant professor is the most efficient means of technology transfer this nation has," says Monsanto's Howard Schneiderman. "The thousands of faculty members who consult for industry accelerate the application and exploitation of the knowledge created by our universities."[6]

Share Facilities to Expand Resources

Sharing costly equipment with universities, or working in their laboratories, makes it possible to conduct experiments that would otherwise be out of reach. Shared learning through contacts with faculty researchers can be an important additional benefit.

The University of Michigan, for example, sells time on its nuclear reactor outlet ports for neutron beam experiments in health care, advanced materials, and other areas. In Switzerland, pharmaceutical makers Ciba-Geigy and Sandoz have contributed 25 percent each toward the cost of a modern tomograph machine at the University of Basel. The university and the companies use the equipment for research. In Sweden companies often have R&D employees serve as adjunct professors, both teaching and maintaining contacts in related research fields.[7]

Increase Contacts to Speed Technology Transfer

Any arrangement that brings company and university researchers together helps speed the flow of knowledge between them, which accelerates R&D progress. This is why research parks—corporate R&D sites located near universities—have been growing rapidly in recent years. A further step in this direction is for a company to donate or share the cost of a building to house its own and university staff dedicated to a particular topic.

Monsanto, for example, contributed most of the funds to build Oxford University's Glycobiology Institute, part of the university's biochemistry department. The institute is directed by an Oxford professor and employs sixty scientists, of whom ten are on assignment from Monsanto's research center in St. Louis.

Understanding Universities' Perspective

Like other alliances, business–university links combine mutual and conflicting objectives. Knowing something about universities' unique interests can help you build more effective relations.

How Universities Benefit

Business sponsorship can provide income, equipment, employment opportunities for students, consulting opportunities, and a keener awareness of applications for faculty. The effects of this understanding may be substantial. Roderic Park, vice chancellor at the University of California's Berkeley campus, maintains that industrial support there has made an essential contribution to the quality of research and teaching.

Industrial projects also give students a valuable glimpse of the world of business. Leo Hanifin, director of the Center for Manufacturing and Productivity at Rensselaer Polytechnic, notes that the coffee maker design project for Norelco "provided great educational experiences for many of our students who thought manufacturing was the last place they wanted to work."

Unlike typical government grants, industrial funds tend to be easier to apply for. They are often awarded in a month or so, as against the better part of a year for government support. Companies often have a clearer understanding of future needs than other sponsors, so corporate support can open new horizons. Monsanto sponsorship has helped university scientists attack difficult, long-term problems that were neither likely to be supported by traditional federal grant mechanisms nor to produce immediately publishable results.[8]

Universities Have Different Needs

Despite these benefits, there are some conflicts. Universities are the world's principal source of scientific progress. As business links have grown, so has the tension between some firms' desires for secrecy and immediately useful results, and the open communications and long-term perspective universities need for basic research.

For the most part companies and universities have been able to work out compromises. Typical university sponsorship rules now respect each side's priorities. Individual project sponsors can be protected by confidentiality from competitors, and academics are assured of the right to publish—after firms have had reasonable time to review articles for proprietary data.

Such rules have not prevented commercial considerations from influencing the choice of research projects, threatening to bias universities away from their basic mission. The intense competition for funds, especially for larger projects, has also caused universities to delay the publication process and has led to secrecy agreements that created serious embarrassments.

University links to business also tend to be closer than to government and other sponsors, which takes more time away from research. For these reasons some professors prefer to steer clear of business funding.

The specifics of a situation also depend on the basic or applied nature of the subject, and on individual university and college policies. Engineering schools have had decades of business ties. They see things differently from colleges of arts and sciences, for whom business links are newer and interest in immediate applications is traditionally lower.

Academics may also have a different time frame from business people. This leads to conflicts if the contrasts aren't accepted. Carnegie-Mellon University withdrew from a research project to develop a metal powder process for this reason. The sponsor had unrealistic deadlines that were impossible to meet with normal graduate student staff.[9]

Managing University Relations

The value a firm gets from a university alliance depends as much on how the relationship is managed as on the funds invested. Imposing one's culture and controls on a university project is as inappropriate as with a corporate partner. Some firms find it hard to accept that faculty members who receive their funds do not in effect become their employees.

Staff Contacts Should Be Mutually Productive

Business–university relations work best when people on both sides believe they are getting equal value. As with other alliances, it takes more than money to build equality.

Researchers are most effective with colleagues who understand their work and make their own contributions, so be sure your contact person is dedicated to the success of the program. Promote a give-and-take spirit. Academic freedom should not be a university scientist's excuse to do entirely as he or she wants. A debate with a closed mind is not a debate.

To foster ties with universities Monsanto assigns a liaison scientist to each university project. This person provides needed technical assistance and support. "Any company wanting to develop a research program with a university without close relations and constant interaction will be disappointed," says Edward MacCordy, associate vice chancellor for research at Washington University. "The interest expressed by sponsor company scientists in our faculty member's research has been an important source of encouragement for them."

Link Organizations, Not Just People

For projects with significant size and duration, seek a relationship between institutions rather than just between your firm and a professor. Relations between organizations are more likely to win university support and help if problems arise. And universities don't change jobs.

A committee composed of peers of the participants should review the work for its technical merit and the value for both organizations. Monsanto has had bad experiences when its funding was regarded as a charity. There was little communication and no peer review. This led to adversarial relations when Monsanto sought to interact with the research.

Making Technology Transfer Work

The quality of staff a firm assigns to monitor university work also determines the quality of technology transfer back to the firm. Arno Penzias, chief scientist at Bell Labs, sees the solution to getting information from academe as being able to give some back. Bell Labs, which has no formal program for university collaboration, works on personal chemistry between individual researchers.

Knowledge transfer people have to be well connected to intended users to understand their interests, and must have the credibility needed to get attention. American firms tend to assign expendable staff to the liaison task. Their foreign competitors have shown more interest and have reaped greater rewards from the same programs.

At MIT, "the Japanese company usually sends one of its staff members as a visiting scientist," observes associate provost Kenneth Smith. "The person will be absolutely first-rate and makes a real contribution to the project. Normally the U.S. company doesn't send anyone. It just waits for the report." Further, MIT is getting considerable value from these contacts—more than money can buy. "We gain far more information from our foreign contacts than we give them," Nicholas Negroponte, chairman of MIT's Industrial Liaison Program reports.[10]

It seems arguable that universities, like any organizations, have an incentive to align more closely with others that offer the most productive relations. Just possibly, the most advanced concepts are first proposed to favored sponsors—not by formal policy, but by individual decisions. More certainly, technology flows are faster and stronger to sponsors that pay the closest attention.

Choosing University Partners

Unless a firm has a lot of money and patience, it is best to look for established competence when building university links. You get much more by leveraging already strong programs. Focusing collaboration at a few universities also raises a firm's visibility for student recruiting.

Bell Labs' collaboration tends to center on a small number of U.S. universities chosen for mutual interests. They may be doing the latest research of concern to Bell or may have a high reputation for the caliber of their students. ICL, the British computer firm, has similarly chosen six universities that are on the leading edge of important fields.

IBM has at times taken more initiative by encouraging university departments to do research in areas where they were not active. This has not worked as well as leveraging existing programs.[11]

THREE

IMPLEMENTATION

14

Scanning for Opportunities

We make grocery shopping a regular part of our business trips to Europe. In this case it helped give us a jump on our bigger competitors. We were like the tortoise beating the hare.

—Grant Wood, marketing vice president of Minnetonka, on finding toothpaste in pump dispensers in a West German supermarket

JUST yesterday, it seems, keeping close to customers was a mark of excellence. It is clearly still important. Today, however, global interdependence requires firms to have similar links to all kinds of organizations, and these may be scattered around the world. Is it possible to do this? Yes, if you know where and how to look for useful resources.

Scanning Is Always Important

Compare tiny Minnetonka, based in Chaska, Minnesota, with AT&T's Bell Telephone Laboratories. These firms are strikingly different. Minnetonka makes specialty soaps for the U.S. market; vaunted Bell Labs is a world leader in many advanced technologies. Yet the two have one thing in common: Both actively look for outside resources.

At Minnetonka, managers regularly go shopping abroad for new ideas. When they happened upon toothpaste in a pump dispenser, they contacted Henkel, the German manufacturer, and the firms brought the concept to U.S. markets together. The product became a major success.

Similarly at Bell Labs, systems engineers routinely scrutinize worldwide research literature for new knowledge and scan widely for the latest developments. Novel ideas and devices are included in their plans, regardless of origin.[1]

Opportunity scanning at any firm—like that at Bell Labs and Minnetonka—can help build strength four ways:

Finding resources. A formal, organized search will locate advanced know-how and capabilities germane to a firm's needs, from around the world.

Strategic planning. Scanning helps a firm plot its course through the competitive forest. Knowing the state of the art on the outside helps focus internal efforts on topics where the firm can be unique.

Early mover advantages. The winning edge in fast-changing sectors often goes to firms able to locate key developments before others.

Partner choice. Starting with the right partner is a key to future success. A poor choice can mean lost time and foreclosed opportunities. Scanning is where partner selection begins.

Scanning is like looking for a needle in a haystack, so it is different from market research, which is more like describing the haystack. It begins with a description of a firm's strengths and objectives. The purpose is to learn of others' products, marketing resources, technologies, and

Overview of Scanning Methods	
Known Firms	*Broad Scans*
Where to Look	
Customers	Visible resources
Suppliers	Leading organizations
Distributors	Where value first appears
Competitors	Leading geographic areas
Other partners	Broadcasts
Scanning Tactics	
Informal contacts	Visits
Formal joint studies	Experts
	Trade shows
	Conferences
	Literature
	Data bases
	Group research
	New venture investments

operating and organizational abilities that could improve the firm's performance.

The process combines two separate thrusts: probing for opportunities with current trading partners and competitors, and searching more widely. These are summarized in the table on page 204.

Scanning with Known Firms

Firms with which you work or compete every day are a critical source of new opportunities. You serve the same general markets, have similar or complementary resources and objectives, and may know enough about each other to have a basis of mutual trust.

Be aware that many new product ideas—in fields as different as scientific instruments, bakery products, and commercial aircraft—come from early users. Such customers are important, because their pioneering interests often set the course of future developments.

Do you know which of your customers are the most innovative? Are you aware of the advances they want from suppliers? Are you willing to experiment with them and to provide early support for their developments? Do suppliers bring new concepts to you first? Are more innovative suppliers familiar with your needs in areas where they might contribute?

Having an open attitude and being receptive to others' suggestions is a good start. More opportunities can be found through formal scans with important partners.

For instance, Black & Decker, the power tool and home appliance firm, has ten advisory councils composed of dealers and other key partners. A testing ground for new ideas, the councils also suggest new products and practices. These arrangements have led to important new products, including a reciprocating power saw proposed by one dealer.[2]

The broader firms' mutual interests, the more ways they may scan together. Take Ford and Mazda. To seek mutual opportunities, the firms share their views on the direction of Asian and European markets, make semiannual comparisons of their product plans, and often share product needs with each other, both for comment and to spot joint possibilities.

Scanning with prospective partners can be an important step in forming an alliance. Often, two firms know they share a potential opportunity but must first explore their mutual abilities. This was how Northern Telecom and Apple Computer created their alliance in the office automation market. The firms' relationship began when they agreed to make their equipment compatible to achieve higher data rates. To develop linked products, they then spent several months studying each other's technology to find the best combinations.[3]

How to Scan Broadly

When Motorola set new quality and productivity goals for its remote paging business to battle Japanese competition, its managers knew they would have to adapt as much off-the-shelf manufacturing know-how as they could find. So they traveled the world looking for "islands of excellence"—not in paging firms, but among the best manufacturers of cars, watches, cameras, and other technology-intensive products.

Motorola researchers spent the most time in Japan, where they found factory managers surprisingly receptive. "When a company is doing something well, they like to show it off," says Motorola's project manager, Scott Shamlin. "We had a fairly free hand, similar to the access the U.S. gave the Japanese to our factories in the 1950s and 1960s." Back home in Florida, the Motorola team combined know-how from Honda, Seiko, and others with its own expertise to build a new production line. Once in danger of being forced out of the business by the Japanese, Motorola has since held firmly to its lead in the U.S. market. The pagers are so good they rank among the top sellers in Japan.[4]

Clearly, there are useful resources beyond the limits of your current relationships. Given the importance of scanning widely, doing so effectively should be a prime consideration. Looking for useful data in every possible corner would be too costly, and you probably couldn't absorb the results. The key to productive scanning is to control the process from the start: Know what you are looking for and where it is most likely to be found. This is determined by the subject's characteristics, such as its visibility and where value first appears.

Some Resources Are More Visible

Locating functional capabilities like operations or a distribution network is easier than finding new products or technologies. The former are more visible in the marketplace. Finding them involves checking industry registers, trade association memberships, and other published lists for firms that are active in a particular sector and location.

In crop genetics, for example, major agribusiness firms have needed seed company partners to provide genes for new varieties, to test the results, to cultivate them in large volumes, and to distribute the product to farmers. But the list of prospective partners is short and is readily available from seed outlets, trade associations, or government agricultural agencies. Agribusiness firms have put far more effort into constantly scanning the world's laboratories and scientific literature to find new developments applicable to their interests.

In smaller markets or developing nations, where published lists are not available, a number of organizations can help locate potential partners. These include commercial sections in embassies; export or economic development agencies; local business groups, banks, and offices of foreign chambers of commerce; and professional groups with special sections or events tailored to the sector of interest.

Target Leading Organizations

By reviewing the press or technical literature, or discussing your interests with experts or observing the marketplace, you will find that certain firms, universities, and government labs excel in specific fields important to you. By keeping in touch with them one can spot new advances before they are widely known.

That is one way food processing firms find new products and keep up with market trends. People from Campbell Soup, for instance, regularly visit pace-setting restaurants to learn of new developments.

The seed for Genentech, the leading biotechnology firm, was planted by venture capitalist Robert Swanson, who was scanning the research literature in the mid-1970s. In his readings, Swanson found considerable growing interest in the emerging field of recombinant DNA. Near the leading edge was Herb Boyer, then a professor at the University of California. Swanson sought a meeting with Boyer, which led to their formation of Genentech.

Kodak's disk camera experience illustrates what can happen when firms don't maintain contacts with key leaders. The camera was planned as an offensive move against Kodak's Japanese competitors. The product used a revolutionary aspheric lens developed by Kodak and not available in Japan. While Kodak was working on the camera, Corning was developing its own aspheric lens, which it marketed in Japan to camera makers and others. Reportedly, Kodak didn't know what Corning was developing and Corning never approached Kodak—although both companies are neighbors in upstate New York.[5]

Look in Places Where Value First Appears

Different products, technologies, and scientific advances first become visible in various ways. Knowing where to look depends on the nature of the target sector.

Some kinds of products, for example, are first publicly evident in test marketing or on retailers' shelves. Others are introduced at trade shows.

Scanning fast-moving technical areas depends on where the state of the art is changing most rapidly. For more basic scientific and engineering topics, this will include leading universities and government labs. Current research literature will point to the leaders. For more applied areas, new or established firms may have the lead, and there may not be anything in the literature until patents are granted. In this situation leaders can be found through discussions with experts and visits to trade shows.

One way to locate experts is by reading general press and professional review articles on the topic. A good reporter will already have made an effort to find, interview, and quote recognized authorities. Also, review papers are typically written by leading experts.

For science and technology, secondary sources such as newsletters and other prepackaged scans offer a broad overview but cannot focus on unique interests of individual firms. Further, the lag between the appearance of original research reports and the availability of these summaries can be as long as several months. Learning of a development is useless if others have formed an alliance with the source before you. In fast-breaking areas, even a week can make a crucial difference.

Investments in new entrepreneurial ventures, like participation in university research groups, can be a useful window on new developments. New venture investments can be direct or through funds managed by venture capitalists. These funds offer a wider scope than individual investments. Some focus on specific sectors if there are enough opportunities and interested investors. Typically, the products of venture funds include periodic reports and opportunities to visit investee firms, plus any financial gains. Direct investing offers closer ties to individual ventures and a chance for exclusivity.

Venture capital goes primarily to firms meeting substantial growth criteria. It usually is not attracted to slow-growth firms that might still have value for particular investors, or to capital-intensive firms such as those with new chemical products, because plant startup costs are too high.

Scan in Leading Geographic Areas

People who live or work in Washington, D.C., benefit from advanced technology developed in the Soviet Union. That is because the Soviets are world leaders in metal welding and casting technology. When the builders of Washington's Metrorail subway system were looking for the latest and best way to weld the rails, they found their way to a technology developed at a welding institute in Kiev.

The Japanese wash their clothes in colder water than Americans. Thus, because Japanese surfactants must work harder to get clothes clean, surfactant technology is more advanced there. On the other side of the world, water in Europe averages more than twice the mineral content of typical U.S. wash water. New water-softening ingredients, which enable surfactants to work better, tend to appear first on the Continent.

Laws requiring seat belt use were passed in Europe several years before similar rules were mandated in the United States. So European firms were leaders in advances like belts that have shoulder harnesses and automatically retract in a crash.

These illustrations underscore a valuable point: Some developments are more advanced in certain places because of local physical, economic, cultural, or governmental circumstances. Scans that focus on such areas can be productive ways to find advanced concepts.

For larger nations, the same kinds of geographic leadership patterns are evident in specific regions. Southern California, for example, is an early trend-setter in U.S. auto buyer tastes. Japanese auto makers took advantage of this by locating design studios there and by forming alliances, well before U.S. firms, with local design schools.

To find leading geographic areas in your field, scan the international literature and note the sources of articles and cited references. Asking experts about leading areas can also help.

When periodic scanning of another locale will meet your needs, you can collect information through regular visits—such as Minnetonka's shopping trips to Europe. However, some places are sufficiently important sources to warrant constant attention.

Many American, European, and Japanese firms, for example, have special technical information collection operations in other countries. These units typically employ a few people who screen journal articles and papers presented at industry association and technical society meetings, translate scientific reports, and answer requests for technical data from company scientists and engineers at home.

Many firms also locate R&D centers in technically active places, both to tap local expertise and to be close to pertinent developments. Procter & Gamble, for instance, developed its Liquid Tide detergent by combining surfactant technology it developed in Japan with water-softening ingredients from its Brussels laboratories.[6]

Consider Broadcasting Your Message

New opportunities can also be located by telling the world what you're looking for. This approach can be useful when the information sought is widely dispersed and when public knowledge of your interest in a topic would not hurt your position or is likely to be known to competitors through other means.

Broadcasting methods include circulating brochures describing company products and abilities, providing information for computer data banks that facilitate communication between prospective buyers and sources and with other potential partners, and advertising.

Honeywell, General Electric, and Sweden's SKF, for example, use newspapers and trade journals to advertise capabilities they have developed and to suggest potential applications in other areas.

Organizing and Managing the Scanning Process

For companies in changing environments, scanning should be part of everyone's job through ongoing contacts, reading, and observations. From the shipping manager who learns of a new procedure for offloading trucks to the executive who discovers a new company at a trade conference, these sources can help keep a firm abreast of developments across its environment.

People at Apple Computer often engage in informal discussions with friends and colleagues from other firms about potential opportunities for working together. Apple regards the informal contacts as an important source of alliances.

At Nippon Steel, each of the firm's nine thousand engineers is expected to exchange information on needs and rough concepts through informal daily discussions with customers and suppliers. To explore opportunities further, Nippon holds periodic technical conferences with specific users or manufacturers to discuss common technological subjects. Ideas from these contacts lead to about thirty to forty joint evaluation and research alliances each year.[7]

Scanning may also require more focused efforts, plus ways to share information collected at one place in a firm with others in the firm. In these cases the people involved and organizational arrangements are important elements of the process.

Choosing People for Important Scans

Scanning is a creative activity that appears deceptively simple. We all scan in some fashion, so it is natural to believe anyone can do it. But knowing where to look, how to anticipate potential value, and how to combine apparently unrelated facts, as well as having the curiosity to probe unusual sources, are uncommon abilities.

People who are particularly good at scanning are naturally inquisitive. They tend to search widely and develop more external information contacts than others.

The breakthrough to high-temperature superconductivity happened just this way. Two scientists at IBM's Zurich Research Laboratory in Switzerland, K. Alex Müller and J. Georg Bednorz, spent three years creating new oxide compounds to test their electrical properties. Then one day Dr. Bednorz read in a French chemical journal about a particular new oxide. The scientists who discovered the compound were primarily chemists, and never tested it for superconductivity. And scientists working in superconductivity don't normally read chemistry publications. It took Bednorz's creative probing to uncover the opportunity.

Effective scanners understand their organization's needs, so know what kind of information is important. Good analytic capabilities are required for data collection and processing. These qualities in a scanner increase the user's faith in the process, which improves the chances that the results will be accepted.[8]

In some engineering fields company-specific requirements and work that involves few outside contacts combine to create a jargon unique to each firm. As a result, it can be hard for people in one firm to appreciate ideas and information from another.

Overcoming this technical language barrier requires a two-step process of finding relevant outside information and then translating it into terms that are more meaningful to those on the inside.

This task is best performed by people who have developed "gatekeeping" skills through their own interests and activities. Such people are typically more creative than their colleagues, are often project-level supervisors who scan and translate as part of their jobs, and are usually recognized for this talent. Significantly, their presence contributes materially to the performance of product and process development projects.[9]

To scan a geographic area, some firms employ people who are already familiar with the locale. In one case a large Tokyo-based construction firm hired an American who had majored in Japanese studies. His job, which first placed him at the firm's headquarters and then at its New York office, is to find new U.S. developments that might be useful in construction.

Other firms train people for such tasks. One French company with long-term interests in the American market has been sending French employees to U.S. universities, both to understand the American culture and to develop contacts.

These two approaches—recruiting people from a locale and training employees to understand it—have different merits. Hiring someone from another culture opens an immediate window on that person's geographic area. This provides closer contacts than a "sensitized" foreigner could easily achieve. Being able to get inside the other culture can be important for scans that require considerable face-to-face discussions to uncover key insights.[10] By contrast, people from another culture must be trained to grasp a firm's particular needs.

Making Organization Arrangements

Information channels from external sources to final users should be as short as possible. Qualitative information tends to degrade and lose its credibility as it gets repackaged and moves through different people, units, and levels.

For these reasons some level of scanning should be done by people in each group, to meet its needs. Those within a unit are most able to interpret the implications of new developments in their field and can read nuances others would miss. They are also exposed to information others never see.

Special groups, such as geographically based technical staffs, can be useful when scanning scale economies exceed individual unit abilities, and when different client units have similar needs.

In the computer industry, software availability is a major determinant of equipment sales. Approximately one-third of all software IBM leases for use on large and medium-size computers comes from outside sources. The firm thus established an Installed User Program Department as a focal point for collecting information on software developed outside the company from its field representatives and directly from customers.

Interesting programs located by this department are referred to relevant IBM divisions, which apply their own evaluation criteria.

Specialized scanning units that serve different client groups run the risk of priority conflicts and organizational distance, which can inhibit understandings or responsiveness and weaken client acceptance. Close internal links are thus essential. GEVENCO, General Electric's wholly owned venture capital unit, reportedly suffered from low visibility within GE and weak understandings of client needs. For this and other reasons it was eventually disbanded.[11]

Using Informal Networks

Larger firms have a dilemma. Size works to their advantage by providing more exposure to outside sources. Yet size may raise barriers to information flows between units that normally do not work together. Clearly, no formal structure can ensure that information picked up by a person in one unit will get to a distant unit. Under these conditions you have to rely on informal contacts.

The experience of U.S.-based Vistakon, a $13-million maker of specialty contact lenses, is informative. Vistakon is a unit of Johnson & Johnson, the big health care firm. Like many small companies, Vistakon's growth was restrained by a limited product line. A breakthrough came when a Danish salesman for Janssen Pharmaceutica, J&J's European drug company, heard of a Danish opthalmologist who had discovered how to make contact lenses cheaply enough to be thrown away after a week, freeing wearers from the trouble of constantly cleaning and occasionally losing a lens.

The salesman had read about Vistakon in J&J's annual report and contacted Vistakon's president, who hopped on a plane and within three weeks had struck a deal. Vistakon developed the new lens, named Acuvue, which it introduced in 1988. Annual sales could reach $100 million by the early 1990s.[12]

Significantly, Vistakon and Janssen are just two of 166 individual Johnson & Johnson companies. Perhaps in many firms, the observations and contacts that led to Acuvue might not be made. Yet the same forces that are driving companies to form alliances compel them to be in constant touch with their environments, often in unpredictable ways. Then, the ability to form internal networks is a decisive strength. Firms that do this well, like Johnson & Johnson, emphasize open organizations as a key part of their cultures.

To be sure, formal structures and processes are appropriate when scanning involves repetitive tasks and constant information flows. Then, as with any organizational arrangement, formality reinforces desired behavior and improves efficiency. However, imposing routine on inherently *ad hoc* activities will stifle the very practices that must be encouraged.

To appreciate this, consider the common practice of circulating publications among people in an office. This arrangement ensures that everyone eventually sees each journal, but it does not reduce the reading burden. Further, the information explosion has become a publications explosion. Adding more journals or more people to the routing slip only magnifies the problem. By contrast, informal networking—where people pass notes or articles to others they know are interested—seems to be far more effective.

For things to work this way, each person should have easy and timely access to publications important to him or her, with the expectation that people will keep each other informed.

Researchers at Minnetonka are expected to review hundreds of journals a month to keep abreast of scientific advances and consumer interests. This is possible only because the task is allocated to many different people who understand the firm's needs and communicate interesting findings to each other.[13]

Recognize Obstacles to Scanning

Scanning is valuable only if it stimulates ideas and produces new perspectives among decision-makers. Yet taking timely advantage of new information isn't easy. The data originate outside the firm, arrive in unsanitized and unanticipated formats, bypass standard information channels, and can challenge the status quo. Being responsive to this kind of input takes an adaptive, cooperative, outward-looking culture. Richard Reever, Minnetonka's vice president of research, says: "The philosophy here is what's happening in the marketplace, what's happening sociologically, how can we generate a product?"

Unfortunately, some corporate cultures are not accustomed to collecting and acting on information that goes beyond routine practice. In other firms internal turf boundaries inhibit people from sharing and benefiting from what others in the firm already know.

15

Choosing Partners and Building Alliances

The more we talked, the more we sensed a commonality of views and values.

—Marty Gibson, Corning's group president, on negotiations with Ciba-Geigy

WHEN France's SNECMA picked General Electric as its partner to build a new class of commercial aircraft engines, some observers thought it was a poor choice. Neither firm was in this market, which was dominated by Pratt & Whitney. Further, United Technologies Corporation, Pratt's parent, held 10 percent of SNECMA's stock, and the firms knew each other well.

Yet SNECMA, which had a strong desire to enter the commercial market, recognized a similar need in GE. SNECMA believed GE's position created a powerful incentive to work harder than Pratt. Also, GE had a solid technical foundation and reputation, and GE and SNECMA had developed a good working relationship through an earlier co-production alliance. And there were strong bonds between Gerhard Neumann, the chief of GE's aircraft engines unit, and SNECMA's president, René Ravaud.

The rest of the story has already been told: The firms' steadfast commitments to their objective and a strong relationship that included high-level executives fused their resources into a winning combination. Their alliance, CFM International, became and remains the world leader in its markets.

Obviously, you must find complementary strengths to justify an alliance. However, as GE and SNECMA have demonstrated, compatibility and commitment are also important. To put it another way, your evaluation of possible partners must consider implementation.

Successful alliances start with partner choice and build from there. From scanning, you know the potential candidates. Next, analysis to find the best match suggests priority firms. Negotiations with your top choice are the launching pad: This is where mutual comfort and commitment begin. Picking the right kind of alliance to use then depends on your mutual objective.

Partner Selection Criteria

The only reason to pursue an alliance is that it is the best way to reach your objective. Thus partner choice must build on a precise definition of your priority needs and what is most critical to meet them. Clearly, no firm will make a perfect match. Similarly, prospective partners will see gaps in what you can offer. So each firm must satisfy its basic requirements and adjust to the rest.

When a pair of Asian and American firms were negotiating to form an alliance, the Asian company found its prospective partner far less willing to share information than it had experienced with other American firms. Yet this firm had exceptional strengths that could give the two a substantial competitive advantage.

From discussions with local banks and some of the firm's trading partners, the Asians learned the American firm's restraint was probably due to its rural, conservative values. They decided it was worth making an extra effort to accommodate this style and agreed to form an alliance. In the ten-plus years since then, information sharing is still a difficult issue. But each firm has made adjustments, and they have built a thriving alliance.

Another example is the small British tool firm that needed a partner to enter the German market. This firm had two credible prospects, one German and one Italian. The Italian and British companies both were owned and run by their founding families. Because of these similar backgrounds, early discussions led to immediate rapport. Yet joint studies suggested that building the market share needed to be profitable in Germany would take more than both firms could afford.

The German firm, on the other hand, was part of a large enterprise with a solid position in its home market. However, the British family was uncomfortable. The Germans were proposing substantial changes in their product line. Further, some family members had an instinctive fear of large organizations. They agreed that the changes might be appropriate to penetrate the German market but believed that making those adjustments would yield too much control to an organization they didn't understand. Even so, the need for more resources persuaded them to work with the Germans.

The alliance ended four months after it began. The discomfort at the start fueled growing misunderstandings, and a good working relationship seemed out of reach. So the British went back to the Italians, and the two revised their plans to go after selected regional markets in Germany.

These examples illustrate a basic principle: The circumstances of an alliance define separate criteria that must be met to reach your objective. Without enough strength, you cannot succeed in the market. Without some level of compatibility, you won't work well together. Also, as CFM International demonstrates, every alliance requires sufficient commitment from each firm. Without that, the needed efforts won't be made. These points are summarized here:

Criteria for Partner Choice

Criterion	Measure
Combined strength	Market requirements
Compatibility	Acceptable trust, understandings
Commitment	Needed effort

For those situations where the match with another firm isn't clear, you can move toward forming a stronger alliance through one or more steps.

This is how Dow Chemical approaches some joint ventures: If questions about appropriate skills or the best way to approach a market can't be resolved, if compatibility isn't clear, or if one party is reluctant to make a solid commitment, then Dow and the other firm sometimes say, "Let's work together on a small, less formal scale and see how it goes." That gives them an opportunity to assess a stronger bond.

Note that a firm's alliance opportunities depend on the strengths it can offer. In the early days of genetic engineering, for example, the technology's value was less proven than it is today. Young entrepreneurial firms had to give up rights to critical know-how, manufacturing, and marketing in exchange for vital capital. Today these firms are introducing major products and are being treated as equals in potentially lucrative deals with the large drug firms. Typical alliances involve even sharing of costs and revenues from global markets.[1]

Meeting the three criteria for partner choice helps reduce opportunism in an alliance. Of course, you must be sure an arrangement is really an alliance—mutual need, shared risks, and a common objective. These factors encourage commitment. Opportunism is further reduced when partners' combined strengths have clear strategic value, when they are compatible, and when their commitments are strong enough to overcome any differences.

Finding Strategic Synergy

A potential partner's competence is judged by studying its strengths, weaknesses, resources, and track record. This is similar to traditional competitive analysis, with more dimensions.

Take a Market Perspective

Look at a potential alliance from the market's vantage point. Include in this picture future combinations of other firms. Might these create more strength than what you are planning now?

Consider Your Partner

Assess a planned alliance from your partner's position, to be sure it will be the best combination for both firms. Don't assume a prospective partner knows enough about your firm to assure a good combination.

In an early Ciba-Geigy alliance with Alza, a California biotechnology firm, Alza committed its broad range of advanced drug delivery systems, which exceeded the range of drugs Ciba could use with it. The mismatch was a significant contributor to the alliance's demise.[2]

Advance Your Independence

Be certain the alliance will increase your independence. Also consider how it will strengthen your partner. Be sure you will not be creating a new competitor or strengthening an opponent at your expense.

If you intend to share key know-how, are you comfortable with how a prospective partner will guard it?

Will Key Resources Be There?

Be explicit about the availability of important resources. If key experts are needed, will they have the time?

In smaller markets and less developed nations, there is some benefit in looking for partners in related areas beyond obvious candidates in the same business. In such cases management abilities may be a more pressing requirement than specific product-market experience.

Think About Expansion

Does a prospective partner have the strengths you will need for later expansion? Also determine whether the other firm has obligations that could inhibit expanding an alliance after its initial success.

For Teamwork, Draw Skills from Both

For teamwork, ensure that each firm contributes strategic abilities. This is crucial to maximize day-to-day cooperation among operating people.

Could Their Troubles Give You Problems?

Identify problems that might be transferred to you. Poor labor relations or a bad safety record, for example, can be like sap on a tree; they stick to whoever gets too close.

Judge Factors They Don't Control

Consider whether circumstances beyond the other firm's control will affect your joint performance. This takes more probing in unfamiliar settings.

For instance, many alliances in China depend on a supporting infrastructure, which isn't always available.

Will You Be Compatible?

A relationship depends on the people directly involved and partners' corporate cultures. Both are important; even long-term employees may have styles that vary from company norms. Each firm's organization and decision-making processes may also affect an alliance.

Get to Know the Key People

Dow Chemical and Corning Glass invest substantial time with a prospective partner's key people. In-depth discussions in the context of negotiating an alliance help them understand individuals' styles and technical competence. Mutual comfort or friction here is a good predictor of future relationships. Dow and Corning have declined potential partners when the chemistry wasn't right.

One measure Corning uses to judge compatibility is whether people can comfortably raise issues with each other. Anything that causes deep discomfort suggests an alliance may not work. People who don't like or accept each other cannot perform well in joint problem-solving.

During the dialogue to plan Ciba Corning Diagnostics, people developed a sense of how their counterparts made decisions and what their tradeoffs were. On most issues they reached the same conclusions, which led to a growing feeling that they could work together. Human resources received ample attention; they were the backbone of the business. "The more we talked, the more we sensed a commonality of views and values regarding how we treat people," reports Marty Gibson, Corning's group president.

Look for a Cultural Match on Key Values

Understanding a firm's culture tells you how most of its people do many things, much of the time. Cultural compatibility is especially important for longer-term alliances or for alliances involving cooperation between several people on each side.

Marty Gibson notes that one important source of bonding between Ciba and Corning is the similarity of the firms' basic values. Both invest heavily in R&D, strongly emphasize employee loyalty and involvement, and are served by long-term executives.

These shared values support understandings that research takes time, a pair of Swiss and American companies cannot be expected to have everything lined up correctly the first day, and solutions to problems come from working issues through with people.

When Corning is entering a new context, it often does background work on the integrity of the lead people. Dow Chemical looks for style differences in how the other firm's executives conduct themselves, in what people say and do about relationships, and in the opulence of corporate offices. The values of a prospective partner's leaders indicate what they are likely to emphasize.

If a firm's leadership "wants to get the last squeal out of the pig," one Dow Chemical manager explains, "if they are opportunistic in everything they do, that's how other employees will behave. Or if they work for long-term mutually beneficial returns for customers and stockholders, that's what employees will do."

Understand How You Will Work Together

Possibly to a significant extent, cooperation will depend on communication and coordination within and between firms. Companies with radically different structures must invest more effort in managing their interface. Also be sure critical internal links exist.

Early in Ford's alliance with Excel, the window maker, Ford's Glass Division and Excel developed a part for a new vehicle. Excel had done a lot of work on this, but Ford lacked the internal coordination links needed to support the alliance. Thus other parts of Ford followed traditional practice, and the business went to a different supplier. On similar deals since then, Ford has included all relevant groups in alliance planning early enough to affect negotiations.

You can avoid discord and be better prepared by knowing something about how a partner works before getting started. Dow Chemical wants to understand how a potential partner makes decisions. Strong central authority, in contrast to appropriate delegation and decentralization, can inhibit operating-level cooperation and affect Dow's ability to work with a firm.

How Have They Performed in Other Alliances?

When Corning is contemplating a joint venture, it often uses third parties to learn how a potential ally conducts itself as a partner. Corning also gets calls from others inquiring about firms with which it has had joint ventures.

It's worth knowing if a prospective partner has been successful with the same kind of alliance you are contemplating. Are they effective with other cultures? Do they always want to have the lead, or expect another firm to be in charge? If you anticipate a 50–50 joint venture, have they had any that failed? If they have litigated with a partner, find out why.

Limit Innovation at the Start

Strategic alliances can blend radically different resources to produce significant innovations. Yet it is worth avoiding substantial internal change at the start. An innovation that disrupts either organization adds to any confusion between firms. If you have large cultural differences or don't know each other well, begin with less radical efforts.

Will Both Firms Be Committed?

An alliance between two firms involves at least four groups of people: those on each side who will be working together, and higher-level executives whose support will be necessary.

Be Sure of Operating Support

At the operating level, alliances don't go far without enthusiasm. Cooperation with another firm—especially a new partner—takes more effort than comparable internal activities where people and routines are familiar.

Even in participative cultures like those at Corning and Dow Chemical, success on any project depends on active support by those involved. People can't just agree to go along; they must reallocate their time, invest their resources, and include the project in their group's priorities.

Whenever an alliance will require significant internal adjustments, there should be a champion on each side who believes in the opportunity and sees the benefit to each firm. This is important in all kinds of companies. In more rigid cultures, nothing new happens without a maverick manager cutting through the status quo.

"I had many hours of arguments with the party apparatus in Moscow," says Vatslav Krotov, president of Applied Engineered Systems, the Soviet–American joint venture with Combustion Engineering, the first to be established under perestroika. "There are people in the Soviet

Union who want joint ventures to fail. The petrochemical bosses are still offended that I took their best workers away."[3]

In more participative firms, every project is competing for resources and attention with others that are also being championed.

It takes a true believer to invest the time to persuade others to add a proposed alliance to their priorities. For Apple Computer the presence of such an evangelist—who may be the person given the lead for an alliance or someone at a higher level—is a clear signal of implementation potential.

Be especially wary of alliances that will involve different units in a firm having weak championing and poor internal coordination. At best, someone from your firm may have to search for the right people inside a partner's organization to keep things on track. At worst, internal conflicts may not be resolved. Apple has learned from experience that such alliances are hard to manage, get weak internal support, and usually do not succeed.

Look for Policy-Level Commitment

Without informed top-level backing, an alliance will die as soon as difficult issues arise. Dow Chemical considers its own willingness to commit top people before it forms an alliance. Corning has pulled out of negotiations when it became evident that a prospective partner's senior people did not actively support an alliance.

How Does the Alliance Fit In?

Also judge likely commitments by understanding how an alliance contributes to each firm's goals. Don't expect to get needed attention if an alliance is inconsistent with a partner's priorities. One test is to determine what other investments or activities will benefit from the success of an alliance.

Among the communications cable manufacturers with which Corning discussed possible optical fiber alliances, it found the most interest at Siemens. Fiber was a potential threat to copper cable, and Siemens was not as heavily involved in this business as the others, so it was more willing to make the change.

Corning wants to know that each firm's need for the other will remain important enough so each can be counted on for an alliance's expected duration.

How Well Do They Meet Their Commitments?

Unfortunately, some firms don't persist even when something is important to them. It is thus worth learning about a prospective partner's track record in this regard. Dow Chemical looks for the kinds of successes a potential partner has had—whether they give up after failures, or try again.

New Alliances with Past Partners

After years of successful cooperation, GE and SNECMA work together as a single team, with substantial joint learning, mutual high regard for each other's skills, and considerable shared understandings about how each firm thinks and works. This compatibility comes from experience, plus specific efforts to build mutual knowledge. Issues get resolved faster and easier now. Overall, there is a great deal of comfort.

This experience, which GE's Aircraft Engine Group has also had with other partners, makes it increasingly easy to develop new programs together. Partner desires therefore carry some weight when it comes time to launch a new effort. "You can't just dump a long-term good partner if it wants to participate in a new program," one GE executive remarks.

Clearly, working together can improve compatibility and make it easier to judge the depth of new commitments. Strategic benefits may also be significant: A joint learning curve leads to lower costs; mutual adjustments shorten response times; familiarity and respect break down "not-invented-here" barriers, promoting higher levels of innovation.

Yet there is good reason to consider a different partner when circumstances change. Each firm is responsible for its own survival. Staying with a current partner isn't wise if it is going to compromise your independence.

If a partner does not maintain its abilities, if significant new resources appear somewhere else, if changed market conditions make other skills attractive, or if a different firm is likely to invest substantially more effort in a new opportunity, you are obliged out of self-interest to consider a change.

As SNECMA demonstrated when it chose GE over Pratt & Whitney, the right partner is the firm that best meets all three criteria of combined strength, compatibility, and commitment.

Negotiating to Build an Alliance

How people treat each other at the start sets the course of an alliance. This is where mutual understandings take root and dedication is built. Significantly, your chief objective should not be to write an agreement. That will be produced along the way. Its value is only as good as your comfort and commitment.

What is most important is to complete discussions in the same spirit as developed among negotiators for IVECO Ford, Ciba Corning Diagnostics, Dow Chemical and Personal Care, Autolatina, and other successful alliances. In each of these, attitudes and understandings cultivated during negotiations became a sturdy bridge into the whole relationship.

This Is Where Your Relationship Begins

Under some conditions negotiations are necessarily a contest: There is just so much pie to divide, and one firm can get more only at the other's expense. With an alliance, the objective is to cooperate to make a bigger pie.

The way you develop understandings and resolve differences thus has to build mutually attractive solutions and improve your ability to deal with future issues. Neither firm can afford to win a point that undercuts mutual trust.

People learn differently from negative and positive experiences. Just one unpleasant incident—such as being misled or pressured against your will—imprints the event on your memory. Like touching a hot stove, you keep your distance after that. A good experience, by contrast, must be repeatedly reinforced before people accept the pattern. Think of how long it takes to become good friends with someone and of how the mistakes we sometimes make inhibit this.

Negotiations between people who haven't worked together thus shape their convictions about each other for a long time to come. One bad negotiation can do lasting damage to a working relationship.[4]

In discussions, don't present your philosophy of strategic alliances. Anyone can read how to do things right and repeat what they read to others. It is better to learn how each firm actually works. Corning, for example, does not discuss what it regards as good joint venture practice with prospective partners. Corning learns about a firm's style before and during negotiations to conclude whether they can work together comfortably.

Explore and Define Your Interests

In the parable of the oranges, two pairs of men are each given an orange, which they must share. As a fair compromise, the first pair quickly agree to cut their orange in half. Each man gets to use his part as he wishes. The second pair begin by exploring their interests. They learn that one of them hopes to make orange juice, while the other wants the rind for marmalade. So they use the whole orange for juice, and have the whole rind left for jam.

A strong alliance builds on finding the best way to meet each firm's needs. To do this, begin with a joint exploration of the various interests and issues involved. What are each firm's objectives? What are the different topics that might be included in an agreement? What are people's initial concerns regarding each subject?

In the process of asking these questions, you may find other interests that are not in conflict, which can lead to creative solutions. Joint exploration is more likely to uncover complementary interests than presentations of gross positions. Significantly, exploring interests also helps generate a problem-solving attitude.

Preparations for a meeting will include discussions in each firm about its objectives and priorities. It is a good idea to talk about what the other firm might need at the same time. Chances are, you will misjudge some of this. Even so, putting their needs on your agenda helps build a "win-win" frame of mind. Also, when you get together, differences between how you perceive their interests and how they describe them make you more sensitive to them. Further, each firm has a different perspective. Your experience may help reveal issues that concern them, of which they were not aware.

The first product of your negotiations should be a brief description of your separate and mutual objectives and the commitments these imply. Knowing what you can achieve together, and that your own interests will be protected, helps you keep going through the more challenging thickets of negotiations.

Ford and IVECO negotiators, for example, had several meetings over about three months to discuss each firm's objectives. They produced a three-page document that described their mutual objective, recognized the consequences of consolidation, and noted their expected obligations to the venture and how related activities would be performed. The document became a common frame of reference for everything that followed. One participant likened it to a beacon that illuminated their path through the high and low points of the negotiations.

Identify True Deal-Breakers at the Start

A productive alliance isn't possible if it violates a basic need of either firm. Describing such positions early permits both firms to decide if these are acceptable.

Dow Chemical, for example, disclosed the price it would need to make its diaper material alliance with Personal Care worthwhile. Dow did so as early as possible to avoid later unpleasant surprises.

Be sure to separate absolute needs from "wants"—those things you would like to have, but which are not critical for reaching your goals. The more conditions you impose on an alliance, the less flexibility there is to find acceptable solutions and the more you lose credibility as a constructive partner.

Isolate Divisive Issues

Some negotiators will probably be working together in the alliance. Topics that may create conflicts of interest among them should be handled by others.

To avoid creating divided loyalties among managers who would negotiate Autolatina and then move into the venture, Ford and Volkswagen worked on a number of key issues separate from the main negotiations. These included net worth valuations to determine how much each firm had to contribute for its share, and export policies, which affected Autolatina's profitability and both parents' domestic markets.

Work Toward Total Clarity

Be willing to work on any issue your partner believes is important. The goal should be to maximize comfort and minimize potential conflicts. Unless you know each other well, don't be misled by agreeing to resolve a major question after the alliance is under way. That may not be possible.

Specifically define the scope, key objectives, priorities, important tasks, milestones, and performance measures for your alliance. Different firms do this in different ways. Omitting this formal step in an alliance can cause serious confusion.

As a check for completeness, discuss and agree on how you will deal with each major uncertainty. The following list, from Chapter 6, summarizes the sources of uncertainty that could affect an alliance.

External Uncertainties	*Internal Uncertainties*
Economic environment	Goals
Market responses	Partner abilities
Other partners' reactions	Latent conflict
Liabilities	Planning gaps
Government approvals	Authority
	Relationships
	Performance
	Benefits
	Commitments
	Opportunism

It is legitimate to ask for and to receive all information relevant to a planned alliance. The more firms are going to depend on each other, the more each needs to be comfortable with its partner's contributions, and possibly its financial strength and other aspects of its business.

Dow Chemical will disclose anything a partner reasonably needs to know to make decisions and expects its partner to do the same.

To protect its interests, Dow's proprietary disclosures go through a sequence of steps. Dow begins with a general description of a technology and what it will do, and discusses business concepts and areas of mutual interest. The purpose here is to determine if there is a basis for a strong alliance by making claims that can later be supported with detailed facts. More information is disclosed as mutual interest, trust, need to know, and the certainty of forming an alliance grow. Sensitive disclosures are backed up with binding agreements.

Avoid Coercive Tactics

If the other firm feels pressured to do things your way, anger and frustration defeat reason, shared understandings are unlikely, there is less opportunity for effective communication, and its representatives will feel their interests and views are spurned. In short, a forced agreement is hard to implement and likely to disintegrate.

Roger Fisher and Scott Brown of the Harvard Negotiation Project point to a crucial distinction between treating a negotiation as a win-lose situation and managing it as a shared and difficult task for partners trying to create a good solution to a difficult problem.[5] To be sure, firms have conflicting needs, emotions may run high, and people will have to change their views to agree. Yet there is a sharp contrast between trying to force a decision against another person's will and using candid persuasion, which convinces the mind.

Above all, don't threaten bad consequences if the other firm rejects your proposals. Agreements made under duress earn little commitment. If you really believe your approach must be followed and can't convince the other side, the best solution is to improve your options for dealing elsewhere.

Be as Open to Persuasion as You Are Persuasive

To build creatively, get out as much information as possible before developing solutions. Then, when describing what you are willing to do, be clear that your suggestion is not the only approach you will accept.

Whether you are proposing how to resolve an issue or responding to your partner, share your thinking. Relate why this is fair and reasonable. But no matter how well you know the subject, let them know that you are open to persuasion with better logic or information.

Discuss objective benchmarks—your mutual goals, other opportunities, or market comparisons—for deciding what is fair. Legitimacy in everyone's eyes is one measure of a good agreement. It is easier to yield to an objective standard than to a rigidly held arbitrary position. Ford's and Volkswagen's desires for Autolatina, for example, emphasized cost, quality, and productivity goals that served as benchmarks for their discussions and decisions.

Be as flexible as possible. Aside from valid deal-breakers, taking an early fixed position limits the other side's options. Think of what that would do to you: It makes you resent being boxed in and may encourage you to respond with a similar tactic. This does more than threaten a relationship. Rigid positions make it hard to work out a better agreement later, when people know more about each other's interests and can jointly explore paths they did not previously see.

Thus on difficult issues, instead of continuing an unproductive debate, try to invent several alternatives. The more options there are to consider, the better your chances of crafting an agreement that reconciles differences and builds synergy from your strengths. Recall that to develop a mutually acceptable business plan for Autolatina, Ford and VW negotiators went through more than twenty versions as each firm's needs and different issues surfaced and became clear.

Avoid Quid Pro Quo Bargaining

The easiest way to agree is to accept a proposal you don't like in exchange for the other firm's accepting one it doesn't like. This tactic produces weaker alliances by reducing combined strength, compatibility, or commitment.

It may be necessary to do something you would rather avoid in order to meet a partner's critical needs. Leaving important interests unmet reduces commitment. Yet if every such move requires a compensating move for "fairness," both firms have weakened their position.

Ford, for instance, wanted to structure Autolatina as a single holding company for more direct management links to the Brazilian and Argentine units. But VW's needs dictated otherwise, so Ford accepted VW's position, which was to have Autolatina Brazil "coordinate" operations in Argentina.

Think of creating an alliance as building a team. On the one hand, you have to adjust to each person's skills and limitations. On the other hand, a team whose members will work for its best interest only if every move is rewarded will find cooperation difficult.

Build Internal Understandings and Commitments

While it is good management practice to give negotiators clear authority, it is hard to delegate what you can't anticipate. Even if all issues could be foreseen, an alliance is only as strong as its backing in each firm. So take the time to be sure relevant executives and operating people fully support the objectives and progress toward them.

Corning, for instance, has muddled joint venture negotiations and has had to backpeddle when its negotiators' objectives were not supported at the highest relevant decision-making levels.

In the process of building support, internal negotiations should build new links that will be necessary and should flush out and resolve dissent. It will be easier to spot internal problems if you use the same decision channels for negotiations and for implementation, provided all players are included. Remember Ford's early experience with Excel, in which Ford had not provided for coordination across different units to support the alliance.

Before Ciba Corning Diagnostics was formed, it "died on the operating table" twice, a senior Ciba executive says. Many issues came up that could not be resolved. At one time, some people in Ciba grew uncomfortable with the emerging strategic concept of the business. The internal negotiations that resolved this strengthened Ciba's support.

Who Should Be Involved?

Managers who will have day-to-day responsibility for an alliance should negotiate it and write the business plan. People expected to produce results are more likely to bring up relevant issues and to be dedicated to an alliance's success. Just as significantly, the earliest partner bonds are among people who get to know each other in negotiations and build a shared vision of the alliance.

Higher-level executives should participate in negotiations to the extent their approvals, support, and understandings will be needed. In Dow's alliance with Personal Care, top executives from both firms met toward the end of negotiations to confirm the major concepts and risks. For Autolatina, which involved important aspects of each firm's business, senior Ford and VW executives led the negotiations.

What Goes into the Agreement

The contents of an alliance agreement depend on firms' knowledge of each other. Corning believes nothing should be taken on trust that can reasonably be formalized. All issues of concern to either party should be included. But details of implementation, monitoring, penalties, and control should be held to a minimum.

There is a difference between defining areas of understanding and concern in an agreement, and putting in all the contingencies. Clause after clause of contingency planning assumes an understanding will not be implemented fairly, which affects the tone of a relationship. Similarly, trying to cover every possible alternative during negotiations implies a lack of trust, which makes it harder to have a win-win attitude.

More detail is appropriate when starting with a new partner or in a new context. For example, the agreement for a U.S. joint venture between Tungsram, based in Hungary, and Action Industries, of the United States, has considerable content resulting from the need to embrace two different legal systems—and the Hungarian corporate counsel's need to become familiar with the American legal framework.

Picking the Best Structure

With alliances, as in other aspects of business, strategy determines structure: The kind of alliance to use depends on your objectives and approach to them. Specifically, this includes the scope and duration of the activity and what each firm's policy and operating roles will be.

Several kinds of alliances are described in earlier chapters: informal, contractual, minority investments, joint ventures, strategic networks, and alliances with universities (a form of contractual alliance).[6] Three of these are summarized in the following table.

	Contract	Minority Investment	Joint Venture
Scope	Individual project	Close to full scope of investee business Multiple projects	May be distinct from partners
Duration	Project	Indefinite long-term	Indefinite long-term
Operating Control	By each firm on its side of interface	By each firm on its side of interface	May be shared
Policy Role	None	Explicit for one, may be for other Must represent all shareholders	Explicit for both Represent own interests

Features of Different Alliances

Informal Alliances

The guideline for informal alliances is simple: With no binding agreement, limit your risks. Any changes in either firm that depend on the alliance should at most be incremental.

Contractual Alliances

These are single-project alliances which may include major risks. For instance, Dow Chemical's investment in the diaper alliance with Personal Care involved several tens of millions of dollars and substantial market uncertainty.

In a contractual alliance neither firm gets a formal role in the other's operations or policies, although informal influence may be significant. To have a contractual alliance with a customer, for example, a firm may make basic changes in its delivery or quality assurance practices.

Minority Investments

Just as contracts replace informal alliances when risks are high, minority investments help build strong policy-level ties when firms have major long-term interests that can't be realized by occasional top-level contacts.

Typically, this involves multiple projects. Operating links are the same as with contractual alliances.

A minority investment makes sense only when the investee's business is focused on products and markets with clear strategic value for its partner. For the sake of independence and other stockholders' rights, a minority investor cannot affect a partner's policies for its own interests. A minority investment is the only kind of strategic alliance that is not feasible between major competitors; conflicting interests get in the way.

Joint Ventures

Like minority investments, joint ventures cement long-term mutual interests and give each partner an equity investment. Compared with minority investments, joint ventures offer more room for defining mutual objectives and for shared control at policy and operating levels. Joint venture partners can, for example, make any mutually agreed-upon changes in the venture. A minority investor must consider other shareholders. Further, a joint venture may have a distinct identity outside the scope of either partner.

To appreciate the difference between minority investments and joint ventures, consider CFM International, the jet engine alliance. Virtually all CFM activities are conducted by GE and SNECMA, but under CFM control. Neither partner can change any work it does for CFM without CFM approval. Further, through CFM, the partners jointly set all policies that affect it. The combination of tight policy and operating control makes CFM perform and compete as a single, integrated, responsive organization.

If the alliance were a minority investment—say by GE in SNECMA— GE would have a limited policy voice and neither firm would exercise significant control over the other's relevant activities.

To be sure, it is entirely possible to have joint R&D, marketing, or other activities without creating a new organization. Dow and Personal Care performed joint R&D; Northern Telecom and General Electric marketed their cellular phone system together. Similarly, joint operations can be managed without a new organization if one partner owns the facility and shares it under appropriate cost and risk allocation terms.

Yet each of these activities offers limited opportunities for shared control. There may be a joint coordinating group, but unless it has real authority over the activities—which would make it a joint venture— it cannot control. Such arrangements work best where the most critical decisions remain in each firm. By contrast, the purpose of creating a separate organization is to provide more opportunity for shared control.

Two conditions which make that desirable are when an alliance requires substantial independence from both firms, and when it involves significant integration of partner activities, as with CFM International.

Strategic Networks

Strategic networks are woven from any or all of the other kinds of alliances. Many firms participate in strategic networks to some extent. The issue here is not just when to use this kind of alliance, but also how to get more out of existing networks.

Other Considerations

While tax, securities, and other financial and legal factors may be important, don't let these compromise your choice of alliance. Otherwise, controls and commitments will not serve your mutual objective. Each kind of alliance has room for flexibility to meet partner's varying needs.

It is sometimes argued, for example, that because smaller companies often lack the capital for joint ventures, minority investments are a better choice for alliances between small and large firms. Yet when Corning and Genentech agreed to form Genencor, the industrial enzymes venture, Genencor needed substantial policy and operating involvement by both partners. But Genentech did not have the cash to invest. So Corning invested $15 million in Genentech for 5 percent of its equity. Genentech used these funds for its share of the venture.

16

Developing Effective
Relationships

*We're not only partners, we're good friends. And we do take into account
all aspects of each other's needs. We may fight like cats and dogs on
how to do a given thing, but when it comes to broad policy issues
we're like partners and friends.*

—Dow Chemical executive vice president Bob Keil,
on his firm's alliance with Schlumberger

IN 1974, soon after CFM International was approved by the French
and American governments, SNECMA's president René Ravaud,
planning a trip to General Electric, mentioned to GE's aircraft engines
chief Gerhard Neumann that he liked Kentucky Fried Chicken.

When Ravaud and his staff arrived near GE's Lynn, Massachusetts,
plant, they were taken to a local KFC outlet, which Neumann had
converted to a French restaurant for one day, complete with white
tablecloths, decor, and wine, and menus in French that featured fried
chicken. Overhead, an airplane towed a streamer acclaiming in French
the CFM product, again Neumann's touch. The affair made a tremendous
first impression on the SNECMA people, indicating GE's willingness
to look after the French firm's interests.

Clearly, how well firms work together determines the success of an
alliance. It can be extremely risky to leave this to chance. Every company
has its own way of working, its own priorities. An effective alliance
requires a smooth interface between partners and a relationship of trust
and understanding which, as GE displayed to SNECMA, confirms their
importance to each other.

235

Planning Interfirm Contacts

The set of connections between firms (or to a joint venture) should be complete. Take into account the resources, the levels and kinds of issues to be involved, geographic separation, and decisions to be made.

Direct Contacts Are Best

An effective bridge between partners comprises people from each firm who represent their separate units and personally furnish strengths important to the alliance. This principle applies to all kinds of close ties between firms. Companies having successful alliances with distributors, for instance, usually have the most competent and best-trained field sales forces in their industries. By involving high-quality people, these firms help distributors do their best.[1]

Having a designated contact person represent several groups to a partner does not work well. One individual cannot grasp the multifunctional expertise typically involved in an alliance. In addition, unless the person is at a high management level, he or she will not be in a position to commit different groups. Even then, this person is more remote from information about the alliance and commitments made at a distance may not hold.

Apple Computer has experienced single-point-of-contact arrangements in some alliances and found them wanting. When a person is there only as a boss or coordinator, he or she cannot make a real contribution and does not earn credibility from the other side.

Be aware that since different firms have different structures, needed connections may not be easily made unless the interfirm links are clearly defined. With CFM International, organizational contrasts at first made it difficult for GE and SNECMA people to find their counterparts.

Also make sure the people responsible for contacts have enough influence or authority in their units to ensure continued progress. At the start of Ciba Corning Diagnostics, the individuals chosen to be liaisons between Ciba's R&D and CCD did not have the power or respect to deliver their organizations. To improve the connection, CCD formed a technology committee of the board, with members from both parents. Chaired by Ciba's head of pharmaceutical research, the committee helped formulate programs to draw more strength from Ciba. CCD has also sent people to Ciba's R&D labs for a year or so to learn more about Ciba and to ease technology transfer.

Those who link their firms in an alliance represent their firms in the alliance and the alliance in their firms. This representation should reach out to customers if an alliance product will directly and significantly affect their ability to use a partner's goods or services.

In Apple's alliance with Digital Equipment, the two firms cooperated to produce a common product interface to integrate Apple's Macintosh into the DEC environment. That permits each firm separately to develop products for its customers in the same market. Each partner cannot, of course, have easy access to the other's sales force to meet with its own customers, yet each must be sure customer needs are satisfied. For this reason, a person from Apple's marketing group is on the DEC alliance team. He contributes in his area of expertise and represents the alliance product to Apple's customers. He makes sure key resources are delivered to customers and works to create customer comfort that the alliance product will be a reliable part of the total package.

How to Cooperate at a Distance

For complex programs, geography gets in the way of easy coordination. Having local representatives can keep things on track.

For Ford and Mazda, Ford's coordination support office in Hiroshima, Mazda's hometown, has proved much more effective than occasional formal meetings, with multiple agenda items, among people who are only acquaintances, and who are pressed for time on short visits from far away. In fact, when Ford has not had representatives in Hiroshima, issue resolution has been more difficult.

An on-site coordination unit is a staff function that serves the line organization. Ford's Hiroshima office, for example, includes people from each Ford business unit involved with Mazda, who make connections as necessary throughout Ford and link through negotiated relations into Mazda.

Still, real authority remains with Ford's operating units, where it belongs. The Hiroshima office cannot require Ford people to work through it, but must earn its value by serving operations. The fact that the office gets about 95 percent of Ford people coming from other locations is one measure of its performance. Individual project links remain between principals in each firm. These people are expected to stay in contact and to meet as necessary.

When staffing a coordination unit, look for people who can be effective in the other culture. They must also have good contacts in your firm. Someone who has been overseas for a long time may have lost his or her credibility at home and may lack the personal ties needed for easy access. Newcomers aren't useful in this role for the same reason.

Include Needed Authority at the Interface

Whether you cooperate informally or have a contractual alliance, minority investment, or joint venture, each firm should give one person the authority and accountability for the alliance. Together, these people lead their respective teams and recognize each other as appropriate contacts for resolving difficult issues.

It generally isn't possible for a team leader to have full authority on all items. But he or she must be high enough to understand and influence related policy questions and, once a program is under way, be able to make or effect all but the most critical decisions. Mutual trust and understanding between firms can't be complete when authority is absent. Corning has made mistakes in its alliances when it hasn't had contacts high enough in partner organizations.

Even as final arbiter, the lead manager should not control day-to-day contacts. This inhibits communications and implies individual ownership of an alliance, which discourages participation.

The way Apple Computer works is typical of firms that build constructive interfirm bridges. Apple does not like individual ownership of projects; this discourages commitments. On an Apple alliance team, which may include a product person, a field person, and a marketing person, each works as appropriate with his or her counterpart in the other firm. Each person takes the group lead on pertinent issues, with no one acting as filter or traffic cop.

Build an Interfirm Team

With a shared vision, the strengths to achieve it, easy contacts with each other, and needed authority, the people who come together at the interface have the potential to become a real team, in which the initial sharp line dividing them is blurred. This offers great power and creative energy; it gives firms uninhibited access to each other's abilities within the scope of their alliance.

This has been a hallmark of the GE–SNECMA interface, the CCD board of directors, and the Dow Chemical–Personal Care team. It also characterizes the Ford and Mazda staff groups that meet regularly to monitor and reinforce their alliance.

To build acceptance and shared understandings, a new team should define itself with a formal mission statement. It should include measurable objectives, key tasks, individual responsibilities, and pertinent interfirm contacts. People from different firms begin with fewer shared assumptions about such matters. Moreover, some members of an interfirm team usually were not present in negotiations that formed the alliance, and some detail is always left to the implementers.

How the leaders work together sets the pattern for others. Close bonds here are particularly important in high-risk alliances. With much at stake, each side has more incentive to hold back. Visible coherent leadership helps people cross the line.

With more substantial alliances, leadership should include the heads of both firms. "The prerequisite for the management of the whole thing is for top management to have the intention of making it work," says Frank Homan, CFM International's executive vice president from GE. "This is fundamental to reaching agreement when difficulties arise."

A Goal: Improve Your Joint Problem-Solving Abilities

To give an alliance a chance, your shared objective must make it worth compromising some of your interests and accepting values with which you disagree. But it isn't enough to share an important objective. You also need a relationship for solving problems along the way.

When a Good Relationship Is Crucial

Partner relations become more critical in proportion to company differences, the value of the alliance, and the degree of uncertainty that affects it.

Consider partner differences. Overall, an alliance must satisfy both firms' needs. Yet the less familiar each is to the other, the less they know what is essential for each other. Each firm has to work harder to understand how the other sees things.

Similarly, for more important alliances, partners must invest more effort to appreciate each other because the risks are greater. You might loan a stranger 25 cents without much thought; you would want to know a lot more about someone who sought a substantial amount.

Larger uncertainties have the same effect. They also pose greater risks, and thus call for a stronger relationship. In the 1970s Ford signed a ten-year contract with Mazda to make Courier trucks. While the agreement had a formula for price adjustments, each firm would have been hurt if they had rigidly followed the terms. At one point the price would have been so high Ford could not have sold any trucks. Another time the formula price was so low Mazda could not have made a profit.

So the firms bent the agreement to meet their real objective, which was selling trucks. "It's almost impossible to put this spirit of cooperation into a contract," says Robert Reilly, Ford's executive director of strategy.[2]

Keep Your Relationship Separate from Other Matters

A good relationship grows only from understanding and acceptance; it can't be bought or coerced. Agreeing for the sake of relations ("we'll go along with you this time in the spirit of cooperation") sets a pattern of evading tough issues. If this continues, bitterness grows as people concede on more positions with which they disagree. Further, bribery reduces respect and the incentive to understand the other's interests.

To be sure, yielding on an issue settles that problem. But don't expect backing down to build a good working relationship. Avoiding arguments does not help develop mutual problem-solving skills. Moreover, it is inconsistent to impose your interests on a partner and simultaneously to advance your joint ability to resolve conflicts. Forcing others to retreat reduces shared commitments.

Thus it is not enough to solve a current problem. You must look ahead to the next one, and the one after that, and develop a relationship that will enable you to manage these more easily. This can be done only by working on your relationship independent of substantive issues.

A Corning internal analysis of a joint venture that failed says it all: "We should be sure in the future that if trouble begins we can at least discuss the problem logically and candidly with our partner. A venture may fall on hard times. A relationship should not."

Use Constructive Arguments

An alliance gains strength from tough, productive debate. Corning, Dow Chemical, GE, Ford, and other successful alliance practitioners have greatly benefited from this. However, they avoid arguments in which tempers get out of hand or that go into heated discussions of fault and blame. These weaken people's desire to raise new issues and may do lasting damage.

The most fruitful arguments are those in which people feel free to raise issues with each other, listen well, make themselves understood, and, based on this understanding, come to a resolution involving creative solutions plus some degree of compromise. Such debates reinforce a relationship because they give partners a strong sense that they can survive conflict together.

Dow Chemical executive vice president Bob Keil offers a description of his firm's oilfield services alliance with Schlumberger that is typical of a healthy relationship: "We're not only partners, we're good friends. And we do take into account all aspects of each other's needs. We may fight like cats and dogs on how to do a given thing, but when it comes to broad policy issues we're like partners and friends."

To develop working relationships across an alliance, problems should be resolved without escalation to higher levels. Getting edicts from above to settle issues weakens people's ability to work together.

You Can Improve Your Relationship

We often take relationships for granted. Either the chemistry is right or it isn't; things go well or they don't. But relationships are not fixed. To be sure, they cannot improve without work. In an alliance, so much hinges on a good relationship it is worth investing the effort.

A good relationship is not one in which it is easy to agree, any more than a good bridge is easy to build. You have to be willing to invest the time to develop understanding, trust, and acceptance.

Even in relationship-intense Japan, it takes time to weld these bonds. Nippon Steel, for example, has scores of alliances with other Japanese firms. Azusa Tomiura, Nippon's general manager for technical planning and development, observes that "in most cases such relationships are established gradually by deepening mutual understanding and distilling the information obtained through daily contact."[3]

A Winning Strategy: Always Be Constructive

"We have had some 'tough guys' as partners," reports Dick Dulude, Corning group president. "Working *with* them made it possible to have a constructive relationship. If you regard another person as impossible, or expect a difficult person to change, you have little hope of building effective relations. You have to change yourself to make things work better, and they generally will. If you treat your partner as a customer you improve the chance that things will work out."

In an ideal relationship each side behaves rationally, fully understands the other's views, communicates well, is reliable, avoids coercion, and respects the other as someone whose perceptions and interests deserve to be taken into account.

Yet no matter how well you conduct yourself, you can't have the same expectation of others. And no matter how poorly you believe they are behaving, doing the same will further damage your alliance. Also, by following suit you give up the opportunity to set the tone of your relationship.

Thus to improve your ability to work together and advance your interests, be unconditionally constructive—follow principles that will improve the relationship and be good for you, whether they use the same principles or not. If they do, your alliance works even better. These concepts, articulated by Roger Fisher and Scott Brown of the Harvard Negotiation Project, can be summarized as follows:

> *Argue constructively.* Even if they try to pressure you, remain open to persuasion and don't try to coerce them.
>
> *Act rationally.* Even if they become highly emotional, use reason.
>
> *Be understanding.* Even if they misunderstand you, work to understand them.
>
> *Communicate well.* Even if they are not paying attention, consult them on items that affect them.
>
> *Be reliable.* Even if you can't count on them, don't mislead them.
>
> *Be accepting.* Even if they reject you and your concerns, accept them as worthy of your consideration.[4]

Recall Dick Dulude's observation: These are the same principles you would use with an important customer.

Work to Understand a Partner

It is a critical error not to realize how differently a partner sees the world. It is easy to believe they should know more about you. It may be harder to recognize you should know more about them. Yet to satisfy both firms' needs, and to deal better with differences, you must understand what these are and appreciate your partner's perception of fairness. The more you recognize each other's attitudes, concerns, and values, the greater your ability to avoid some problems and resolve others.

Just as better products come from clearer understandings of customer

needs, a stronger relationship grows from improved knowledge of a partner. To work through an issue, explore their thinking. The less you
know, the more likely you will underestimate how little you know. So
keep peeling back the layers of misperception. One important benefit
is that being open to learning encourages your partner to do the same.

Know the People and the Company

There are two critical sets of relations in an alliance: between individuals
and between companies. Understandings have to be developed by both.
Dow Chemical, for example, had worked with Personal Care before
the diaper alliance was formed, but that involved other people in other
units. Those involved in the new alliance still had to become comfortable
with each other.

Similarly, companies having effective relations with distributors build
company-to-company and interpersonal ties. They become familiar with
distributors' histories, keep up with their training needs, and work to
understand and resolve problems as they occur. To reinforce the working
partnership, these firms also promote close ties between their lead
sales and marketing people and counterparts in distributors' organizations.[5]

At Corning there is an unwritten rule that whoever has the internal
lead for an alliance is responsible for keeping others up to date on the
other firm's direction, needs, and interests. For joint ventures with Siemens and other partners where Dick Dulude has the lead, he circulates
the latest press on a firm's activities and sees himself as the local expert
on each partner.

"You have to work the relationship—understand your partner, its
markets, technologies, strategic direction, key people, and power structure," says Dulude. "You have to understand the people and organization
you're working with." These understandings within Corning help its
people know how to frame and raise issues with a partner constructively.

Understandings Grow from Good Communications

Good communications take time. The Ford and Mazda staff groups responsible for monitoring and managing this alliance meet every month,
alternating between Dearborn and Hiroshima. That's a lot of travel,
but it has paid off handsomely.

At CFM International, the executive vice presidents from GE and
SNECMA (who are based in the United States and France, respectively),

meet at least three or four times a year. For months at a time, they have met in person about every three weeks.

Again, listen to Dick Dulude: "Good relations call for lots of communications. You can't just go to meetings. You have to spend a lot of time talking to your partner. This involves much more than words. You have to spend time together on social occasions, go skiing, or whatever you both like to do. But you must go way beyond the protocol requirements of partner contact."

Corning's optical fiber partner in Britain is BICC, the large cable and construction firm. Dulude makes a significant effort to get to know Sir William Barlow, BICC's chairman. That includes always stopping by whenever Dulude is in London. The attention gives their venture additional importance within BICC, even though it is a relatively small part of BICC's business.

Once, when Dulude was in France, he traveled to London before returning home instead of going back directly via Paris. He did this for the sake of a brief visit with Sir William. No major issues were present—the purpose was just to keep up contact. In their discussion Dulude invited Barlow to visit Corning on his next trip to the United States. As it turned out, the only feasible time was when Corning had a meeting with security analysts. Barlow agreed to that date.

During the meeting one analyst was pressing Corning about its optimistic outlook for optical fiber. Following its own response, Corning suggested that BICC's chairman might have another view. He had previously chaired British Telecom, one of the world's largest phone companies. His observation regarding growing demand for fiber added substantial credibility to Corning's projections.

The experience was as rewarding to Barlow as it was for Corning. He gained new insights into U.S. business practice. For both firms, the event led to much closer relations.

Good communications with a partner keep it informed, give it more opportunities to respond, reduce suspicion, and—as with BICC and Corning—let it know it is important to you.

To appreciate this in a wider context, look more closely at the alliances some firms have with their distributors. In these, communications are two-way at multiple levels and use a variety of channels.

Several manufacturers, such as DuPont, use newsletters to complement personal contacts. The mailings inform distributors about new products and applications, personnel changes, distribution news, and human interest stories. Many manufacturers, including Parker Hannifin, the leading fluid power products manufacturer, communicate with distributors via video casettes which contain messages from the manufacturer's senior management, describe training programs, and more.[6]

Overcome Barriers to Open Communications

Rather than assume there is no need to communicate, keep your partner informed on all alliance activities. This helps avoid surprises, which can weaken trust. Further, always consult before making a decision that could affect them. To be sure, their agreement isn't needed if you have the authority to act. However, by informing them, requesting their advice, listening well, and taking them into account in your decision, you promote better understandings and trust, and demonstrate that their interests and views deserve consideration.

Even though IVECO has operating responsibility for IVECO Ford, its practice of keeping Ford informed on all matters and consulting Ford on a wide range of issues that IVECO can decide has been a key source of strength in their alliance.

Once when a problem occurred in CFM International with a test engine, one partner moved quickly to analyze it. This was the firm's normal response to internal problems, and part of its strength. When it found the cause, it proposed a solution, even though the responsibility for the problem belonged to its partner. This produced some hard feelings. Meanwhile the second firm, moving at its own pace, developed a different, and more constructive, solution.

That experience, while awkward at the beginning, stressed the value of consulting before acting and led to increased mutual respect and understanding between GE and SNECMA.

Formal communications are incomplete paths to good relationships. You have to move beyond discussions of specific tasks to candid conversations about why each firm does things the way it does, and what really concerns people. To encourage candor, think about why the other side might be reluctant to talk, then say things that will make them more comfortable. For instance, reveal a bit about your own situation, then be ready to listen.

It is easier to have candid conversations if you allow time for informal one-on-one talks or hold separate meetings for this purpose.

Autolatina board members have dinner together without an agenda before each board meeting. The talks are off the record. People thus feel more at ease about what they discuss. Being able to converse freely helps them get nuances out, understand each other better, and appreciate each other's thinking. There is more time to explain positions. Subsequent formal board meetings do not refer to anything said at the dinners.

Another way to develop better understandings, especially about your firm, is to include a partner's people in relevant conferences. Ford, for instance, holds internal events for key technology partners to improve mutual understandings.

Assigning people to work in a partner's facilities for several months builds even deeper insights, eases know-how transfer, and offers direct exposure to the other firm's thinking and style.

Obviously, it is harder to solve a big problem than a small one. If you are thinking about a partner-related issue but don't discuss it soon enough, misunderstandings may expand as you increasingly view the question from your perspective. By the time you finally discuss it, you first have to work through polarized views. So rather than wait until a problem worsens, make it a practice to raise and resolve issues quickly.

Corning's Dick Dulude often senses when he has not been talking to a partner enough and will telephone his contact. He has learned that when he gets out of touch, issues have grown out of proportion.

Communications are also affected by attitudes. For most people it is difficult to remain open and to feel constructive with someone who is stubborn, makes contemptuous remarks, tries to score points, or ascribes blame. Telling a partner what you want it to stop doing has the same effect. Instead, reinforce its constructive behavior by suggesting what it might do more of. And talk in terms of your shared objective—not what your firm wants, but what you hope to achieve together.

Effective communications are hurt by inactive listening. Do your people talk more than theirs? When they are talking, are you silent or do you ask questions to draw them out and increase your own understanding? To confirm what they have said, use your own words to summarize what you have heard. Ask them to do the same.

Communications get confused when people give mixed messages to an audience or conflicting messages to different audiences. As in American presidential elections, when candidates tell each interest group something different, the overall theme is lost. With alliances, the top authorities—a steering committee, board members, or corporate leaders—should send coherent signals to interface teams, internal units in both firms, and others who are involved.

If you have inconsistent priorities, acknowledge this to reduce confusion. It is better to admit your own conflict than to give changing signals.

Unless you agree on a position, keep alliance issues private. Once a firm makes a public statement it is inclined to support it for the sake of consistency. Airing views tends to harden different positions and inhibits constructive communications.

When AT&T and Olivetti began having trouble with their alliance, each side shared its views with the press. That led to an escalating series of charges and counter charges, which didn't help them solve their problems.

How to Be Trusted—and When to Trust

When Dow Chemical and Personal Care planned their diaper alliance, they knew that uncertainties prevented them from being absolutely sure Personal Care would use the new material or that Dow would meet its commitments. So they agreed on a strategy if things didn't go as planned.

Clearly, one can trust too much. No firm can have everything under its control; unexpected events may force a change in plans. To limit damage, make arrangements—agreeing to end an alliance, to grant additional rights, or to pay compensation—if a major commitment isn't met. Such provisions also create an incentive to work harder for success.

However, too little trust will backfire: It creates ill will and reduces the incentive to work harder at being reliable. As Harvard's Roger Fisher and Scott Brown explain, a reasoned level of trust promotes trustworthy behavior.

A trusting relationship also expands your horizons. Dick Dulude tells of the time Corning wanted to build an optical fiber plant in West Germany sooner than Siemens, its partner there. Corning believed if a plant were not built quickly, someone else would enter the market. Siemens accepted the recommendation, based on trust, and the partners gained needed speed.

Trust grows from honest and reliable conduct. Being able to trust each other means each firm can take the other's statements at face value. But trust goes beyond this. You want to believe that when tough issues are raised constructively, the response will also be constructive. Otherwise, communications are threatened. Further, since you can't monitor every aspect of an alliance, you want to rely on each other to do things in a way that considers your mutual interests.

In the early years of CFM International, people lower down in GE would occasionally step out and "try to win one for GE" by getting more out of the venture at SNECMA's expense. When those issues were raised to higher levels within GE, however, they were always resolved in the spirit of the partners' mutual commitment.

High levels of trust do not require full disclosure. Each firm must protect its separate interests. Even competitors can build trust if they segregate their basic rivalry. Harvard's Fisher and Brown observe that conflicting objectives are less of a problem than deception about them. Honesty does require clarity about where full disclosure should not be expected. The more you can share, the easier it will be to solve problems and manage your differences.

Trust can be defeated by surprise, which reduces predictability. One way to avoid this is to plan your next steps together in more detail than you might use for internal activities. Chances are, you know less about how each other works than about your own firm. So there is more room for surprise in an alliance. It is easier to express concerns in advance than to fail on a task when others depended on you to suc- ceed. Be open about problems before they happen. If you're not sure you can meet a commitment, let your partner know as early as possible.

Rather than expect a partner to raise all issues that affect its interests, bring such items to its attention when you spot them. Executives and board members of Autolatina and Ciba Corning Diagnostics, members of the Ford–Mazda joint staff team, and people in other successful alliances routinely do this for each other. Issue-spotting reduces the possibility of surprise and helps build a partner's confidence that you are looking out for its interests.

To have a solid relationship, trust has to flow in both directions. Don't just think in terms of your ability to trust them. Consider how your behavior affects their willingness to trust you. Be aware that differ- ences between you leave a margin for misinterpretation. A pledge you make lightly may be significant to a partner, so be clear about whether you are making a commitment or not. And work to understand its needs. When you behave reliably—from a partner's perspective—it will give more weight to your statements and you have more opportunity for influence.

Accept Them As Equals and Work on Their Needs

To be effective together you have to accept each other as people who are equally legitimate, equally involved in the situation, and equally deserving of having your views taken into account. Unless you listen to a partner's ideas, and accept its right to have perspectives that differ from yours, it is not likely to be that way with you.[7]

Accepting others as equals does not mean you have to agree with their values or perceptions or approve of their conduct. But to have a productive relationship, you must be willing to deal with people as they are, to hear their views, and to respond to their needs.

General Electric and SNECMA, for example, have readjusted their revenue-sharing formula from the original agreement when exchange rates and inflation changed beyond expectations. "We don't do this for altruism," one GE executive says. "We all know that, if we hurt our partner, we could damage the relationship and thus hurt ourselves."

One way to show a partner's importance to you—and to build high-level communications and understandings—is through regular senior management contacts, such as Jamie Houghton's and Dick Dulude's meetings with top executives of partner firms.

Dayco Corporation, a manufacturer of engineered plastic and rubber products, does the same with its distributors. Each year, all its distributor marketing managers, the president, and even the board chairman make selected calls on distributors to emphasize each firm's value to Dayco.[8]

To accept others, understand what makes them different and demonstrate your respect for this. If they use more analysis before deciding, find ways to accommodate them. Also, hold alternate meetings at each other's locations. If their culture is different, look for ways to honor it when they are with you—as Gerhard Neumann did for his SNECMA guests with the converted restaurant and French streamer overhead. When you are their guests, know what is and is not acceptable conduct in their culture, and how to be effective there.

You may not be able to make large adjustments in any of these areas, but even small steps, if sincere, say you care. You can, for example, recognize a partner's national holiday when its people are visiting you and respect other events that are significant to them.

Demonstrating care for others' ways becomes a self-fulfilling prophecy. Most likely, practices that first seemed strange will make sense when you understand them. Further, you will find more areas where their strengths complement yours. And as you get to know them, you will almost certainly find your perceptions were more biased than you had thought.

When you cooperate to reach a shared objective and treat each other as equals, lasting friendships often grow to reinforce the working relationship.

For some time now, CFM International staffers have informally organized an annual GE–SNECMA soccer game with SNECMA employees
and their families based at CFM's Cincinnati headquarters. Further,
both GE and SNECMA people have been invited into each other's
homes when overseas. This is an uncommon practice in France, so it
is more of an honor. Families have also exchanged children for weeks
or months.

Even if you are ending an alliance, it is worth finding ways to respect
a partner's interests. One American firm, which had a minority investment in a partner, sold its stock and stopped the alliance without consulting the partner. This action so damaged relations that years later, when
the Americans wanted to share the same firm's new technology, they
couldn't get it and had to settle for a distant second best.

Continuity Is Important

Bob Keil, Dow Chemical's executive vice president, knew he was somewhat overstating the point for emphasis when he said, "The spirit of a
transaction lasts as long as the original participants are involved."

The president of a large Japanese tool maker voiced the same concern
about his American partner, which had gone through three ownership
changes over the preceding decade. "We never know who we are dealing
with," he complained.[9]

Their message is clear and critical. Relationships require understandings and trust. To a significant extent, this depends on the individuals
involved. When people change, partner bonds will not last unless continuity is arranged through overlapping multiple contacts or in other
ways.

In Ciba Corning Diagnostics, both partners recognize the need for
continuity. Thus as Ciba and Corning people have changed jobs or
retired, they have usually remained on the board. The CCD executive
committee, where relationships are the most crucial, has been even
more stable. Three years after CCD was formed, it was still important
that the core group of people who planned the venture remained involved.

For a particularly critical transition, you can build trust and smooth
the change by involving your partner in the process. When Chuck
Lucy, who had formed a crucial relationship link with Siemens, announced his plans to retire, Dick Dulude talked to Siemens about candidates to replace him at the same time he was discussing this with others
in Corning.

Keep Working on Relationships

You are building a relationship to handle future issues more easily. The benefits can be substantial: Growing trust and understanding speed joint activities, ease shared innovation, and expand mutual horizons.

So look at troublesome conduct as a shared concern, not a sin. Think about it as a chance to find ways to reduce such incidents in the future. To be constructive, accept responsibility rather than shift blame. Be careful to talk about conduct rather than people. It's hard to be productive when under personal attack.

When there are problems with a relationship, discuss them constructively as with any other issue. Openly reviewing your own performance if it appears to be unsatisfactory can enhance trust. Don't interpret their poor behavior as characteristic. Such an attitude can infect a relationship. And let people know when their conduct is particularly appreciated. Sincere compliments reinforce good performance.

The table below may help assess the quality of a relationship.

Some Measures of a Relationship	
Stronger	*Weaker*
Fundamentals	
We clearly need each other and are willing to make compromises to reach our mutual objective	Our interests are not well aligned, or one of us is much more exposed than the other
We are working to improve our relationship separate from other matters	Our relationship depends on our substantive gains
Problem-solving	
It has become easier to raise issues, resolve our differences	Key issues are not raised
Conflicts are a normal part of our relationship and get resolved by discussion	Conflict resolution is by acquiescence, coercion, or reference to rights
Understanding	
We have a growing awareness of each other's interests, abilities	They do not appreciate our needs, skills, priorities

Some Measures of a Relationship (Continued)	
Stronger	*Weaker*

Communications

We have extensive formal and informal communications	We are limited to infrequent formal discussions
Issues are raised early	Problems tend to get worse before we discuss them
We always consult before making key decisions	We have been surprised by their decisions

Trust

We can always rely on each other when it counts	It is risky for us to rely on them

Acceptance

Their actions tell us we are important to them	They treat us as less than equal
We actively work on each other's needs	The relationship has caused significant frustrations
We are becoming adapted to each other's culture	We are as uneasy with their style now as when we began
Some real friendships have grown	We feel like strangers to each other

Outlook

We are exploring new opportunities together	Our scope is the same or has narrowed since we began

17

Working with Other Cultures

I find it amazing that people can work together so well who didn't know each other before. People on the board genuinely like each other. The more we understand each other the fewer gut cultural differences there are between us. We fundamentally look at the same factors in arriving at our decisions.

—Lynn Halstead, Ford's vice president and
lead representative on the Autolatina board

TO create Autolatina, Ford and Volkswagen had to work through two corporate cultures, four different languages (English, German, Portuguese, Spanish), and four national cultures (American, Argentine, Brazilian, West German). These contrasts were reflected in numerous practices—work styles, labor relations, accounting methods, and many more—all of which had to be reconciled and integrated.

Autolatina came together because "people knew building [it] wasn't going to be easy," Ford's Lynn Halstead says. "We knew we had to work on our relationship from the very start."

Halstead makes a crucial point: Being effective with another culture starts with your relationship. This involves the same practices of communications, understanding, reliability, and acceptance described in Chapter 16.

Those practices must be used in concert. To work with people from another culture, it isn't enough to accept them as worth dealing with, to communicate, and to be trustworthy. You also have to understand how they see things and what is important to them. Effective cooperation builds on an informed respect for your differences.

Why Culture Is Important

Think of culture as a set of habits and values shared by a group, which guide much of its behavior. The longer people live or work together, the more their culture will affect their perceptions, thoughts, and activities.[1]

The patterns that make up a culture are deeply ingrained. People are more effective together when they have learned to rely on each other. Success together creates a shared intuitive understanding of what causes such accomplishments. People become emotionally committed to those values, which provide a sense of continuity. They view the world through the lens of their mutual beliefs. Any attempt to change these meets confusion and instinctive resistance.

This is one reason why IBM (which has been a business products firm) had a hard time developing personal computers for consumers, and why Apple Computer (which began with consumer products) had early difficulties penetrating business markets. Each firm had ways of doing things that made it successful in its original markets but inhibited the changes needed to enter new ones.

There is a great deal of evidence that shared values have an important bearing on group performance. People invest more energy when they work with others having similar values. Priority setting, individual tasks, and coordination are easier, because people with the same values can more readily agree on actions to be emphasized and how these are to be done. Such groups are better able to cope with work pressures, and achieve their objectives more frequently, than culturally dissimilar groups.[2]

Significant differences in a group thus reduce its performance. People are conditioned by their culture to see things as they expect them to be. When something unusual happens, they may get confused or disagree.

For instance, former Corning executives in Ciba Corning Diagnostics had learned to make decisions through an informal consensus process, while Ciba people on the CCD board were accustomed to using formal documented procedures. Each group saw the other working in ways that caused confusion. As a result, needed decisions were inhibited.

Anticipating Cultural Issues

It is easy to foresee cultural differences between firms with contrasting religious, ethnic, or national backgrounds. But no matter how similar another organization seems, don't make the mistake of assuming there are no differences. Some cases will illustrate:

- A once highly proclaimed alliance between ad agency Young & Rubicam and financial house PaineWebber joined two New York–based global service firms. Yet it failed because of an irreconcilable clash of cultures. In advertising, a former executive of the venture says, "you're selling a long-term relationship. Investment banking is far more deal-oriented—and that creates a fundamental difference in philosophy that has prevented the venture from achieving all that it could."
- When Caterpillar, the construction equipment firm, transferred the manufacture of some parts from the United States to Scotland, it assumed the Scots used the same machining location points used in the United States. They don't, so Caterpillar received large quantities of a part that had to be junked.
- In an alliance between Du Pont and Rensselaer Polytechnic Institute, to develop a new metal powder, the two never discussed that researchers would be part-time graduate students, as is usual in university research. So Du Pont was surprised when expected progress wasn't uniform, even though graduate students, busy with courses, work sporadically.[3]

Obviously, many situations involve sharper contrasts than these. To prepare for an alliance, it can be helpful to know how much cultural issues will be involved. This depends on three parameters: the difference between partner cultures, the extent of their interaction, and the amount of uncertainty in an alliance.

Judging Cultural Differences

Every company is unique, so there are always cultural contrasts between firms. Some aspects of these differences can be foreseen by comparing their environments.

We know, for example, that a German electronics company and an American electronics firm will have some common practices characteristic of the electronics business, plus some distinctly German or American attributes. A German electronics company and an American furniture chain will probably have greater differences between them.

More generally, the habits and attitudes that constitute a firm's culture are shaped by three forces: the routines developed in its marketing, operating, and other activities; its employees' backgrounds; and the values and practices introduced by its founders and reinforced by later leaders.

Firms in the same sector (such as electronics or furniture) serve the same kinds of customer needs and have similar products, operations, and technologies. Companies located in a given region or nation draw their employees from the same population, so reflect the culture of their locale. Thus a firm's culture depends significantly on its industrial and social environment.

A Culture Has Several Parts. To judge the cultural separation between firms, think of each firm's environment as having different parts: its particular industry, its operating locale, attributes it shares with a parent corporation, its national background, and other nations with which it has a common ethnic or religious heritage. Further, many people belong to professional groups that impart their own values. Accountants, for example, have some habits and practices different from engineers.

Thus one measure of cultural separation is the contrasts between environments, of the kinds listed here, to which each firm belongs:

Work Environment	*Sources of Work Values*
Individual function	Professional practices
Business unit	Competitive strategies
Market or industry	Customer needs, technologies
Parent corporation	Corporate structure
Operating locale	Ethnic, regional attributes
Nation	Shared history, ethnic roots
Group of nations	Ethnic, religious backgrounds

As an example, consider the cultural difference between Young and Rubicam and PaineWebber. Although both have the same local and national backgrounds and both are in the business of providing services, broadly defined, each has a decidedly different market from the other and thus has distinct practices. These differences are behind the firms' cultural contrasts, which evidently were not recognized when their alliance was formed.

As another example, compare Ciba-Geigy and Corning. These firms also have much in common: They are research-intensive, advanced materials–oriented global corporations that place great emphasis on human resources. Yet of the two, Ciba is much larger and more multinational. Although Swiss-based, 98 percent of its revenues come from other countries.

Ciba thus developed a formal decision-making process that emphasizes documentation. Corning, by contrast, has stayed closer to its upstate New York roots and retains an informal style.

Older Elements Are More Rigid. A second, related, measure of cultural differences comes from the fact that some parts of a firm's environment are older and more durable. Values shared by a nation's or region's population reflect ethnic and religious traditions, plus a common history, which are passed along by families as children are raised; reinforced by schools, employers, and public policies; and shared by other firms in that environment.[4]

These conditions affect a wider range of attitudes, which are more deeply held. Contrasts here present more of a challenge for alliances.

Depending on where you come from, you have probably heard about or experienced cryptic British reserve, irreverent American informality, Italian chaos, French protocol, German rigidity, Japanese vagueness, or Latin American disregard for punctuality. Many cross-border alliances have been upset by these differences, which have strong roots going back centuries.

Most significantly, these sometimes annoying traits we display to each other are surface manifestations of more basic differences between us. A firm's national and regional origins shape its people's beliefs about many aspects of business, including how discussions are interpreted, how meetings should be conducted, the content of commercial transactions, appropriate negotiating style, how organizations should work, good management, what gets priority, what it takes to get ahead, government's role in the economy, and more.[5] Consider these illustrations:

- Most Americans and people from northern Europe value frank, emotion-free communications about the specifics of a deal. Some Asian and Latin cultures prefer wider-ranging discussions that include ideology, accept emotional expression, and evolve through subtle changes in positions. In these, meaning is conveyed both in words and between the lines.

- In France, meetings will not start on time if the most senior person is late. No time is allotted to the various topics, with all matters being discussed at once. In Germany, everyone is on time, and there is a schedule for each subject.

- In New York, a commitment is made on paper. In Texas, an oral agreement is binding. The difference cost Texaco $3 billion when it thought it had made a deal for Getty Oil; the court decided Pennzoil's "gentlemen's agreement" with Getty should be honored.
- In East Asia, where group membership often takes priority over individualism, if you tell people they will be treated fairly they hear you saying they will be treated equally. In other places, the same statement means each person will be rewarded according to his or her performance.
- People in France and Japan prefer more rules and more structure, and give more respect to hierarchy in their organizations, than people in Germany. American and British firms place less emphasis on structure than German companies. Swedes are among the least formal of all.

Such contrasts caused some mutual discomfort at the start of CFM International. The French were more formal than the Americans, and some GE people suspect that SNECMA employees first regarded them as "hipshooters." The differences were compounded by dissimilar organization structures and problem-solving practices.

As another example, firms in California's Silicon Valley have a different style from firms in other U.S. regions. Because of its agricultural past and heterogeneous population, the valley has a more informal, individualistic, participative culture than other parts of the country. This leads to attitudes about delegation, dress, performance incentives, and other matters that contrast with other regions.[6]

Here is now such contrasts affect alliances with Apple Computer, which is based in Silicon Valley. At Apple, lower-level people have more authority than their counterparts from other places. Prospective partners' representatives at meetings may be vice presidents, while Apple's people are project managers. Other firms often assume this means the project is less important to Apple. Cultural discomfort is magnified when Apple people arrive at meetings in bluejeans and plaid shirts.

The Special Case of R&D. Around the world, scientists and engineers in a given discipline are educated with the same principles, use the same texts, read the same journals, and share the same jargon. They practice the same techniques in their corporate, university, or government labs, and go to the same conferences. Thus, more than any other disciplines, science and technology share many values that cut across other cultural boundaries.

Science is even less confined than technology by other cultural traits, because it is more removed from markets and operations. Scientists from different cultures thus feel a closer affiliation with each other than do others from the same backgrounds.[7] Science comes close to being the one true global culture.

For these reasons R&D alliances in general, and more research-oriented alliances in particular, work more easily across cultural distances.

Judging Cultural Distance. Every firm's culture is a blend of values that reflect its goals, strategies, and practices, and values that come from its environment. What gets emphasized also depends on how a culture was shaped by its founder. Strong entrepreneurs reject traditional values in favor of ones they believe more important.[8]

With so many variables, our measure of cultural distance is a guide, rather than an absolute. Still, it is a useful predictor of cross-cultural difficulties. Most firms that share a cultural heritage have many attributes in common that separate them from others. Such is the nature of culture.

The cultural separation between two firms is indicated by the contrasts between their environments and between their individual practices, and suggests the effort needed to bridge their differences.

Consider Britain's Celltech, which has drug development alliances with American Cyanamid and Japan's Sankyo. With Sankyo, "we have had to work three or four times as hard," says Celltech's chief executive, Gerard Fairclough. "Communications take longer because of [national] and medical practice differences. We've had to put in more effort than we planned."[9]

How Interaction Affects Intercultural Relations

The cultural challenge of an alliance depends on partners' cultural distance and on how much the firms will interact, as suggested by the figure on page 260. This serves as a qualitative framework for anticipating cultural issues, choosing partners, and designing alliances for increased compatibility.

Larger cultural distances or more interaction expands the amount of confusion or conflict to be dealt with. Each step in this direction requires more attention to communications, mutual understandings, and adjustments to new ways.

Separation Presents the Least Conflict. If an alliance involves only initial contacts between one or two people on each side to set the plans,

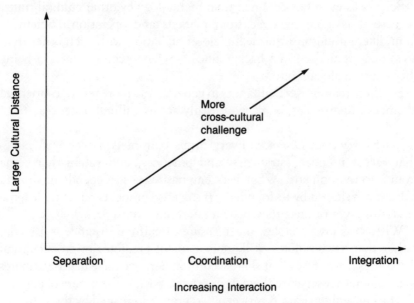

How Cultural Distance and Interaction Affect Cultural Challenge

with all work done separately in each firm, then cultural problems will appear in negotiations and in expectations about each other's performance. This was the situation of Caterpillar and its Scottish supplier, and of Du Pont and RPI. In each case, misconceptions based on cultural assumptions about how people work led to confusion and disappointment.

When cultural distances are larger, there will be more contrasts between practices. This requires more effort to negotiate and to build understandings about what each firm will do for the other.

Coordination Calls for Cross-Cultural Teamwork. Ongoing coordination involving several people from each firm compounds the challenge of cross-cultural relations, compared with initial contacts followed by separate activities.

When partner activities are linked, the way each normally works might not mesh with the other. And if partners don't share the same assumptions, they have to learn how to interpret each other's judgments. An engineer from one firm needs time to understand the forecasts of a sales manager from the other. The sales manager has to learn to interpret the engineer's cost estimates.

Further, having more people involved takes more effort to build mutual trust and understandings. In a small group it is easier to get to know others as individuals, to break down stereotypes, and to ensure that all voices will be heard. You may even be able to choose people with some consideration for their cross-cultural skills. These conditions disappear as the number of people increases.

Poor intercultural coordination almost undermined an alliance between an Italian manufacturer and a Swiss engineering firm to develop materials handling software. Although early meetings were cordial, relations deteriorated after three months. The Swiss complained their creative Italian colleagues always changed their minds and didn't meet deadlines. The Italians had invariably returned soon after interim specifications were set, seeking adjustments that would optimize performance but delay completion.

For their part, the Italians regarded the Swiss as inflexible, always insisting on getting results by fixed dates. They could not understand why the Swiss were so committed to conditional specifications, when a brief delay would lead to better performance.

Both sides eventually recognized their problem was due to culturally different views of time. The Swiss regard time as a precise commodity. For them, events should happen within a specific time scale. The Italians, by contrast, believe deadlines can be moved in the interests of a better product since, in their culture, quality receives a higher priority than time. Building a cross-cultural team resolved these differences.[10]

Integration Takes the Most Effort. The greatest challenge comes when people from each firm are to be assembled under one authority, with one consistent set of practices. In addition to cultural issues that appear in short-term teams, people have to learn to work together as a coherent organization.

If differences are small, integration may be easy. Cultural issues in Pekin Energy, formed by Texaco and CPC International, have been limited to occasional items of compensation and management development. Both parents are large, conservative, capital- and production-intensive firms based in the eastern United States. Both had managed the same kinds of activities before, using the same basic techniques. The venture involved a buy-in by Texaco of a CPC plant, so only a few new people were involved.

Autolatina was a different story. To create this alliance, Ford and Volkswagen combined elements of their contrasting organizations, decision-making routines, quality assurance and cost accounting procedures, bonus systems, supplier and labor relations practices, and product development methods. The goal was to forge a new organization with a complete set of values and practices out of both firms' prior ways. Each partner's techniques had roots in its distinct corporate and national cultures. Argentine-Brazilian contrasts were another factor.

Before Autolatina began, Ford and Volkswagen engaged in a massive year-long effort starting with discussions about how each firm normally works—which were at first inhibited by culture-based misunderstandings—and the development of cross-cultural planning teams. The creation of these teams and the high-level mutual commitment they represented were a necessary precursor to successful integration. Still, Ford and VW expect it will take some years for integration to approach its full potential.

There Are Limits to Integration. Beyond some cultural distance, people's differences simply overwhelm their ability to accept and understand each other and to adjust to new ways.

Too much integration was an early problem for Samsung Corning. Believing its management of the TV glass business would be critical, Corning insisted on running operations for the first three years. Samsung agreed, reluctantly. Corning installed a U.S. president, controller, sales manager, and manufacturing head, plus several technical people to transfer know-how.

After less than a year, Samsung Corning was in trouble. In addition to Korean–American differences, the president could not speak Korean and could not get things done through Koreans on his staff and in Samsung. Further, Samsung had a top-down management style, while Corning's emphasized strong participation and consensus decisions.

The firms' lead representatives had long arguments about who could run Samsung Corning better. To keep it alive, Corning eventually agreed that the Koreans could more easily adapt systems Corning wanted than the Americans could adapt to working in Korea. Except for the accounting unit, the Americans pulled out. H. C. Shin, who became the venture's president, kept Corning's accountants; he felt the standard cost system was an improvement over Samsung's then current method. Corning's financial controller stayed long enough to set up the new system.

Since these changes in the early 1970s, Samsung Corning has grown to become a world leader in its industry.

The activities required for different interactions are outlined in the table below.

	Separation	Coordination	Integration
Nature of Cooperation	Contacts between one or two people	Interfirm team of several people	Units from each firm blended into new organization
	Work done separately in each firm	Work done separately	
	Work follows set plans	Ongoing mutual adjustments	
Needed Skills, Tasks	Intercultural communications	Intercultural communications	Intercultural communications
	Understand partner's performance	Understand partner's performance	Understand partner's performance
		Cross-cultural team development	Cross-cultural team development
			Change individual and group norms

Activities Involved in Cultural Interactions

How Uncertainty Magnifies Differences

One objective for a British–French alliance was to create an innovative product. Since new technologies and markets were involved, neither firm could anticipate all the issues that lay ahead. When unexpected problems surfaced, the firms, each consistent with its normal practice, proposed contrasting ways to solve them. This added new conflicts to an alliance already burdened with cultural differences. The resulting confusion stopped further work; the alliance ended soon after that.

Every alliance is immersed in questions that weren't resolved at the start. For instance, partners may have unproved abilities, relationship issues, or—as in the British–French alliance described above—innovative performances that cause problems later on. Such uncertainties may overload an alliance.

To some extent, the need to cope with unfamiliar situations prods us to experiment and learn. But too much uncertainty creates confusion and anxieties that sap our energy and reduce performance.[11]

Further, resistance to change is proportional to the discontinuity induced by the change. The natural reaction to unexpected events is to stay with what has worked before. The greater your differences with a partner, the more likely it is that your responses will differ as well. Increasing uncertainty thus magnifies the confusion caused by cultural differences.

Designing Alliances to Reduce Cultural Conflict

The challenge of working with a partner from a different background grows with more remote cultures, more interactions, and more uncertainty. It can be reduced by controlling any of these.

Limiting Cultural Distance

Partly because of cultural similarities, Koreans often prefer to obtain technology from Japanese firms. The two are neighbors, many older Koreans speak Japanese—a legacy of Japan's colonial rule through 1945—and the nations share many cultural traits and industrial strategies.

Similarly, it is relatively easy for British and American firms to cooperate. These nations enjoy what their press and political leaders have long called a "special relationship." That is one reason why Britain has more foreign investment in the United States than any other nation.[12]

Alliances need mutual aspirations, compatible practices, and clear understandings. The closer your cultures, the easier it is to build those bridges.

By contrast, working intensely with a new partner, in a different business, and in a strange land, to develop a wholly new product that combines your technology and their marketing know-how may be more than you can manage. Such multisector, multifunctional, interaction-intense, high-innovation alliances have a better chance across shorter cultural distances.

If the strengths you seek are available in more than one firm, and integration or significant uncertainty will be involved, consider choosing a partner with a similar background, or one with which you have already learned to cooperate (particularly if the same people will be included). As an alternative, find a partner with superior intercultural skills. Some firms are better at it than others. A track record of successful international alliances is one indicator of this ability.

Cultural distance may also be reduced by giving a local operation lead responsibility for an alliance. Corning does that with Iwaki Glass, its joint venture with Asahi Glass. Corning's oversight of Iwaki is through its Japanese headquarters. In addition to easing cultural and administrative matters, Corning's interests in Iwaki, plus its other activities in Japan, are sufficient to warrant a single strategic locus for all its business there.

Shape Interactions to Reduce Conflict

Another way to reduce cultural conflict is to limit the number of cross-cultural contacts. Corning and Samsung did so when they changed Samsung Corning from U.S. to Korean management. Now, rather than expect Americans to manage a Korean workforce and to interface with the Samsung bureaucracy, cultural interactions are limited to policy-level contacts on the executive committee and to links with Corning's technical support staff in the United States.

Samsung's executive committee representatives have substantial experience working with Westerners, so there is little cultural conflict at this level. The technical support links connect professionals in the same disciplines on each side, largely free of organizational interference.

If significant integration is essential, consider starting with a new "greenfield" organization separate from both firms instead of bringing one partner's employees into the other's organization. Beginning at a new site eases blending both firms' styles by putting some organizational distance between the people involved and partners' cultures.

That was part of the motivation behind General Electric's "skunk works" on the campus of Rensselaer Polytechnic Institute, to develop automation software with RPI. Having a separate organization eased the integration of GE engineers with RPI faculty and students, and insulated the work from other GE activities.[13]

Be aware that close cooperation can lead one firm to impose its style on another. This may or may not be constructive. You may want to help a supplier improve its quality control programs. You may not want to push a small entrepreneurial partner toward your more bureaucratic ways.

So pay attention to the kinds of requirements you would like a partner to meet. Think about whether you want them to do something because that is how you do it, or because it strengthens both firms. The latter approach will meet less resistance and cause fewer cultural problems.

Reduce Uncertainties to Limit Confusion

When General Electric and SNECMA launched CFM International, their first product involved little innovation by either firm. One benefit was less internal confusion at both firms, allowing them to focus more effort on their alliance.

Uncertainties can overwhelm an alliance with unresolved problems that become dominant later on. To be sure, you cannot eliminate all uncertainty. But you can decide which issues will be kept open, and which ones merit extra effort to reduce.

Thus part of planning a cross-cultural alliance is to agree on how uncertainty will be controlled. The greater your differences, the more vital this task becomes. Remember, you can expand an alliance to include more innovation or other kinds of uncertainties once mutual understandings have grown.

Begin with Clear Objectives. When planning an internal project for your firm, some of the objectives go unstated because they are already understood. You have to be more explicit with an outsider because there are fewer shared assumptions.

Here is one way Acme-Cleveland, a machine tool firm, has built bridges to new startups in which it invests: B. Charles Ames, Acme's chief executive, found discussions with the entrepreneurs to reach an understanding on values and goals before deals were signed helped resolve cultural differences and enhanced alliance performance.

Take More Time to Plan. Don't expect good cooperation on tasks where each firm has traditionally different practices unless you first resolve your differences. The larger the cultural distance, the more you benefit from understanding how each key detail of an alliance will work.

Start with a Narrow Scope. A small scope limits the issues to be dealt with. Restricting the number of markets, products, or other activities involved frees energy to invest in your relationship.

Use a Weaker Form of Alliance. Joint ventures and minority investments involve both policy and operating matters, so can present more issues than contractual alliances. One way to reduce uncertainty is thus to avoid equity arrangements.

Racal, a British electronics firm, took this approach in China. The firm was concerned about potential difficulties and misunderstandings regarding labor and salaries, the need for future investment, and how tax liabilities and other regulations would evolve. Consequently, rather than set up a manufacturing joint venture, Racal formed a contractual alliance which provides for technology transfer, training, and the supply of components for assembly by its Chinese partner.[14]

Of course, there is a tradeoff here. On the one hand, using a contractual alliance avoids questions of shared control and external uncertainties in an unfamiliar context. On the other hand, equity alliances offer more opportunities to control, and to learn about working locally, which may be important for the longer term.

Various design tactics for reducing the demands of working with another culture are summarized in the table.

Design Tactics to Reduce Cultural Conflict

Limit Cultural Distance	Shape Interactions	Reduce Uncertainty
Choose partner with similar background	Avoid integration	Invest more in defining objectives
Work with familiar firm	Limit number of people involved	Take more time to plan
Choose partner having superior intercultural skills	Choose adaptable people	Start with narrow scope
Give lead to local unit	Begin with new organization	Limit innovation
	Weigh effect of requirements on partner	Use weaker form of alliance

Developing Cross-Cultural Understandings

When American manufacturers began touring Japanese plants in the 1970s, the Japanese described the importance of such human factors as worker participation and training. But the Americans, who had long assumed labor was a cause of their productivity problem, did not accept this. They were looking for technological reasons for the growing Japanese success.[15]

Similarly, when some people view a football game, they see a meaningless confusion of players running around on the field. Others, who appreciate it, recognize an intricate pattern of strategies and plays that make the game exciting to them.

People understand what they are conditioned to understand. This may lead to confusion and conflict when you are working with another culture. Clearly, the road through this forest has to be built with more communications. But that isn't enough. You also have to realize that a partner's reasons for doing things its way are as legitimate as why you do some things your way. And you must be willing to adjust your assumptions about what is best.

Learn About Them Before You Start

Knowing something about another culture before contacting it is like having a map of an unfamiliar city. There is a lot the map doesn't tell you, but at least you won't get totally lost.

Prepare for National Differences. It is good business to have some minimum competence in a host culture. This is particularly important for national differences. Knowing the local rules of protocol avoids some early confusion and embarrassment, and tells a prospective partner you care enough to be sensitive to its ways.

Corning's practice with its foreign optical fiber ventures is an example. The technology managers Corning sends to them go for two to four years. Even where English is widely used, some prior knowledge of the local language and social norms helps them get accepted as well as pick up nuances in meetings and discussions. It also signals each person's commitment to the host culture. Managers and spouses are sent to Berlitz and other schools for six to eight weeks of full-time language and cultural training.

Cross-cultural education should include factual information about a nation and its history, which provides a framework for understanding the culture. It should also break down stereotypes, describe local business practices, and simulate future experiences to give people useful tools and realistic expectations before they go. A large percentage of people who transfer to a foreign culture perform poorly there because of inadequate preparation and unreasonable expectations.

At Japan's NEC, managers going to the United States get elaborate training in Western customs. This includes differences between Japanese and American decision-making, several periods of simulated negotiations with non-Japanese, and a course in English conversation so intense that teachers are replaced every few days. Even U.S. social etiquette is covered—table manners, cocktail party conversations, and English-language jokes.[16]

The best training helps people understand how their views are colored by their background, how their behavior can interfere with a successful cross-cultural experience, how to recognize cultural influences in others' conduct, and how to adapt more productive thoughts and practices.

Many people suffer culture shock—the anxiety that follows the euphoria of entering another culture. It is due to losing familiar patterns of social behavior. The most effective people work their way out of it. Rather than blame the host country and people for problems, they recognize that understanding the other culture helps their own adjustment.

Anticipate Company-Specific Differences. You can learn about a firm's particular culture from its unique patterns: strategies that have succeeded and ones that have not; how people handle relationships with each other; practices that have survived more than one product cycle or CEO; and why people get promoted.

For example, if a large number of executives in a manufacturing firm have a financial background, you can safely bet the firm's culture is financially oriented. Quantitative analysis will probably have a large role in its decisions. More generally, practices that have been in place long enough to become set patterns will be ingrained in a culture.

Understand Them in Their Context

The easiest way to view another culture is to compare it with your own. This is also the wrong way to understand it. Judging others' behavior by relating it to yours foregoes the opportunity to see the complexity of their ways. This, in turn, inhibits your ability to interact with them. If you have an engineering background, how well would you learn marketing by comparing it with engineering?

To Understand Each Other, Break Down Stereotypes

The tendency to see what we expect to see causes us to prejudge others and damages a working relationship. Since attitudes are shaped by experience, people tend to form the most biased images of competitors and of firms with starkly different cultures where ethnic or religious contrasts have created negative views.

To overcome a stereotype, learn more about each other to appreciate why your preset ideas aren't valid. Look for ways your actions might invalidate falsely held beliefs. Demonstrate your willingness to cross this bridge by recognizing their interests and taking them into account.

When Honda and BL (now Rover Group), the British auto firm, announced their plan to build a new car at an English plant, the local workforce felt betrayed. Some harbored bitter memories from fighting the Japanese in World War II. Fearing violence, union leadership warned BL management to keep Honda people out of the plant. Yet when a team of more than forty Honda engineers arrived, the workers' animosity quickly turned to admiration. Instead of the pinstriped suits favored by BL executives, the people from Honda wore the same green overalls as hourly employees.[17]

Always Explore Your Differences

You don't have to be an anthropologist to spot cultural contrasts. If people on the other side are accepted as responsible members of their organization and have good communication skills in their own context, then any surprises, conflicts, confusion, or behavior that appears strange to you but not to them probably has cultural roots.

When this happens, it is as valid and useful to talk about your differences as it is to discuss technical, marketing, or financial items in an alliance.

The best time to resolve cultural issues is during negotiations. However, some discord simply has to be left to work on after an alliance begins. Furthermore, some problems won't be visible until then.

Frank Homan, CFM International's executive vice president from GE, tells of the time he proposed to SNECMA that GE have the system responsibility for a new project. To his surprise, Homan met a lot of resistance. He had assumed his words meant the same to both firms. In his mind, GE would write the specification, and SNECMA would get that part of the work where it was strong. However, taking responsibility had a different meaning at SNECMA. Its people heard Homan saying GE would be doing all of the work. The issue was resolved when the firms discussed their views in more detail.

Discussing Cultural Differences

When you suspect cultural differences are behind an issue, discuss this face to face. Culture is woven into people's beliefs about how things should be. Meeting in person provides a chance to invest more time on a question, to read each other's body language, and to build the kind of mutual comfort that makes it easier to explore your differences and reach new understandings.

This is a major reason for Ford's and Mazda's monthly joint staff meetings, where relationships and cultural issues are discussed with substantial comfort.

In reviewing cultural questions, be particularly sensitive about politics, religion, or personal or family matters. Raising these topics may expose unnecessary conflicts. Save such topics until you know people well.

If a person does something you don't like, don't attribute the action to stupidity or ill will. An unpleasant experience may only indicate language or cultural differences.

William Madia, senior vice president of Battelle Memorial Institute, the private global research group, says language barriers often leave his staff feeling confused and angry, and have threatened to destroy projects. For instance, a staffer will go to him and report, "Helmut said it was a dumb idea." Only after several meetings do they realize Helmut basically liked the idea but had a few concerns—and didn't have the vocabulary to explain that.[18]

You will be better understood when you avoid jargon. Many people use sports terms, company slang, or colloquial expressions to make their conversation more interesting. A person might say, for example, that he will "quarterback" a job. Unless the listener is a fan of American football, the statement is meaningless.

Mutual Understanding Is a Shared Responsibility

Since culture is part of all relationships, you can form stronger links with others by accepting the resolution of your differences as a mutual responsibility. Don't wait for them to become confused or withdraw because they can't understand you.

From experience, you may be aware of how your culture affects others' understandings. Describing pertinent aspects of your ways to a new partner can help avoid this. Also, try to sense when your actions cause confusion. Then take the initiative to probe for clarity.

Dow Chemical, for example, makes an effort to explain its culture to prospective partners. Apple Computer does the same. Ford and Mazda formally analyzed their differences to find ways to improve their cooperation. A Mitsubishi unit published a brochure to help Western firms understand its customs.

Here are some techniques Apple uses to move beyond cultural differences. Often, when Apple project managers first meet with representatives from another firm (who typically are higher in their organizations), Apple's representatives see expressions on their faces which suggest they are not sure the level of contact is appropriate. Apple's people then explain how Apple works, and that they really are the right people and do have the necessary authority. Any lingering misunderstanding about roles disappears if real mutual interest develops.

To further soften cultural contrasts, Apple has learned to talk about differences from the start. When a visitor is walked across Apple's campus, he or she is told, "You will see people doing things differently from what you may be accustomed to. Apple employees may be laughing, running, and appear very informal. Please don't mistake this behavior for carelessness. It is simply our style."

Another cultural problem Apple experiences is a contrast between the way it plans and how many of its partners plan. Apple uses what it calls "back-to-the-future" planning, which involves painting a picture of where it would like to be at a future time, then working back from that point to develop plans to get there. Many other firms plan forward: They begin with where they have been, and extrapolate from that. To get past such differences, Apple shares its vision to help partners understand where it is headed and how it will get there.

Include a Cultural Interpreter

Appreciating a partner's culture is as critical as understanding a market: You can't be effective without it. Just as marketing is everyone's job—in the sense that a firm performs better when product developers, operating people, senior executives, and others understand customers' needs—each person in a relationship should be culturally aware and resolve conflicts as they arise.

Like marketing, cultural interpretation is even more effective with the help of someone who has the expertise to understand each side, who can more easily spot issues and explain differences.

Two Americanized European executives, Doug Watson and Max Wilhelm, who work for Ciba and understand Swiss culture, help bridge Swiss–American differences in Ciba Corning Diagnostics. Doug Watson sees this as an important part of his role. For instance, when he is discussing an issue with Corning's Marty Gibson before a meeting, he may see the need to explain different Swiss and American perspectives. He does the same with Ciba people as well.

Similarly, in Ogilvy & Mather's alliance with Charls Walker Associates, Ogilvy's vice chairman, Jonathan Rinehart, serves as a cultural interpreter. Advertising people and Washington lobbyists have different styles. Mr. Rinehart has worked in the advertising and public relations worlds, so is able to interpret each firm to the other. Like Ciba's Doug Watson, Rinehart sees this as a natural part of his job.

Cooperating with Another Culture

To work with another culture, one or both firms has to make some adjustments, based on understandings about their differences. Recall how Caterpillar and its Scottish supplier did not realize they had conflicting practices for machining points, and so failed to adapt.

For a successful alliance, partners need a healthy problem-solving relationship to reach their objective. That requirement, and the nature of culture, suggests three guidelines for adjusting to cultural differences:

Maintain the spirit of equality. Each partner should make changes to accommodate the other.

Serve the objective. Changes should create the combined strength that will best meet partners' objective.

Recognize limits to change. Each firm's culture defines its ability to adjust.

How these guidelines apply depends on the context. Within one partner's culture, local norms usually prevail. When GE engineers visit SNECMA, they have learned to follow SNECMA's hierarchy. When SNECMA people are at GE, they use GE's more informal style. Similarly, Ford's investment in Mazda has a low yield, consistent with equity investments in Japan. Firms there traditionally retain more earnings than in the United States.

Following local norms is more than a courtesy. You choose a partner because of its strengths. Wanting it to work your way in its environment— unless this will strengthen it there—may compromise the abilities you sought. For example, asking a Japanese firm to increase its dividend payout beyond its normal range may invite new pressures on its prices and labor rates.

You have to accept the fact that employees of your Mexican partner will be absent for family obligations. You can't change the job-hopping nature of the Silicon Valley population. You have to endure slow decision-making by a more bureaucratic partner.

Better yet, appreciate why such traditions give a partner value in its context. Even if a cultural change would be good for them, it isn't likely to happen quickly.

Both firms have more freedom to adjust in a setting where neither culture dominates. Here, both should make changes to maximize their combined performance. An example is Autolatina, which operates in Brazil and Argentina—away from each parent's home culture. Ford and Volkswagen both made major compromises to reach their objective. Criteria for selecting resources and practices to be adapted were based mainly on the partners' goal of improved quality, costs, and productivity. In a few cases elements from one company or the other were kept to maintain a sense of fairness.

Cooperation When Most Activities Are Separate

For a relationship involving initial contacts to make plans, followed by separate work in each firm, cultural issues may appear in business etiquette, negotiations, and expectations about each other's performance.

Follow the Host's Protocol. Most people would feel silly going to the office barefoot. They might be comfortable, but others wouldn't accept it.

More generally, people in different places have different ideas about appropriate conduct: how to make introductions, show respect for authority, display feelings, express disagreement, entertain, dress, and so on.

It helps to know what is right where you are. In England, using given names at first is rude. In the United States, not using given names inhibits further discussions. People who work in both nations learn to adjust their conduct. For the same reason, people from Apple Computer dress casually at Apple but wear more formal clothes when visiting other places.

Knowing what is and is not acceptable, and how to be effective in another culture, is critical for initiating and maintaining relationships. Many people are offended by strange habits. Following local rules helps avoid misunderstandings and is a clear signal to your counterparts that you care enough to have learned their ways.

Understand How They Negotiate. Some firms want to get to specifics quickly. Some want to develop a relationship before reaching agreement. Others send representatives who can make commitments. Still others' delegates must return home to build a consensus. Some want to develop far more detail before they agree. And some try to gain an advantage by waiting until the last possible moment for better terms.

To avoid confusion, understand how your opposites negotiate. Even better, recognize their style as an outpost of their culture. This is how they have learned to get what they need from the outside world.

Remember that negotiation is where an alliance begins. Problems should be solved to build mutually attractive solutions, and the process should improve your ability to deal with future issues. No matter how they negotiate, strive to understand them, accept them as equals, avoid coercion, be reliable, and work on any issue they feel is important.

Be Clear About What Is Expected. By working separately you escape continuing disruptions. Yet each firm's results have to meet the other's needs. So make sure you agree on what will be delivered in terms of specifications (such as machining points), quality, timing, and so on. Don't assume they do things the same way as you.

Cross-Cultural Coordination

The need to adjust grows with the amount of interaction. With separation, conflicting styles require adjustments to follow protocol, agree, and meet each other's expectations. By contrast, coordination may entail further changes as new developments surface in the course of the work. Moreover, the closer interfirm links of a coordinated effort raise the potential for cultural conflict, increasing the need to adjust.

In one industrial product alliance, both firms began with joint market research and cooperated through product design, development, manufacturing, and marketing. Close coordination and continued mutual adjustments were essential. Yet early work was often delayed and went off track. People in one firm who had to support the alliance, and even members of its alliance team, were not kept informed of progress.

When two meetings on the subject failed to produce change, the other firm's team leader realized that his partner's weak internal communications reflected its culture. His co-leader did not have the strength to overcome this. To compensate, he advised his team members to assume their counterparts would not learn of progress through internal channels. He suggested that their regular contacts include updates on the total effort. These adjustments largely corrected the problem. The project was completed successfully.

Since cultural forces are strongest within an organization, it is most difficult to adapt there. GE and SNECMA, for example, have had different philosophies regarding hours needed for engine testing and related procedures—tasks performed by them for CFM International. Both firms knew their differences were cultural. Neither would accept the other's way, so they negotiated a compromise.

Adjustments are easier at the interface between firms. Fewer people are involved there, and people making outside contacts are free of some internal constraints. Adjustments are also easier in a neutral setting where partner cultures are less dominant. Changes in either context should get the best from each firm in support of your alliance objective. These settings provide opportunities to create real intercultural teams.

In the Italian–Swiss software project, the Italians' desire for flexibility confronted the Swiss' preference for predictability. To overcome the conflict, the teams conducted a role-playing experiment to understand each other better. Each worked for a short period according to the sense of time in the other culture.

From this experience, the Swiss learned to be more pliant with time and to give interim deadlines a lower priority. The Italians developed a new respect for the discipline of precise time. When project work resumed, the Swiss agreed to deliver a provisional program, to give the Italians a chance to innovate. For their part, the Italians committed themselves to producing an agreed-upon final specification on a fixed date.[19]

Cultural Integration

With integration, both cultures are blended into a new organization. Adjustments here can be the most extensive of all.

If an alliance is to operate at one partner's location, integration can be frustrated by cultural limits on its flexibility. Then, for a good relationship, partner equality should be preserved at the policy level but cannot be expected in operations. Recall the start of Samsung Corning, when Corning people could not adapt to Samsung's ways.

In a more neutral place, equality demands a fair combination of both firms' people and talents across the organization. The case of Autolatina shows how this works. Cultural differences here made integration a substantial effort. At the start, negotiators from each firm could not even understand how their opposites worked.

One of many differences regarded decision-making. Delegation of authority was well defined in Ford's Brazilian and Argentine units, consistent with typical American business practice. By contrast, Volkswagen's units had supervisory boards which, typical of German business, made decisions by consensus. Another difference involved the weight technical management had in decisions. While both firms regard technology as important, technical management in Volkswagen had a stronger voice than at Ford.

As a result, Ford could not at first comprehend how VW evaluated the importance of new technology in its decisions. VW had just as much trouble grasping why more authority was necessary for decisions.

To help form these understandings, Volkswagen brought in a senior manager from VW of America, who had earlier been with Ford. He gave VW people insights into Ford's corporate culture as well as U.S. language and mentality. As necessary, and when he sensed confusion, he translated "Ford English" into "VW English."

During a year of intense negotiations the firms worked through all of their differences, selected practices to be kept, and produced a comprehensive plan for the business. It described how Autolatina would operate and how decisions would be made. With one or two exceptions, everyone supported the new structure. There was wide agreement on the need for a merger and thus on the need for it to work. Ford's Wayne Booker, Autolatina's first chief operating officer, regards the year-long planning and negotiating effort, which included Autolatina's future executives, as having built critical understandings that sped its progress.

Still, people were not sure how easily they could make the changes. Some of these conflicted with long-held cultural patterns. The consolidation also produced substantial stress: 30 percent of former Ford and VW employees in Brazil and Argentina had to be terminated; those who remained were moved into offices and units that were integrated vertically and across the organization (see Chapter 10). Everyone had to learn new practices.

But there was now a clear shared vision. People understood how they got to where they were, recognized the need to make it work, and were willing to try. To reinforce this understanding, Autolatina's operating committee (the top functional heads) crafted a statement of the new firm's mission and objectives. Everyone on the committee contributed and all accepted it. The statement was regarded as an important way of communicating with employees what Autolatina was to become: how it would be distinct from Ford and Volkswagen, how employees would be treated, the quality and technology levels of its products, and more. This statement became a constant guideline for developing the organization.

Once Autolatina began, integration progressed under the leadership of Wolfgang Sauer, its chief executive, and Wayne Booker. Autolatina's board reinforced the process through its own monitoring and controls.

Those top-level efforts focused on Autolatina as a unique organization. Management never talked about what Ford or VW needed, but only what was best for Autolatina in its markets. At times this included rejecting parent requests. The practice of making decisions in the best interests of Autolatina set a constructive pattern for its other executives.

Both parents and Autolatina's executives recognize that, to aid integration, the mutual need which drives their alliance has to be understood well down into the organization. It is also essential that people know where things stand. Thus financial information, future product and manufacturing programs, human resource plans, and management's appraisal of external conditions are shared with all management levels to paint a clear picture of policy directions and the new company's progress.

Integration is monitored through periodic employee attitude surveys and by comparison of progress against plans. Autolatina also created a method to measure a manager's performance. Among other things, it requires managers to help their people understand each other.

Some individuals had a hard time with the changes. One or two initial management appointments were ended because the people could not adjust to the cultural change or to the pressures of consolidation.

There was also an undercurrent of discontent, particularly in the first several months, until Autolatina made progress people could be proud of. Ford and VW employees have separately felt they were taken over, and the Argentines felt they were taken over.

Before Autolatina, each parent's Argentine units reported directly to corporate headquarters. In the new structure the Argentines report to Autolatina headquarters in Brazil. The two nations have distinct ethnic backgrounds and economic histories. Those differences, and the new reporting relationship, created morale problems and reduced the efficiency of the decision-making process.

Integration has been reinforced by a bonus system that combines elements of the Ford and VW systems. It encourages hard work and progress toward integration even if there are no profits; it also provides additional rewards for profits.[20]

Once every quarter, Autolatina's operating committee meets off-site for several days with a consultant to expose, discuss, and resolve conflicts. They also go through exercises to help people appreciate the value of participation and cooperation. Those forums offer a better opportunity than the day-to-day work environment for people to get to know each other and are seen as valuable experiences. Similar off-site meetings are held by each functional group to help it integrate.

By the end of 1989 all key Autolatina executives were people who had come from Ford and VW after the alliance began. Both parents recognize continuity as an important issue, yet the kinds of executives needed in Autolatina are also in short supply in Dearborn and Wolfsburg. So turnover at the top has been inevitable. Only time will tell whether or how much this has impeded Autolatina's progress.

18

People and Practices: Getting More Value from Alliances

In the old culture, Ford people probably would not have been willing to work with Mazda.

—Bob Reilly, Ford's executive director for strategy

A FEW months after Ciba Corning Diagnostics began, the original business plan was voided by major technological changes, new regulations that limited price increases, and a rapidly rising dollar. The plan called for more R&D and larger gross margins to pay for it; both were not possible under the new conditions. In a series of CCD board meetings the parents reviewed their objectives, wrote a new mission statement, and did major surgery on the budget.

Corning yielded on its original desire for a short-term earnings turn-around for the sake of building for the long term, which was the partners' basic goal. The toughest part of the 1986 CCD budget negotiation was an intense one-on-one discussion between Corning's Marty Gibson, then CCD chairman, and Corning's chairman, Jamie Houghton. Houghton agreed to accept a revised budget to favor the long term. The resulting increased R&D has made a substantial contribution to CCD's continued rapid growth.

How well a firm benefits from alliances depends on how it works on the inside. Firms like Corning that get the most value take a long-term perspective and adopt practices that promote cooperation.

279

Delegation Is Essential

Alliances cannot function with top-down management. Compared with arm's-length transactions, they take more effort. Much of it has to be invested by people who are absorbed in the day-to-day work. Except in cultures where employees have an unwavering allegiance to their firms, real dedication comes from those directly involved. For this, they must participate in the spirit of an alliance: They recognize a need for each other and are sharing risks to reach a mutual objective.

Further, alliances have to be found, and commitments made, by units close to the action. They are in the best position to sense, understand, and respond.

One General Electric venture, with Huntsman Chemical, was born over lunch and quickly spurred more projects between the firms. Under the old centralized GE management system, "I just don't think it would have happened," says Glen Hiner, head of GE's plastics and materials business. "By the time the proposal had got through the process, someone else would have done the deal ahead of us."[1]

Back when Corning was getting started with foreign joint ventures, it created a high-level corporate committee to pursue them. In one country the commitment to proceed was made without effective participation by Corning's regional operations. The committee consequently chose a partner who was hard to work with.

Corning was also insensitive to its partner's needs and management style, and was slow to read and react to the changing market. The wrong products were introduced, and the venture lost money. Corning sold out at a loss. Since then, Corning has learned to rely on its operating groups, which are better positioned to find the best partners and which understand local conditions.

The person who has day-to-day responsibility for an alliance should be close to the relevant market and technology. To be effective, he or she also needs political credibility—in both firms. This begins at home, with clear understandings and acceptance of who has the lead and is the spokesperson. He or she should also understand the alliance in the firm's strategic context: how it fits in, strengths the firm hopes to gain, how these will be transferred, and the location of proprietary limits and other boundaries. Internally, open vertical communications are necessary to support this role.

Alliances thus work best in flatter, leaner organizations where people have more authority and more opportunity to use their abilities. Such organizations have short communications paths and responsive control systems, which help people direct their attention to customers and other partners. These conditions also support internal teamwork.

Make Internal Cooperation a Strength

At the start of Ford's alliance with Excel Industries, the car window manufacturer, Ford had to change its own internal connections. The alliance was to work with a number of Ford groups; close coordination among them would be essential.

Traditionally, vertical communications were part of horizontal relations at Ford. People had to go up their own hierarchical "chimneys" to coordinate across different units, which inhibited cooperation. This style was changing at Ford, but internal coordination was still difficult, and the need to work with Excel made it important to accelerate the process.

More authority was therefore delegated to Ford's Glass Division. In addition, Ford Glass introduced changes to support horizontal cooperation. One change was that the division acknowledged its mission was to satisfy the internal customer. Related to this, Ford Glass developed a clearer understanding of how the vehicle design process worked. Previously people had seen just their own small island. Now they needed to appreciate how their work tied in to other parts of Ford.

Another change focused on internal communications. To avoid surprises and to build trust, people are now informed of issues that affect them as soon as they surface.

Ford Glass also pushed authority down to lower ranks. Decisions and attendance at meetings could no longer be by management level, but rather by whoever was best informed and in the best position to act. Project managers were given more authority to oversee the progress of the work and to cut through the organization to get the job done.

It is obviously impractical to restructure a firm for each new task. Yet there is a definite need to optimize the organization for customers and other major partners. Many of these activities crosscut a number of internal units, in different ways for each project. With the growing importance of outside links, effective organizations need a hierarchy for corporatewide decisions, overlaid by flexible project management arrangements, with considerable authority vested in people close to the action.

These arrangements are necessarily supplemented by improved communications and understandings about other parts of the firm, as Ford

Glass achieved to support its alliance with Excel. Hierarchies must be flatter, which is consistent with more delegation, to shorten information paths and to enhance vertical understandings.

Delegation clearly involves some dispersal of authority from a few people to many. Just as clearly, this raises opportunities for conflict. Some conflict can be resolved by more effectively communicating objectives and priorities throughout the organization. Still, that leaves room for interpretation on many issues. Thus consensus-building skills are a necessary complement to delegation. Further, with more responsibility to act and authority dispersed, people have to rely on each other more.

Significantly, all these practices necessary for internal cooperation are needed for alliances: authority close to the action, good communications, mutual understandings and acceptance, the ability to build a consensus, and an emphasis on trust. The parallel with alliances goes even further. People work together best when they need each other and share the risks to reach a mutual objective.

Maintain Internal Continuity

Ford people, like those in most firms, move on to new assignments. So when newcomers arrive at key contact points with Mazda, they have to develop understandings about the alliance. This has led to some awkwardness at transition times. Moreover, new people tend to introduce new concepts into the relationship, which is not always desirable.

Turnover at Ford has also placed a burden on Excel to keep the spirit of its alliance healthy. Excel's chairman, Jim Lohman, notes it took three years to develop mutual understandings about the value and potential of the alliance. Then a key Ford purchasing executive with whom Excel had negotiated moved on. In addition, Ford buyers working with Excel changed several times in the first few years of the alliance. A steering committee, formed with the alliance, met every quarter for a while and then lapsed because of personnel shifts. With no committee meetings, the spirit of the alliance waned more rapidly.

Lohman believes such factors cause Ford to underuse the alliance. New people do not understand what they can get from Excel. No one at Ford is "pounding the drum" for the alliance, he says. This attitude gets translated into a lack of trust in Excel abilities and recommendations. Lohman reports that Ford has taken Excel suggestions about work it is qualified to do to others, creating new competition for Excel. He says the firms spent two years developing "formula pricing" to cover their transactions. As a result, Ford knows Excel's costs in detail, yet Ford has pressed for price cuts beyond the formula.

Excel's chairman sees a strong desire within Ford, fostered at the highest levels, to develop long-term relations with suppliers. This is driven by an unrelenting need for continued improvement in all aspects of quality, technology, and cost. He notes that Ford is doing dramatic things to strengthen its supplier community. But he feels Ford has not yet educated people who must conduct those relations.

Corning had a similar problem early in its relationship with Siemens. After the launch of their West German joint venture in the early 1970s, Corning went through several management changes at the level above Chuck Lucy, who had championed the alliance. So the only relationship link the firms had was between Lucy and Berndt Zeitler, who had supported the alliance at Siemens.

When it came time to consider a U.S. venture, the person to whom Lucy reported had been exposed to the alliance for only a short time. Like anyone who is new in a position, he had not had a chance to develop enough background or faith in the arrangement. Besides, Corning's senior management was not as deeply involved in joint ventures then as it is today.

Since the decision to form the venture involved a large commitment, Corning began an extensive review of its optical fiber business, including an evaluation of potential partners for the American market. This caused a great strain in relations with Siemens, which believed it had already demonstrated its merits. Eventually the decision was made to go with Siemens, but for a long year, the relationship was in jeopardy.

One way to ensure continuity, which Corning practices today, is to maintain close relationships at more than one management level, reaching high enough in both firms to ensure some overlap and to secure longer-term understandings and commitments. A second approach is to have key contact people stay at their positions for longer periods. Corning does that with key support staff for major ventures.

A third strategy is to keep people involved after their positions change. For this to be effective, they must continue to have access to relevant internal resources. Corning has done this with the CCD executive committee.

Another way to achieve continuity is to expect people who will assume contact responsibilities to accept their predecessors' commitments. This is the most generally useful approach; it tolerates job rotation, which is necessary for internal learning and breaking down organizational walls.

However, the tactic is effective only if it is widely practiced. To the extent people see themselves as free to ignore colleagues' agendas, alliances are threatened at each transition. By contrast, when people share a strong mutual obligation and understand each other, they are more willing and able to adopt each others' commitments.

Thus continuity with alliances depends on the strength of a firm's internal bonds. Like other good alliance practices, this is a matter of corporate culture.

Develop a Culture for Cooperation

The mechanical tasks of alliances can be easy: recognize mutual need, agree to share risks, replace short-term contracts with long-term arrangements, and so on. Yet these steps don't take you far without understandings and commitments that bridge differences with a partner and keep both firms moving toward the same objective.

Notably, the skills a firm needs to build relations with others are also needed to innovate and respond to its environment. To appreciate this, think about how innovation works.

At the most innovative firms organizational borders are not barriers to cooperation. Harvard's Rosabeth Moss Kanter observes that in such firms, new ideas are more easily blended and adapted because people feel integrated with the whole, rather than with the organizational box of the moment, which can change. Innovation here is a cooperative process, supported by values that encourage individual initiative, mutual commitment, and risk taking. In these firms people are more action-oriented and accept more responsibility for their actions.[2]

Human resources in these firms are recognized as the most critical asset. People are important enough to warrant top management time and to be worth continued investments in training. Guided by a shared vision of the future, employees place their faith in colleagues' competence above loyalty to turf. People feel encouraged to raise issues regardless of whether they fit organization compartments or current practices.

Innovative cultures are also more cosmopolitan. Their ease of working across internal boundaries and their high concern for people make firms with innovative cultures more inclined to scan their environments for opportunities, more adept at responding to these, and more able to accept diversity.[3]

Such cultures nourish stronger relationship-building skills and are more capable of adapting to others than inward-focused firms where participation is weak. Members of these cultures view themselves as part of an enduring community of owners, customers, suppliers, other employees, and local communities.

Keeping these attributes in mind, look again at Corning. With one-half of its corporate earnings coming from joint ventures, Corning may be the most successful alliance practitioner in the world. It also has a long tradition of innovation. Corning launched one of the first industrial research laboratories in the United States. Before that, it produced the lamp bulb for Thomas Edison; since then, it developed the first glass television bulb and invented the commercial optical fiber for telecommunications.

Consistent with its innovative performance, Corning's style is open, nonbureaucratic, and participative; it emphasizes consensus decisions. Even difficult issues surface more readily than in less open firms. For example, an internal memo prepared by midlevel staff after a failed alliance noted shortcomings in Corning's practices, including some at the highest executive ranks of the company.

Further, Corning management levels are more easily crossed. Corning people on joint venture boards, for instance, have come from several different levels. In many firms, doing this deters lower-level people from being effective. To be sure, senior Corning people carry more weight on a board. But lower managers feel they have ample opportunity to contribute, without having to play corporate politics.

Corning's emphasis on people is reflected in its reputation as an exemplary employer. It has been a leader in offering progressive benefits, including child care and flex-time schedules. Its pursuit of equal employment opportunities for women and minorities ranks Corning among the more aggressive U.S. firms.[4]

By their nature, Corning's open, participative ways include the outside world. Its approach to international business has always been one of flexibility: to seek full ownership or form alliances, depending on the need for total control and the location of needed strengths. Corning's style also drives it to spend more time working on relationships than its partners. Yet it has no policies about this. The values are imbedded in its culture.

Ford, under the initiative of chairman Donald Petersen, has been moving its culture in the same direction, to become more flexible in the marketplace. Ford people describe their past culture as strongly top-down, with a rigid hierarchy. The auto maker tended to manage external relations unilaterally. A Ford decision was final and was not explained even when the other party was not satisfied. As a major international firm, Ford was culturally nearsighted. U.S. nationals were in charge of most overseas divisions.

Today Ford explains more and listens more. Internal barriers to cooperation are breaking down. Teamwork is easier. People have begun to feel there really is a "Ford Motor Company" and to see how they fit into the picture. Overseas, each of Ford's fifteen European companies is headed by a European executive. Virtually all have either worked in or are nationals of other countries. Moreover, an increasing number of Europeans are moving to senior management posts at Ford headquarters in the United States.[5]

Ford people believe the cultural change still has some distance to go, but they share real pride of accomplishment over how far they have come. Changing one of the world's largest employers has been a mammoth task.

The cultural changes already achieved have substantially and positively affected Ford's participation in alliances. Ford people now are generally willing to commit to alliances and are better at building effective relationships.

Bob Reilly, Ford's executive director for strategy, notes that in the old culture Ford people probably would not have been willing to work with Mazda. Today, Ford has made changes to satisfy Mazda and has learned from the alliance. As an example, Ford units supplying Mazda's Flat Rock, Michigan, plant have gained valued insights regarding focused teamwork in supplier–purchaser relations.

Overcome Internal Resistance

The problem is as old as cooperation. Other people, other firms don't seem to have strengths as good as those developed at home. Or others' competence is recognized, but the opportunities still get low priority. Either way, alliances are rejected, or at least resisted, as unwise.

To be fair, there are times when such attitudes are in a firm's best interest. A new project may not create a real advantage; another firm may benefit more; internal activities may deserve more attention. Often, however, opposition comes from wounded pride or a fear of being displaced. People don't want to admit that others are equally able, or feel their work will be judged inadequate, or, worse yet, believe cooperation will lead to lost jobs.

Such attitudes are highly destructive. The world has never been as interdependent as it is now, and all trends point to cooperation as a fundamental, growing force in business.

Corporate Leaders Set the Stage

The offensive against "not-invented-here" has to start at the top—not just because leadership is needed to set new patterns, but also because these patterns are critical.

Corning's chairman, Jamie Houghton, tells of how his father, who was then chairman, boarded the train four times a year in the early 1940s to travel from upstate New York to upstate Michigan for Dow Corning board meetings. At the time, Dow Corning annual revenues were only $200,000. But the senior Houghton's active support set a crucial example for others at Corning. More recently, Corning executives spotlight Jamie Houghton as having built up more steam behind alliances since he became chairman.

Ford's most visible alliance (with Mazda) had early backing from Donald Petersen when he headed international operations. Later, as chairman, Petersen repeatedly communicated the importance of the alliance to lower management levels. Today, a group of top executives led by chairman Harold Poling meets quarterly with other Ford executives having an interest in alliances, to review opportunities as well as to discuss and improve Ford's alliance management process.

Balance Championing with Participation

Some championing is almost always necessary for alliances. It takes more work to link with another firm, even when authority has been delegated to lower levels. And champions help overcome internal resistance. Yet there can be too much of a good thing. The advocate who makes an alliance a personal project breeds resentment and indifference in others.

Thus champions must be negotiators and cheerleaders, not owners. Their job is to promote the project, build a groundswell of support, and give others room to make it theirs as well.

Before an alliance is approved at Dow Chemical, managers involved in its development must win the formal backing of units that will contribute. A good deal of preselling goes on to get relevant functions involved in the planning process. Giving them a voice in design helps win their commitment.

Participation may also be used to sway a reluctant unit by expanding the internal boundaries of an alliance. For instance, if an R&D group resists working with a partner on a new product, you might ask marketing to join the team and help develop joint product policies and specifications to get things going.

Formalize Expectations About Cooperation

To complement high-level leadership and participation, make sure plans and performance reviews stress effective use of inside and outside resources. If an alliance will build more strength, and you can protect your interests, that's the way to go. For maximum impact, communicate these criteria widely. Then stand behind them. If unit management people talk about adding internal resources when an alliance is preferable, impress upon them the advantages of cooperation. Eventually, people see the light.

Ford generally compares alliance opportunities with internal possibilities. The firm's use of alliances, and its working with Mazda as a favored partner, is backed by corporate staff groups, which challenge plans that seem to have overlooked these outside links. Ford's drive to cooperate is reinforced by people in its car, truck, and geographic units who know Mazda well enough to bring it to the attention of planners in each unit.

Focusing a Business Reduces Resistance

Concentrating a firm's efforts on its core strengths will also lower internal resistance. People in a focused company have to work more with outsiders to complement their own abilities. The wider exposure and greater need to cooperate offer a more balanced view of outside skills.

Moreover, a sharp focus better defines an organization's priorities. Employees can concentrate on niches where they excel. With this, and knowing their work is critical to the firm's success, they are less likely to feel threatened by cooperation. And people working near the frontiers of their disciplines have more reason to respect each other, which helps break down internal resistance.

Cultures That Promote Cooperation Discourage Resistance

Outward-looking, participative cultures are natural enemies of "not-in-vented-here." At Corning, for example, the priority is to move the company ahead rather than advance individuals to the company's detriment. Internal resistance seems to be much less of an issue at Corning than at many other firms.

Like most companies, Corning has a statement of philosophy about participation and being market-oriented. But in many firms there is a difference between such statements and reality. Chuck Lucy, who joined in 1952, and others who have been at Corning for many years, report the philosophy was there well before it was expressed in writing.[6]

People who easily share ideas with each other are more inclined to learn from outsiders; learning is a habit that can't be turned on or off with each new encounter. It is also a critical skill.

Emphasize Organizational Learning

In this age of constant change, having a competitive product is not the same as being a competitive company; tomorrow there will have to be new products and new ways of doing things. The winning advantage comes from an organization's ability to learn and apply new skills ahead of its opponents.

High-learning organizations have a strong propensity to search for and adopt new ideas from all sources. Every outside contact is seen as a chance to find useful practices to be applied at home. On the inside, high-learning firms are woven together by countless informal networks that build collective understandings with new information from experience, partners, customers, classrooms, and the literature.

Learning Is More Important with Alliances

Alliances expand the value of learning because the close interfirm ties they foster create more opportunities to find information than many other outside contacts. Whether cooperation helps or hurts depends on how well a firm learns compared with its partners.

More emphasis on learning, for example, has given some Asian manufacturers clear advantages over their Western partners (see Chapter 4). But the challenge isn't limited to manufacturing.

The unfolding story of alliances between American and Japanese financial institutions shows the same pattern. Nippon Life has linked with Shearson Lehman Hutton, Yasuda Mutual Life with PaineWebber, Sumitomo Bank with Goldman Sachs. The Americans' purpose is to get needed cash, new business, and contacts in Japan. The Japanese want to learn about U.S. financial markets and investment banking practices.

The Japanese have not hidden their interest in moving onto the Americans' turf. Their investments suggest the importance accorded to learning. At Shearson, two dozen Nippon Life employees get fifteen months of intense classroom training and on-the-job apprenticeships.

Setting up the program was one of Nippon's primary goals when it invested $538 million in Shearson in 1986.

Further, while Japanese firms' group orientation causes rapid adoption of new organization practices, fragmentation in the American firms works against this.

Koji Nakatani, a Nippon Life trainee, comments on analysts in Shearson's bond department: "They're working for their own principle, their own future. [We] are working for an organization." Another trainee, Tomiaki Amano, is more explicit. After watching people go home whenever they finished work with their own clients, Amano observed, "In Japan, if we finish our job and another guy has a job, we help him."

Such individual-versus-group contrasts are magnified by another practice. In American firms, in the financial community and elsewhere, people with the most expertise often leave to start their own businesses. This has been an enduring source of strength in emerging industries where new ideas and entrepreneurial vigor create a healthy advantage. But when a combination of large size and expertise is needed to win, as in many manufacturing and service sectors, valuable opportunities to keep learning walk out the door with each new entrepreneur.[7]

Build a High-Learning Organization

Learning is so crucial it should be a formal, ongoing activity. In high-learning firms, part of every manager's job includes encouraging experimentation and helping people find better ways to do things. Failure is not only tolerated; it is expected to lead to new insights and add to the organization's knowledge. Assumptions are regularly revisited to avoid the trap of yesterday's wisdom.

Continued learning is so important to Corning that everyone up to and including the chairman is required to receive one hundred hours of formal training a year. This emphasis on training is led from the top. On one occasion Corning's top six officers, including chairman Jamie Houghton, traveled to Boston for classroom training in computer applications to planning and decision-making. Another time, when plans were being set for training in quality, the schedule did not have room for top management to go first—which was Houghton's intent. To keep this commitment he arranged for their training to be over a long weekend. Giving up personal time for learning sent a compelling message to the rest of the organization.

Ford's powerful thrust into organizationwide learning is moving on several fronts. First, its cultural transformation into a more open, participative company is supported by an intense senior executive training program that builds cross-functional, cross-cultural, multilevel teams to help break down internal barriers to cooperation. Like Corning, this effort is also led from the highest ranks. The regular instructional staff has included Donald Petersen and other top corporate executives. This development program dovetails with Ford's extensive participative management effort, which includes employees from the shop floor on up.

Another part of Ford's conversion emphasizes organizational learning, which is distinct from learning by individuals. Organizational learning works through the development of shared insights and adjustments. Change is blocked unless major contributors learn and adapt together.

Choosing People to Build Alliances

Alliances connect companies; the relationships so essential to their success must be shaped by individuals. Clearly, some people are more adept at this than others. Choosing representatives for key positions is thus a vital step in alliance planning.

Select People with Strong Relationship-Building Skills

In addition to suitable technical abilities, representatives should have:

Negotiation skills. The talent to explore differences creatively, to locate common ground, and to find solutions

Flexibility. The skill to adopt different responses and approaches according to the needs of a situation

Humility. The ability to accept others as equally worthy

Risk acceptance. A willingness to make mistakes

Repair skills. The competence to rebuild damaged interpersonal relations

Integrity. Being by nature honest and reliable

Sensitivity. The facility to listen and observe well, to glean subtle cues from conversations and nonverbal communications, and to know when and how to raise issues

Patience. The aptitude to tolerate unfamiliar and uncomfortable situations

Curiosity. An abiding interest in learning about others

These traits are always important for alliances. They are even more valuable with larger risks or significant cultural differences, because the potential for discord and confusion is greater.

Dick Place was Ford's resident director at Mazda from 1983 to 1987, the period of strongest growth and change in this alliance. By agreement, the resident director is a member of all Mazda senior management committees and has the number four position in Mazda—highly significant in rank-conscious Japan. This role, which carries no formal authority, is to advise each firm of the other's interests, to ensure that Ford gets all the information it needs and is entitled to, and to make sure joint projects are implemented with minimal misunderstandings.

When he took the assignment, Place had only minor Japanese language skills. In the few months between his appointment and departure for Japan, he studied Japanese intensively at Berlitz. (To put this in context, a Westerner needs several years or more to approach fluency in Japanese.) While in Japan he learned significantly more, yet he still needed to work through interpreters.

Despite his language handicap, Dick Place was expected to take a key role in strengthening the firms' mutual understandings. There were numerous complex projects at that critical time.

Unlike many people on foreign assignment, he recognized that his duties would have to include appreciating the culture. "If you're going to be sympathetic with their ways, you are going to have to know what is driving them, and what is important to them," Place observes. "This can only come from studying and talking to people. If you show an interest in their culture, they sense that and bring new information to you to help you understand even more. It is also an important sign that you really care about their ways and their interests."

During his stay, Place developed close personal relations with many Mazda people and others outside Mazda. He knew people well enough for them to tell him when he was wrong, which helped shape his understandings. Many of his conversations with top Mazda executives pertained to Japanese culture. Knowing he was interested, they brought up the subject and recommended readings on key topics. One time, to help him understand traditional Japan, Mazda friends invited Place to visit some of their friends in a rural town. Such opportunities are rare for foreigners.

A significant part of his role was serving as mediator to build trust between the firms. Ford and Mazda both wanted a forthright relationship. The broad contacts and comfortable understandings Dick Place developed at Mazda paralleled his already wide acceptance at Ford. This "has been an extremely great help in doing my job," he says.

One joint program involving Ford's Escort and Mazda's 323 was in danger of collapsing when Place attended a critical meeting in San Francisco with Yoshihiro Wada and Lou Ross, both executive vice presidents of their firms. Dick and Lou were old friends, and Dick knew Wada on a personal basis. These close relations made it possible for him to speak more freely than otherwise and to play a role that helped them reach agreement.

When Possible, Look for People with Similar Backgrounds

It is easier for strangers to build a relationship when they start with something in common. Alliances with universities, for example, work better when company representatives have attended graduate school and understand academic ways.

Similar experiences contributed to the rapport between GE's Gerhard Neumann and SNECMA's René Ravaud. Each was European-born. During World War II each had served in his nation's military with exceptional accomplishments to his credit.

In planning Autolatina, Ford and Volkswagen chose people with compatible backgrounds for key positions. For a top manufacturing slot, Ford picked a German national from Ford of Europe who had worked in Spain. He thus could relate more easily to VW people and understood working in a Latin culture. He also had good cross-cultural skills. VW made similar staff selections, for example, for Autolatina's technical director.

Developing the Skills Pays Off

In this age of alliances, companies have every reason to develop people with relationship-building and cross-cultural skills. A good bit of this comes from hiring appropriate people and from a corporate culture that nourishes cooperation. Still, substantial exposure to different environments helps people become more adaptable to different contexts.

The Emerging Corporation

We are in the midst of basic long-term structural changes in the world economy. As technology flows increase and nations become more alike, competition grows more intense. To remain effective, businesses must also change.

One central feature of the emerging company is a facility for sharing resources and know-how with others to build more strength. To do this well, firms need substantial cooperation skills. Several dimensions of this ability stand out: more delegation, fewer organizational levels, and easy horizontal coordination, all of which speed responses to opportunities, promote mutual commitments, and improve internal understandings. Other key attributes include participative cultures that nourish relationship-building and ready acceptance of others; an aptitude for seeking and adapting outside ideas; and a relentless emphasis on learning by individuals and by the organization as a functioning whole.

Making full use of cooperation recasts a firm from an individual performer into a more powerful, more independent, *and* more interdependent enterprise. At the firm's center is a focused core competence that enables it to attract partners and to continue bringing unique value to its customers. The emerging firm regards all others as both friends and opponents. Specific relations depend on how each opportunity affects the firm's central core.

For such firms generating new growth is easier because opportunities for understanding related products, markets, technologies, and other activities are close at hand. Moreover, focusing on a few core strengths increases a firm's ability to keep up with change and to invest for the long term.

To be sure, strategic alliances must be complemented by internal activities, arm's-length transactions, and acquisitions. Even so, each of these arrangements works best with the same practices and conditions needed for alliances: participation; acceptance of others as equals; clear trust and understandings; and cooperation that is driven by mutual need, shared risks, and a common vision.

The future corporation will be the hub of interrelated networks of businesses and activities with a wide range of ownership structures tailored to its needs for commitment and control in each market. How this hub functions will be quite different from the way many firms work today. A central brain and authority will still be required to look ahead, establish priorities, and allocate resources to ensure the continued strength of the firm's core competence. But relationships within the network will be egalitarian, conducted for mutual benefit. Control will emphasize shared goals and values.

Notes

Preface

1. "Collaborative Ventures: A Pragmatic Approach to Business Expansion in the Eighties," a joint study by Coopers & Lybrand and Yankelovich, Skelly & White, 1984, p. 10, found that twelve out of thirty-eight collaborative ventures met or exceeded partners' expectations. In a study by McKinsey and Coopers & Lybrand, 70 percent of the joint ventures broke up. See "Corporate Odd Couples," *Business Week*, July 21, 1986, p. 100.

   Of 126 U.S. auto suppliers that entered joint ventures with Japanese partners to supply Honda, Nissan, and Mazda—as well as GM and Ford—in the United States, almost all are losing money. Stephen Phillips, "When U.S. Joint Ventures with Japan Go Sour," *Business Week*, July 24, 1989, p. 30.

An Introduction to Strategic Alliances

1. Azusa Tomiura, "How Nippon Steel Conducts Joint Research," *Research Management*, January–February 1985, p. 22.

2. Terry Dodsworth, "Telecoms Partners Grow Apart," *Financial Times*, June 10, 1988, p. 8.

3. Susan Helper, "Vertical Relations in the U.S. Auto Industry," unpublished manuscript, Department of Economics, Harvard University, 1984.

4. Eugene Carlson, "McDonald's Kroc Bloomed Late but Brilliantly." *Wall Street Journal*, May 23, 1989, p. B2.

Chapter 1
Why Alliances Have Become So Important

1. Japanese quote: Amal Nag, "Fuji, Isuzu Are Planning to Jointly Build Cars, Trucks in U.S. at $480 Million Cost," *Wall Street Journal*, May 19, 1986, p. 53.

Thirty-fold growth: Michael Hergert and Deigan Morris, "Trends in International Collaborative Agreements," in Farok J. Contractor and Peter Lorange, eds., *Cooperative Strategies in International Business* (Lexington, Mass.: Lexington Books, 1988), p. 101. Eastern Europe: "Joint Ventures Double in Eastern Bloc," *Financial Times*, April 14, 1988, p. 3.

India: Nicholas D. Kristof, "Curbs Give Way to Welcome for Multinational Companies," *New York Times*, May 5, 1985, p. 1. William J. Holstein *et al.*, "Suddenly U.S. Business Is Banging on India's Door," *Business Week*, June 3, 1985, p. 54.

2. National Science Board, *Science and Engineering Indicators—1987* (Washington, D.C.: National Science Foundation, 1988), p. 236. The observation refers to long-term R&D growth.

3. The total number of articles from each nation is from unpublished data produced by Computer Horizons, Inc. ("19-Apr-88 Pub Counts & Percent of World 1973 Journal Set") for the National Science Foundation, and graciously provided by NSF. The count of institutionally co-authored articles is from National Science Board, *Science and Engineering Indicators—1987*, p. 285. Data for the years before 1973 do not exist. The data base is dominated by research publications, because much development work is proprietary and is not published. Yet available data (same source as above) show the same basic trends in cooperation in development. The research data are used here because development data are not available for nations other than the United States.

Jointly authored review articles often do not reflect joint research. But this is an insignificantly small fraction of all published articles. It is possible, of course, that there is some national or discipline bias in the choice of journals. It is also possible that the data over- or underrepresent some sectors. But this may not be significant. The levels and growth rates of international cooperation involving U.S. universities, and separately involving U.S. industry, were quite similar between 1973 and 1984. And the time series represented in the text illustrations are continuous over the period 1973–84 even though the data base changed from 2,100 journals in 1973–80 to 3,500 from 1981 on. See *ibid.*, p. 286.

The measure of a nation's R&D effort used here is the number of scientists and engineers employed in R&D. This measure avoids the problem of adjusting for inflation and salary changes in each nation if we were to use R&D expenditures as a measure of effort. Data on national science and engineering employment levels are from *ibid.*, p. 228.

Note that published articles are a measure of R&D *output*, while R&D employment measures *input*. Dividing one by the other may thus seem illogical for our purposes. But output lags input, so including some appropriate adjustment for lag would overcome much of this problem. Further, both factors have been steadily rising at approximately constant rates for each nation. Dividing the slopes to get the growth rate ratios makes our result relatively insensitive to the lag issue.

International cooperation data are from *ibid.*, p. 286. If the comparable rate for individual nations is also slower, then the denominator we have used is too large. A smaller number here would give us a larger growth rate for R&D cooperation.

4. For the past hundred years productivity levels among industrial nations have been converging as know-how—the driving force behind advancing productivity—has rapidly spread around the world. See William J. Baumol, "Productivity Growth, Convergence, and Welfare: What the Long-Run Data Show," *American Economic Review*, December 1986, p. 1072.

5. Caught up or moved ahead: See National Science Board, *Science Indicators 1980* (Washington, D.C.: NSF, 1981), p. 237.

Foreign competition: *The Technological Dimensions of International Competitiveness* (Washington, D.C.: National Academy of Engineering, 1988).

World trade growth: General Agreement on Tariffs and Trade, *International Trade 1985/6* (Geneva: GATT, 1986).

6. In the United States, investments in information technology leaped from 16 percent to 40 percent of all new plant and equipment between 1975 and 1985. *Technology and the American Economic Transition* (Washington, D.C.: Office of Technology Assessment, 1988).

7. Hazel Duffy and David Churchill, "Britain Unveils Plan for Growth to Offset Declining Oil Revenue," *Financial Times*, January 13, 1988, p. 1.

8. Expropriations: United Nations Centre on Transnational Corporations, "Transnational Corporations in World Development: Trends and Prospects," (New York: UN, 1988).

Ecuador's Finance Minister: Nicholas D. Kristoff, "Curbs Give Way to Welcome for Multinational Companies," *New York Times*, May 11, 1985, p. 1.

9. Microsoft and Ashton-Tate: Alan Farnham *et al.*, "Linking Up: Olsen's DEC and Scully's Apple," *Fortune*, February 15, 1988, p. 8.

Aetna: "Aetna and Hospital Group Set Health Plan Venture," *Wall Street Journal*, April 2, 1985, p. 18.

Wendy's: Ronald Alsop, "Why Wendy's Has a Fondness for Baskin-Robbins Ice Cream," *Wall Street Journal*, February 19, 1987, p. 31.

Chapter 2

Employing Strategic Alliances

1. IBM quote: John Markoff, "I.B.M.'s Top Scientist," *New York Times,* July 9, 1989, p. F5.

   Kubota: David E. Sanger, "U.S. Parts, Japanese Computer," *New York Times,* September 7, 1988, p. D1; "Maxtor Forms Venture with Kubota to Make Optical Disk Drives," *Wall Street Journal,* March 2, 1989, p. B11.

2. Acquired firm's strength: More successful acquisition strategies involve the purchase of highly profitable companies. Buying low-profit or losing companies because they are cheap in the hopes of achieving a turnaround involves high risks that are not adequately compensated for in reduced acquisition prices. John B. Kusewitt, "An Exploratory Study of Strategic Acquisition Factors Relating to Performance," *Strategic Management Journal,* April–June 1985, p. 151.

   Benefits: Relatedness is not sufficient for acquiring firms to earn above-average returns. Rather, only when acquirers enjoy uniquely valuable synergistic cash flows with targets does acquiring a related firm produce abnormal returns for shareholders of bidding firms. Jay B. Barney, "Returns to Bidding Firms in Mergers and Acquisitions: Reconsidering the Relatedness Hypothesis," *Strategic Management Journal,* Summer 1988, p. 71; see also Dosoung Choi and George C. Philippatos, "Post-Merger Performance Among Homogeneous Firm Samples," *Financial Review,* May 1984, p. 173.

   Mergers generate abnormal gains for stockholders of acquired firms. The competitive nature of the bidding marketplace and the buyer's apparent optimism make any gain to its shareholders small at best and highly questionable. There is no discernible difference between the systematic risks of merged firms and those of matched control groups. Thus a stockholder with a well-diversified portfolio should not expect the merged unit to yield more than the premerger individual returns. The postmerger profitability experience of acquisitive companies has been either less successful, or not significantly more successful, than the experience of otherwise comparable nonacquisitive companies or the average of the acquisitive firms' industries. Allen Michel and Israel Shaked, "Evaluating Merger Performance," *California Management Review,* Spring 1985, p. 109.

   Firms acquired in conglomerate mergers and those acquired in horizontal mergers were both found to experience substantial losses in market shares relative to control group companies following the mergers. Dennis C. Mueller, "Mergers and Market Share," *Review of Economics and Statistics,* May 1985, p. 259.

   Acquisitive firms generally achieve more rapid sales and asset growth than similar nonacquisitive firms. But this results from adding the parts, not from any change in the merged components' basic growth rates. Sayan

Chatterjee, "Types of Synergy and Economic Value: The Impact of Acquisitions on Merging and Rival Firms," *Strategic Management Journal*, 7 (1986): 119.

Executive departures: One study found that more than 60 percent of corporate top executives leave firms during the first three years following their acquisition. Study by Mitchell & Co., cited in "Running Scared," *Wall Street Journal*, May 6, 1986, p. 1.

A study of senior executives whose companies were among the 150 largest corporate acquisitions found that 47 percent sought other positions within one year. Similarly, 75 percent left or planned to leave within three years following a takeover. "Senior Executives at Takeover Companies Leave Earlier, Faster than Before," Lamalie Associates, Inc., 101 Park Avenue, New York 10178.

3. "IBM Buys Another Key to the Automated Office," *Business Week*, June 27, 1983, p. 27; "Why IBM Snapped Up the Rest of Rolm," *Business Week*, October 8, 1984, p. 48; David E. Sanger, "Rolm Chief Says He Sought I.B.M. Link," *New York Times*, October 10, 1984, p. D4; "IBM and Rolm Cope with Prenuptial Jitters," *Business Week*, November 19, 1984, p. 166; Stuart Gannes, "IBM Dials a Wrong Number," *Fortune*, June 9, 1986, p. 34; John Markoff, "IBM to Sell Rolm to Siemens," *New York Times*, December 14, 1988, p. D1; Hugo Dixon, "IBM to Take Loss on Rolm Sale," *Financial Times*, December 30, 1988, p. 13; Robert D. Hof and John J. Keller, "Behind the Scenes at the Fall of Rolm," *Business Week*, July 10, 1989, p. 82.

4. European supply relations: *Enduring Corporate Success* (Brussels: Management Centre Europe, 1986).

American auto executive: "How to Regain the Productive Edge," *Fortune*, May 22, 1989, p. 92.

5. Ian Hamilton Fazey, "Japanese Tint to American Windscreens," *Financial Times*, March 16, 1989, p. 21.

6. Chaparral: Gene Bylinsky, "America's Best Managed Factories," *Fortune*, May 28, 1984, p. 16.

IBM chips: Andrew Pollack, "G.E. and IBM Sign Chip Accord," *New York Times*, December 10, 1987, p. D5.

7. Paul B. Carroll, "Rivals of IBM Plan to Create Their Own 'Bus'," *Wall Street Journal*, September 6, 1988, p. 4. Paul B. Carroll, " 'Gang of Nine' Unveils a Chip Set That Rivals IBM's Micro Channel," *Wall Street Journal*, July 11, 1989.

8. Based on interviews with Mitsubishi Heavy Industries and information shared by JADC, plus Roy J. Harris, Jr., and Bernard Wysocki, Jr., "Venture with Boeing Is Likely to Give Japan Big Boost in Aerospace," *Wall Street Journal*, January 14, 1986, p. 1.

Some observers have suggested there could not be a serious commercial aircraft threat from Japan, since Boeing did not object to the FSX deal. But Boeing may have seen things differently. Boeing's main commercial competition through the end of the century is likely to be Airbus. Since suppliers provide a high percentage of the value added in an aircraft, a large part of Boeing's competitive strength depends on its suppliers' continued technology, cost, and quality advances, its relations with them, and their willingness to share the risks. From this perspective having strong Japanese suppliers is in Boeing's interest. For the longer term, however, a strong supply community with substantial overall design and systems integration capabilities may face lower entry barriers to full airframe production.

Takaaki Yamada, executive vice president of Mitsubishi Heavy Industries, tried to dispel U.S. concerns that the FSX deal would contribute to a commercial aircraft capability by observing that military and civil aircraft design are distinct. Stefan Wagstyl, "Trade Hawks in Dogfight Over the FSX," *Financial Times*, April 13, 1989, p. 7. Yet Yamada's boss, MHI president Yotaro Iida, exposed deeper commonalities: "The technology we will develop and accumulate during the project will be instrumental in developing next generation planes, such as hypersonic and supersonic transports," *Japan Economic Journal*, January 21, 1989, as reported by Joel Kurtzman, "The Flaw in the FSX Deal," *New York Times*, May 7, 1989, p. 1F.

Other experts have pointed out that although many aspects of military aircraft technology are not readily transferred to civilian applications, what is learned from avionics integration, team assembly, and other processes could be the nucleus for developing a civilian industry. In fact, nations with the strongest civil aviation presence today are generally those with the strongest military base. See Clyde Farnsworth, "Japan's F-16 Plan Gets Bush Support," *New York Times*, March 16, 1989, p. D3.

To be sure, cooperation is not new to the world's aerospace firms. Yet in sector after sector, Japanese firms have proven highly adept at linking their organizations to share R&D and manufacturing information. Katherine T. Chen, "The State of Japan's Military Art," *IEEE Spectrum*, September 1989, p. 28.

9. Michael Waldholz, "Merck and Johnson & Johnson to Form Venture for Over-the-Counter Medicines," *Wall Street Journal*, March 29, 1989, p. A4.

10. Pharmaceutical firms: Michael Waldholz, "Squibb Seeks Johnson & Johnson's Aid In Blood-Pressure Drug War with Merck," *Wall Street Journal*, December 11, 1987, p. 4; "SmithKline, DuPont Set Accord to Increase Sales of Ulcer Drug," *Wall Street Journal*, December 11, 1987, p. 4.

Genetics Institute: David Stiff, "Genetics Institute and Genentech Agree to Cross-License Drug for Hemophiliacs," *Wall Street Journal*, March 22, 1989, p. 35.

Coke and Schweppes: "Coca Cola, Schweppes Launch Joint Drinks Company," *Financial Times*, December 9, 1986, p. 9. Gary Hector, "Yes, You Can Manage Long Term," *Fortune*, November 21, 1988, p. 64; also *Financial Times*, October 12, 1988, p. 16.

11. Charles C. Snow and Lawrence G. Hrebiniak, "Strategy, Distinctive Competence, and Organizational Performance," *Administrative Science Quarterly*, June 1980, p. 317. More recently Meyer and Roberts have shown that developing a distinctive competence in a core technology is critical to the growth of technology-based firms. See Marc H. Meyer and Edward B. Roberts, "Focusing Product Technology for Corporate Growth," *Sloan Management Review*, Summer 1988, p. 7.

12. Vertical integration in U.S. auto-making, British candies and Italian textiles: Sergio Mariotti and Gian Carlo Cainarca, "The Evolution of Transaction Governance in the Textile-Clothing Industry," *Journal of Economic Behavior and Organization*, 1986 p. 351; Richard Waters, "Price Is Not the Only Criterion," *Financial Times*, June 2, 1989, p. 17.

L. M. Ericsson: Jules Arbose, "Ericsson Turns to Alliances in Hunt for More Growth," *International Management*, October 1987, p. 54.

U.S. farm equipment: Betsy Morris, "Tractor Firms Are Changing Old Practices," *Wall Street Journal*, October 27, 1983, p. 33; Kevin Quinn, "Farm-Machine Firms Turn to Marketing," *Wall Street Journal*, October 29, 1984, p. 35.

Department stores: Ann Hagedorn, "Apparel Makers Play Bigger Part on Sales Floor," *Wall Street Journal*, March 2, 1988, p. 31.

13. Bro Uttal, "Compaq Bids for PC Leadership," *Fortune*, September 29, 1986, p. 30.

Chapter 3
Cooperating for Competitive Advantage

1. Lee Adler, "Symbiotic Marketing," *Harvard Business Review*, November–December 1966, p. 59.

2. Leif Soderberg, "America's Engineering Gap," *Wall Street Journal*, January 30, 1989, p. A14.

3. Harris: "Competitive Alliances," *Business International* (New York), 1987, p. 14.

McKinsey results: Brian Dumaine, "How Managers Can Succeed Through Speed," *Fortune*, February 13, 1989, p. 54

Hitachi and Texas Instruments: David E. Sanger, "Texas Instruments, Hitachi in Chip Venture," *New York Times*, December 23, 1988, p. D1;

Elisabeth Rubinfien, "Hitachi, Texas Instruments Agree to Jointly Develop Memory Chip," *Wall Street Journal*, December 23, 1988, p. B2.

National Semiconductor and Xerox: John W. Wilson, Todd Mason, and Otis Port, "Now Chipmakers Are Playing 'Let's Make a Deal,' " *Business Week*, October 6, 1986, p. 90.

4. Barnaby J. Feder, "Ambulatory Patient Care," *New York Times*, March 2, 1982, p. D2.

5. IBM selling team: Steven P. Galante, "Helping Service Firms, IBM Helps Itself," *Wall Street Journal*, January 25, 1988, p. 33.

Lincoln Electric: James A. Narus and James C. Anderson, "Turn Your Industrial Distributors into Partners," *Harvard Business Review*, March–April 1986, p. 66.

6. Taylor Publishing: Edwin McDowell, "Turning to the Big Guys for Help," *New York Times*, July 26, 1987, p. F19.

Bloomingdales: Lynn Asinof, "Business Bulletin," *Wall Street Journal*, January 19, 1989, p. 1.

7. DEC and Unisys: "Digital Equipment, Northern Telecom Plan Compatible Products," *Wall Street Journal*, October 29, 1982, p. 16.

DEC in Europe: Richard L. Hudson, "DEC Links Up with European Concerns in Bid to Win Computer Sales from IBM," *Wall Street Journal*, June 20, 1985, p. 33.

Philips and Sony: E. S. Browning, "Sony's Perseverance Helped It Win Market for Mini-CD Players," *Wall Street Journal*, February 27, 1986, p. 1; Shawn Tully, "A Competitor Who Smells Gunpowder," *Fortune*, August 3, 1987, p. 43.

8. Tagamet versus Zantac: James Buchan, "Enough to Give Medicine Men an Ulcer," *Financial Times*, July 28, 1988, p. 13; Richard Koenig and Randall Smith, "Drop in Tagamet Sales is Putting SmithKline in Danger of Takeover," *Wall Street Journal*, January 13, 1989, p. 1.

DuPont and Merck: Richard Koenig, "DuPont Signs Agreement with Merck in Effort to Speed Up Drug Marketing," *Wall Street Journal*, September 29, 1989, p. B3.

Magazines in fragmented markets: Cynthia Crossen, "McCalls and People Form an Ad Venture," *Wall Street Journal*, April 29, 1988, p. 28.

9. Philip Rawstorne, "How Partnership Put Paid to 'Primeval' Advertising," *Financial Times*, March 10, 1988, p. 13.

10. Nick Garnett, "Fiat and Hitachi Launch Assault on Europe's Excavator Market," *Financial Times*, February 18, 1987, p. 11.

11. Allied-Lyons and Suntory: Paul Hemp, "Allied-Lyons Agrees to Form Venture with Suntory to Sell Liquor in Japan," *Wall Street Journal*, October 13, 1988, p. 19; Barry Cohen, "How to Craft a Cross-Border Alliance," *Financial Management*, December 1988, p. 47.

Herman Miller: Kenneth Labich, "Hot Company, Warm Culture," *Fortune,* February 27, 1989, p. 74.

12. H. B. Thorelli, "Networks: Between Markets and Hierarchies," *Strategic Management Journal,* January–February 1986, p. 37.

13. David J. Jefferson, "Boeing, Facing Delays in 747 Deliveries, Turns to Lockheed for Loan of Workers," *Wall Street Journal,* March 8, 1989, p. A3.

14. Xerox: Elizabeth Tucker, "Corporate Gumshoes Spy on Competitors," *Washington Post,* March 30, 1986, p. F1.
    Owens: "Owens-Illinois Forms Venture with Heye, West German Firm," *Wall Street Journal,* July 12, 1983, p. 25.

15. Intel: "Is the Semiconductor Boom Too Much of a Good Thing for Intel?," *Business Week,* April 23, 1984, p. 114.
    MAN: Peter Gumbel and George Anders, "GM Unit, MAN of Germany Eye European Accord," *Wall Street Journal,* September 6, 1984, p. 33.

16. Lee Berton, "Electronics Project Slashes Paper Work, 45 Companies Say," *Wall Street Journal,* January 20, 1984, p. 14.

17. AGA and Nippon Sanso: Sara Webb, "Swedes Agree Technology Deal with Japanese," *Financial Times,* November 20, 1986, p. 2.
    Nissan and Martin-Marietta: Tracy Dahlby, "U.S. Firm, Nissan Swap Arms, Robot Expertise," *Washington Post,* August 26, 1982, p. 1.

18. Jonathan Kapstein, "Enough with the Theory—Where's the Thingamajig?," *Business Week,* March 21, 1988, p. 154.

19. Imperial Chemical Industries and DuPont: Ian Hamilton Fazey, "ICI and DuPont to Link in European Car Paint Deal," *Financial Times,* March 10, 1988, p. 21.
    International Partners in Glass Research: Andrew Pollack, "A New Spirit of Cooperation," *New York Times,* January 14, 1986, p. D1.

20. Elizabeth A. Haas, "Breakthrough Manufacturing," *Harvard Business Review,* March-April 1987, p. 75.

21. David E. Gumpert, "Corporate Big Brothers Lend a Hand," *New York Times,* April 17, 1988, p. F17.

22. Ronald Alsop, "Why Wendy's Has a Fondness for Baskin-Robbins Ice Cream," *Wall Street Journal,* February 19, 1987, p. 31.

23. Hotel fire: Lawrence J. Tell, "United They Stand—At the Defense Table," *Business Week,* May 30, 1988, p. 102.
    Hercules investment risks: "Hercules: A Joint Venture Puts It Back on the Growth Track," *Business Week,* June 27, 1983, p. 50; Alexander F. Giacco, "Meeting Challenge in the Chemical Industry," *Research Management,* January–February 1986, p. 86.

24. Robert Taylor, "SAS-Swissair Partnership Takes Off," *Financial Times,* September 29, 1989, p. 21.

Chapter 4
Protecting Each Firm's Interests

1. Gary Hamel, Yves L. Doz, and C. K. Prahalad, "Collaborate with Your Competitors—and Win," *Harvard Business Review*, January–February 1989, p. 133.

2. GM apparently lost in other ways as well. To get Toyota to accept the deal, GM gave it the lead for car and plant design and for design changes. Both cars built by NUMMI—the Chevy Nova and the Toyota Corolla FX—are variations on the same model and have the same quality, but Toyota limited GM to a four-door body of an older design. The FX came as the popular two-door hatchback.

   The actual sticker price difference between the Nova and FX when comparably equipped was just $23. But with the unattractive design and GM's image behind it, consumers were not attracted to the Nova. Nova sales were thus far below expectations, except when GM offered low-cost financing. Buyers were waiting in line for the FX, and paid as much as $2,495 above its sticker price. Thus when NUMMI was losing money from weak Nova sales, even though GM and Toyota divided the loss equally, GM's effective share of the loss was much higher. "Toyota Motor Corporation-General Motors Corporation Memorandum of Understanding," February 17, 1983; John Holusha, "G.M.'s Big Burden in Toyota Venture," *New York Times*, May 7, 1987, p. D1; Christopher Lorenz, "Joint Ventures May Damage Your Health," *Financial Times*, September 9, 1987, p. 8; Melinda Grenier Guiles, "GM's Chevrolet Nova Is Part Japanese, But Car Buyers Prefer the Real Thing," *Wall Street Journal*, December 13, 1985, p. 33; Warren Brown, "Joint Venture Autos Present Sales Puzzle," *Washington Post*, May 4, 1986, p. F1; Wendy Zellner, "GM's New 'Teams' Aren't Hitting Any Homers," *Business Week*, August 8, 1988, p. 46.

3. Licensing practice: See John A. Quelch, "How to Build a Product Licensing Program," *Harvard Business Review*, May–June 1985, p. 186.

   Mustang: Paul Ingrassia, "Perhaps Ford Could Rechristen the Old Model 'Mustang Classic,' " *Wall Street Journal*, June 25, 1987, p. 27.

4. Agis Salpukas, "American Air Venture Is Reported," *New York Times*, July 13, 1987, p. 21.

5. Hamel et al: Hamel, Doz, and Prahalad, "Collaborate with Your Competitors," p. 133.

   RCA: "The Hollow Corporation," *Business Week*, March 3, 1986, p. 57; Robert B. Reich and Eric D. Mankin, "Joint Ventures with Japan Give Away Our Future," *Harvard Business Review*, March–April 1986, p. 78.

   Kodak: John Holusha, "Beating Japan at Its Own Game," *New York Times*, July 16, 1989, p. F1.

ICL and Fujitsu: *Competitive Alliances* (Business International Corporation, New York), July 1987, p. 114.

6. Hamel, Doz, and Prahalad, "Collaborate with Your Competitors," p. 133.
   Apple: G. Pascal Zachary, "At Apple Computer Proper Office Attire Includes a Muzzle," *Wall Street Journal*, October 6, 1989, p. 1.

7. Rolls and GE: "Rolls Royce Stands by GE Link," *Financial Times*, September 3, 1986, p. 8; Michael Donne, "Battle Builds Up for Aero-Engine Markets," *Financial Times*, November 21, 1986, p. 7.
   Korean steel: Bernard Wysocki Jr., "Weak in Technology South Korea Seeks Help from Overseas," *Wall Street Journal*, January 7, 1986, p. 1.
   SGS and AT&T: *Competitive Alliances*, p. 45.

8. "IBM Buys Another Key to the Automated Office," *Business Week*, June 27, 1983, p. 27; "Why IBM Snapped Up the Rest of Rolm," *Business Week*, October 8, 1984, p. 48; David E. Sanger, "Rolm Chief Says He Sought I.B.M. Link," *New York Times*, October 10, 1984, p. D4.

9. Asian-Western learning differences: Hamel, Doz, and Prahalad, "Collaborate with Your Competitors," p. 133.
   Genex: Nell Henderson, "Biotech Firms Reach Overseas for Partners," *Washington Post*, May 19, 1985, p. H1.

10. RCA and the VCR: Kenneth Dreyfack and Otis Port, "Even American Know-How Is Headed Abroad," *Business Week*, March 3, 1986, p. 60.
    Honeywell and Ericsson: *Competitive Alliances*, p. 34.

11. Thomas C. Hayes, "IBM Sets Joint Deal in Automation," *New York Times*, September 26, 1989, p. D1.

12. Alan Cane and Hugo Dixon, "Marathon Ends on the Final Green," *Financial Times*, August 1, 1990, p. 20.

Chapter 5
Cooperating with a Competitor

1. Brenton R. Schlender, "Apple Digital Equipment Outline Pact to Devise Ways to Link Their Computers," *Wall Street Journal*, January 18, 1988, p. 6; Leslie Helm and John W. Verity, "DEC's New Plan: If You Can't Beat PCs, Join 'Em—To Each Other," *Business Week*, February 1, 1988, p. 83.

2. Margaret Genovese, "JOA," *Presstime*, August 1985, p. 16.

Chapter 6
Using Alliances to Build Market Power

1. Evelyn Richards, "Search for U.S. Strategy at Crossroads," *Washington Post*, January 8, 1989, p. H1.

2. A firm's technological progress is synonymous here with its productivity growth. See F. M. Scherer, "Inter-Industry Technology Flows and Pro-

ductivity Growth," *Review of Economics and Statistics*, November 1982, p. 627; Albert N. Link, "Interfirm Technology Flows and Productivity Growth," Center for Applied Research, University of North Carolina, Greensboro, Working Paper Series no. E821002, October 1982.

3. IBM president quote: Louis Kehoe, "The Hidden Giant Shares Some of Its Secrets," *Financial Times*, June 14, 1989, p. 37.

    Robert Bosch: Charles F. Sabel, Gary Herrigel, Richard Kazis, and Richard Deeg, "How to Keep Mature Industries Innovative," *Technology Review*, April 1987, p. 26.

    NTT: "The Inroads Japan Is Making in Fiber Optics," *Business Week*, May 21, 1984, p. 176.

4. Thomas Moore, "Would You Buy a Car from This Man?" *Fortune*, April 11, 1988, p. 72. See also James A. Narus and James C. Anderson, "Turn Your Industrial Distributors into Partners," *Harvard Business Review*, March–April 1986, p. 66.

5. Business funding of university R&D: National Science Board, *Science Indicators—1987* (Washington, D.C.: NSF, 1988), p. 243; David Thomas, "Business Doubles Spending on University Research," *Financial Times*, July 31, 1989, p. 4.

    SRC: Evert Clark and Todd Mason, "A Surprise Hit: High-Tech Research Consortiums," *Business Week*, June 23, 1986, p. 138; Philip Stephens, "Industry Foots a Vital Bill," *Financial Times*, August 21, 1986, p. 10.

6. Fuji Xerox: Ken-ichi Imai, Ikujiro Nonaka, and Hirotaka Takeuchi, "Managing the New Product Development Process: How Japanese Companies Learn and Unlearn," in Kim B. Clark, Robert H. Hayes, and Christopher Lorenz, eds., *The Uneasy Alliance* (Boston: Harvard Business School Press, 1987), p. 337.

    McKesson: Russell Johnston and Paul R. Lawrence, "Beyond Vertical Integration—the Rise of the Value-Adding Partnership," *Harvard Business Review*, July–August 1988, p. 94.

7. Providence Journal: Albert Scardino, "A New Way to Print News," *New York Times*, November 11, 1985, p. D3.

    British advanced materials network: Lynton McLain, "Molecule by Molecule Towards 2000 AD," *Financial Times*, November 3, 1988, p. 16.

8. Paul Betts, "St-Gobain Buys into Essilor Optical Group," *Financial Times*, November 8, 1988, p. 21; Paul Betts, "French Glass Group Does Not Throw Stones," *Financial Times*, January 17, 1989, p. 22.

9. In the West, corporate equity is often seen as a commodity that is traded among owners with little vested interest in individual firms. Even when outside stockholders can look past short-term gains, their separation from a firm's activities limits their view to easily measured performance, which typically is financial.

In Japanese *keiretsu*, by contrast, a sizable percentage of each firm's equity is held by other group members—including some of the firm's commercial partners. Overall, an average of 15 to 30 percent of a group member's shares are held by other firms in the group. Among the leading firms in each group, however, the percentage of ownership by group members is double this amount.

Share cross-holdings among group companies thus create a structure of close, stable relations among trading partners and symbolize these relations, rather than represent investments for their own sake. Moreover, although group firms are publicly owned, with much of their stock held by affiliates, there is no room for outside investors to impose their will on a firm's performance. Hostile takeovers are virtually impossible.

For these investors, each of which usually holds only a small percentage of another firm's shares, that firm's long-term viability as a growing, reliable customer and supplier is far more important than alternative uses of the investment. Returns on investments in group firms come only from collective advance. Member firms see each other as resources to be preserved and protected.

Estimates of holdings by "stable shareholders" run between 60 and 80 percent of total shares on the Tokyo Stock Exchange. Yet liquidity is high because these holders account for only 10 percent of total share transactions. See Michael Gerlach, "Business Alliances and the Strategy of the Japanese Firm," *California Management Review*, Fall 1987, p. 126.

Perhaps most significantly, each *keiretsu* has a central bank—such as the Mitsubishi Bank or the Sumitomo Bank—which serves as the main bank for every member and which has a large equity stake in each firm. A bank's close ties to its group closely link members' major source of capital with their overall performance.

The banks play a powerful role in group behavior by promoting and helping finance new business and long-term growth. Moreover, during hard times, the banks defer interest and principal payments, reduce compensating balances, roll over loans, arrange favorable trade terms among group members, and when necessary, intervene in individual firms' management.

The help Mazda (which is affiliated with the Sumitomo group) received from the Sumitomo Bank seems typical of what can happen. For several years up to the mid-1970s Mazda invested heavily in developing the rotary engine—which has size advantages over other internal combustion engines. However, when oil prices rose after 1973, the engine's low fuel efficiency killed its promise. With no hope for a return on its investment, Mazda faced economic collapse. At that point the Sumitomo Bank took the lead in extending new credits, arranging for special terms on sales and purchase agreements from other group companies, and arranging for other group members to buy additional shares of Mazda stock.

Gerlach, "Business Alliances and Strategy," p. 126; Ronald Dore, "Goodwill and the Spirit of Market Capitalism," *British Journal of Sociology*, 1983, p. 459.

10. Nakatani compared the performance of forty-two large members of *keiretsu* with a matched sample of forty-two loners for the 1970s. The loners had higher growth rates and higher average profit levels for this period, but they also had a considerably higher dispersal around the means. Group firms were far more homogeneous in growth and profit levels. I. Nakatani, cited in Dore, "Goodwill and Spirit of Market Capitalism," p. 459.

11. Japanese firms have long had the highest debt-to-equity ratios for all developed countries. The price of a firm's stock is thus less central (compared to Western firms) to its ability to raise new capital. The primary role of credit in Japanese firms' capital structures gives the group bank sizable leverage over members' finances. This, plus the bank's large equity stake compared to other group members, creates a strong reason for the bank to look after individual firms' broad interests. Further, its dependence on the group's collective performance focuses the bank's concern on each member's long-term viability. The lead bank also acts as a signal to other banks regarding the financial health of the company, ensuring the firm will be able to get loans from others.

   One result is that new market entry by Japanese firms has been dominated by larger and older companies. The nation's basic steel firms, for example, have moved aggressively into advanced materials with bank help. Thus, while the Japanese have been slow to invent in some fields, they have had a commanding position from which to capitalize on others' inventions as these progress to the stage where massive development, manufacturing, and marketing investments are needed. See Gerlach, "Business Alliances and Strategy"; Dore, "Goodwill and Spirit of Market Capitalism."

12. George R. Heaton, Jr., "The Truth About Japan's Cooperative R&D," *Issues in Science and Technology*, Fall 1988, p. 32.

13. John Markoff, "Experts Warn of U.S. Lag in Vital Chip Technology," *New York Times*, December 12, 1988, p. A1.

14. William J. Holstein, James B. Treece, and Neil Gross, "Why Mitsubishi Is Right at Home in Illinois," *Business Week*, May 30, 1988, p. 45.

15. Caterpillar–Mitsubishi: Thomas Hout, Michael E. Porter, and Eileen Rudden, "How Global Companies Win Out," *Harvard Business Review*, September–October 1982, p. 98.

   Intel and Siemens: Craig M. Watson, "Counter-Competition Abroad to Protect Home Markets," *Harvard Business Review*, January–February 1982, p. 40.

   Proctor & Gamble: "Utterly Absorbing," *Business Week*, January 12, 1987, p. 125.

Intel vs. Samsung: Andrew Pollack, "Big Chill on Asian Chips in U.S.," *New York Times,* September 6, 1988, p. D1.

Intel and Texas Instruments: Brenton R. Schlender, "Intel and Texas Instruments Inc. Set Design Swap," *Wall Street Journal,* July 8, 1987, p. 4.

GE's advanced turbines: Watson, "Counter-Competition Abroad," p. 40.

Chapter 7
Working with Informal and Contractual Alliances

1. Informal exchange of proprietary know-how: Eric von Hippel, "Trading Trade Secrets," *Technology Review,* February–March 1988, p. 58.

   Microsoft and Ashton-Tate: Paul B. Carroll, "Ashton-Tate/Microsoft Accord Shows Unusual Teamwork in Competitive Field," *Wall Street Journal,* January 14, 1988, p. 30.

2. This discussion benefits from Ian R. MacNeil, "A Primer of Contract Planning," *Southern California Law Review,* 1975, p. 627. For a basic grounding in contracts see *Restatement (Second) of Contracts* (American Law Institute, 1973).

3. The concept of value used here is different from Williamson's definition of a transaction-specific investment tied to a relationship with no alternate use for the investment. Here only the relative worth of a resource from each firm's perspective is considered. Alternative uses of an investment have different values and may be uncertain in advance. The possibility of alternatives is thus included in the treatment of uncertainty. High uncertainty about alternatives approaches Williamson's condition of transaction-specificity.

   Another way to view this is to consider a transaction-specific investment as having opportunity costs. But these are governed by uncertainties. Stripping out the uncertainties leaves what this text refers to as "value." See Oliver E. Williamson, "Transaction Cost Economics: The Governance of Contractual Relations," *Journal of Law and Economics,* 1979, p. 233.

4. With cost-plus, the performer is reimbursed for defined costs, plus a sum for profit. Expected performance may be to deliver a specified result, or to work on a best-effort basis. Some argue that cost-plus contracting is inefficient. But it can lead to different results from having set prices. In the face of substantial performance uncertainty, it can be hard to say what approach would be best. Cost-plus pricing with high performance uncertainty thus doesn't so much cause inefficiency as it supports innovative problem-solving. The keys to effective conduct here are careful partner selection and controls, such as a price ceiling or a time limit.

5. "Synergen, DuPont Agree to Develop Protein Uses," *Wall Street Journal,* February 5, 1987, p. 12.

6. Merck and Repligen: James B. Stewart, "Merck, Repligen Joining Forces in Race to Develop and Market AIDS Vaccine," *Wall Street Journal*, May 28, 1987, p. 34.

   Nuclear power: Matthew L. Wald, "Building Reactors the New Way," *New York Times*, July 17, 1989, p. D1.

7. Here is how GE's revenue sharing works. First, GE and a partner negotiate the parts and percentage of an engine for which each will be responsible. Allocations are on the basis of direct labor hours, machine time, and material costs for each firm's effort. GE and its partners consider one person equivalent to one person at equal functional levels, regardless of pay, in each firm.

   Each partner's representation is taken on faith by the other. The firms usually don't know each other's actual costs. Negotiations are intended to put each in a position to make a profit the best way it can. GE and its partner share the risk of the deal in two ways—through each firm's ability to make its allocated parts efficiently, and the marketing risks for the engine.

   Revenue sharing is easier when partners are in the same business. This simplifies agreement on correlating the value of each firm's contribution— and thus its revenue share—with its work share. Moreover, firms in the same business can usually estimate each other's costs with some confidence.

   In revenue sharing the lead firm is generally expected to disclose more program information. This can limit the appeal of revenue sharing for competitors.

8. Jackson Diehl, "Eastern Europeans Turn to West in Effort to End Technology Gap," *Washington Post*, February 28, 1988, p. H1.

9. Emily T. Smith and Evert Clark, "Now, R&D Is Corporate America's Answer to Japan Inc.," *Business Week*, June 23, 1986, p. 134.

10. Peter Montagnon, "An Entree to Difficult Markets," *Financial Times*, January 4, 1988, p. 9.

11. Even so, strong relations are no substitutes for contracting. In relationship-intense Japan, suppliers with oral contracts are more likely to have goods returned than those with formal written agreements. See Ronald Dore, "Goodwill and the Spirit of Market Capitalism," *British Journal of Sociology*, 1983, p. 459.

12. Client–contractor relationship: Sir Alistair Frame, chairman of the RTZ Group—the global natural resources company—notes that most large construction projects get in trouble in the relationship between client and contractor, not in the technical complexities that characterize such efforts. David Fishlock, "Sir Alistair's Four Rules for Success," *Financial Times*, September 4, 1986, p. 22.

   Fast food business: Joseph P. Guiltinan, Ismail B. Rejab, and William

C. Rodgers, "Factors Influencing Coordination in a Franchising Channel," *Journal of Retailing,* Fall 1980, p. 41.

Chapter 8
Using Minority Investment Alliances

1. James P. Miller, "Micron Acts to Protect Chip Dominance," *Wall Street Journal,* October 5, 1988, p. B4.
2. "AT&T and Olivetti Unsheathe a Strategy to Win Europe," *Business Week,* July 16, 1984, p. 41; David Manasian, "AT&T: Down but Not Out in Europe," *International Management,* October 1987, p. 62; John Rossant and Thane Peterson, "Olivetti Spews Out Some Grim Numbers," *Business Week,* October 10, 1988, p. 60; Richard L. Hudson and Laura Colby, "AT&T, Olivetti End Partnership Dating Since '83," *Wall Street Journal,* July 17, 1989, p. A3.
3. Lawrence M. Fisher, "U.S.–French Wineries in Stock-Swap Accord," *New York Times,* February 10, 1988, p. D4.
4. For more on this, see Victor Brudney and Robert Charles Clark, "A New Look at Corporate Opportunities," *Harvard Law Review,* March 1981, p. 997.
5. Geraldine Fabricant, "Time and Whittle Form an Alliance," *New York Times,* October 21, 1988, p. D1.
6. William Hall, "Ciba-Geigy in $200m Offer for US Group," *Financial Times,* May 27, 1987, p. 29.
7. The research literature describes 30 percent as marking the line between "strong" and "weak" control. Yet there is no precise voting share below 50 percent that gives effective control. An investor's influence depends on the size of its holdings, how ownership is distributed, shareholder participation in voting, interests of other large stockholders, and the probability of winning votes on specific issues. Thus effective control can be achieved with a small share of the vote in some situations and may require more in others.

   In fact, according to Palmer, the source cited by later authors, the choice of 30 percent was "somewhat arbitrary." See John Palmer, "The Profit Performance Effects of the Separation of Ownership from Control in Large U.S. Corporations," *Bell Journal of Economics,* 1973, p. 293.

   For a theoretical treatment of control where ownership is widely held, see John Cubbin and Dennis Leech, "The Effect of Shareholding Dispersion on the Degree of Control in British Companies: Theory and Measurement," *Economic Journal* (UK), June 1983, p. 351. See also the articles by Bothwell and Stano cited in Cubbin and Leech.
8. Janet Guyon and Laura Colby, "AT&T and Its Partner Olivetti Are Spatting Again," *Wall Street Journal,* April 15, 1988, p. 6.

Chapter 9
Making Joint Venture Commitments

1. *Competitive Alliances* (Business International Corporation, 1987), p. 94.
2. Stephen Phillips, "When U.S. Joint Ventures with Japan Go Sour," *Business Week*, July 24, 1989, p. 30.
3. Caroline E. Mayer, "Hechinger, K-mart Scrap Deal," *Washington Post*, April 28, 1984, p. D9; "K mart, Hechinger End Plan to Form Retailing Venture," *Wall Street Journal*, April 30, 1984, p. 2.
4. Sarah Bartlett and Richard A. Melcher, "Credit Suisse First Boston: The Honeymoon Is Over," *Business Week*, April 25, 1988, p. 112; Leslie Wayne, "First Boston's Lesson for the Street," *New York Times*, September 4, 1988, p. 1F; James Sterngold, "2 Top Securities Firms to Merge, Giving Swiss a Big Wall St. Stake," *New York Times*, October 10, 1988, p. 1; Stephen Fidler and Janet Bush, "First Boston in Talks on Merger with European Affiliate," *Financial Times*, October 10, 1988, p. 1. Paul Abrams, "Astra to Form Joint Venture with Merck to Market Drugs in U.S., *Financial Times*, December 6, 1991, p. 21.
5. Kathleen Deveny, John E. Pluenneke, Dori Jones, Mark Maremont, and Robert Black, "McWorld?" *Business Week*, October 13, 1986, p. 78.
6. The GECARS board has four directors from GE and one from Ford Credit, reflecting ownership shares. Even so, the venture is governed by consensus. Ford contributes to the expansion plans as well as to decisions regarding how best to operate and improve the auctions. The senior board member from GE Capital makes sure Ford is comfortable with a position before he concurs. Other GE directors follow suit. Routine operations are managed by GE, so Ford does not have to be involved in day-to-day management. This helps reduce concerns that other auto makers or dealers might withdraw their cars if they believed they were not being treated fairly.
7. William H. Davidson, "Creating and Managing Join Ventures in China," *California Management Review*, Summer 1987, p. 77; W. H. Davidson, private communication.
8. Guy de Jonquières, "Too Many Pilots in the Cockpit," *Financial Times*, July 8, 1988, p. 11; Susan Cary, "Airbus Industrie Seeks Its Independence," *Wall Street Journal*, August 10, 1989, p. A10.
9. Note that a "shotgun buyout" is in effect a formula, because one party defines a price, which the other may accept or exceed.

Chapter 10
Organizing and Operating Joint Ventures

1. Paul Betts, "Aero-Engine Consortium 'Will Not Withdraw From Market,' " *Financial Times*, June 11, 1987, p. 3.
2. Zachary Schiller, "What's Deflating Uniroyal Goodrich," *Business Week*, November 30, 1987, p. 35; Ralph E. Winter, "Ames Bids to Pump Up Uniroyal Goodrich," *Wall Street Journal*, February 22, 1988, p. 27.

3. Elizabeth Tucker, "US Sprint Firing Is Linked to Billing," *Washington Post*, July 14, 1987, p. E1; Mark Ivey, Todd Mason, Frances Seghers, and John J. Keller, "Sprint's New Chief Has a Lot of Wires to Untangle," *Business Week*, July 27, 1987, p. 29.

4. Richard G. Hamermesh and Roderick E. White, "Manage Beyond Portfolio Analysis," *Harvard Business Review*, January–February 1984, p. 103; see also White's dissertation "Structural Context, Strategy, and Performance," Harvard University, 1981.

5. *Competitive Alliances* (New York: Business International, 1987), p. 63.

6. Losses Prompt Fairchild to Rethink Saab Partnership," *Air Transport World*, October 1985, p. 131.

7. Mark Maremont, Frederic A. Miller, and John Wilke, "GTE's Problem Children: Help Is on the Way," *Business Week*, January 27, 1986, p. 45; John J. Keller, Frances Seghers, and Mark Ivey, "AT&T Is Eating 'Em Alive," *Business Week*, February 16, 1987, p. 28; Ivey, Mason, Seghers, and Keller, "Sprint's New Chief," p. 29; Mark Ivey, Frances Seghers, and Todd Mason, "Will Sprint Ever Get Its Lines Untangled?," *Business Week*, April 25, 1988, p. 64; Calvin Sims, "GTE to Sell Telecom Most of Sprint," *New York Times*, July 19, 1988, p. D1.

8. Guy de Jonquières, "Too Many Pilots in the Cockpit," *Financial Times*, July 8, 1988, p. 11.

9. Calvin Sims, "New Atlantic Cable Makes More Calls Possible," *New York Times*, December 14, 1988, p. 1.

Chapter 11
Governing Joint Ventures

1. Jonathan B. Levine and John A. Byrne, "Corporate Odd Couples," *Business Week*, July 21, 1986, p. 100.

2. See Stratford P. Sherman, "Pushing Corporate Boards to Be Better," *Fortune*, July 18, 1988, p. 58.

3. In Japan and Korea corporate boards take a less active policy role than elsewhere. Board membership carries important salary and retirement benefits, so is a key career goal for managers. Further, cultural forces in these nations more closely align managers' interests with those of their firms than in Western companies. Consequently boards in these countries usually include management. Key policy questions are addressed by executive committees and go to boards for routine approval.

4. David E. Sanger, "Key Merger in Phone Industry," *New York Times*, January 17, 1986, p. D1; Mark Maremont, Frederic A. Miller, and John Wilke, "GTE's Problem Children: Help Is on the Way," *Business Week*, January 27, 1986, p. 45; Janet Guyon, "GTE Comes Full Circle After Expansion," *Wall Street Journal*, February 13, 1986, p. 6.

5. Matthew Winkler, "First Boston Venture with Swiss Thrives," *Wall Street Journal*, April 29, 1987, p. 26. CSFB later came apart when the parents' failure to define a scope led to bitter conflicts. See Chapter 8 for more on this.

Chapter 12
Governing 50–50 Joint Ventures

1. Equal participation is possible with unequal governance if the majority parent goes out of its way to meet its partner's needs. This calls for unusual abilities. Most often, equality in control is necessary for the give-and-take that brings the best out of both firms.

    A joint venture may have unequal ownership (typically 51–49) to allow one parent to consolidate the finances. To assure equality in governance, the shareholders' agreement then requires a consensus on all major issues.

    Consolidation can, however, affect venture performance. For example, a large venture may have losses for some time to invest in R&D or build market share. Consolidation here will hurt the consolidating parent's financial performance and put pressure on the venture to reduce its investments. Similarly, a highly leveraged venture could hurt the balance sheet of the consolidating parent. This parent might then want restrictions on venture debt level and type, or more cumbersome capital review and authorization processes, because of the potential impact on its financial reporting. Such measures could reduce venture flexibility.

    Alternatively, not consolidating a major venture denies a parent the full financial benefits of its performance.

2. An executive committee's work depends on a venture's maturity. Dow Corning, for example, is a billion-dollar company with far more expertise in its field than its parents. Dow Corning no longer has strategic or operating links to them.

    With Dow Corning, the board acts as a whole; there are no partner issues. A four-member executive committee meets on demand, usually to consider an investment or compensation issue. The committee has designated a person from each parent whom the CEO can access easily if necessary. Unlike newer joint ventures, there is no significant difference between board and executive committee, other than ease of getting together.

3. Up to this point Corning's overseas experience was limited to licensing and technology transfers in exchange for equity. It had not operated jointly internationally. Even the process of forming domestic joint ventures was much easier in earlier times. Corning's first joint ventures, including Dow Corning and Pittsburgh Corning, began in the 1930s and 1940s. Corning's chairman, Jamie Houghton, points out that back then, "business was like a small club. People from different firms knew each other and it was easy to make contacts." Mutual trust was often strong at the outset.

Chapter 13
Alliances with Universities

1. Schneiderman quote: Howard A. Schneiderman, "Research Universities as Research Partners: How to Make It Work," remarks at The Conference Board, R&D/Technology Meeting, New York, March 3, 1987.

   Bell Labs and universities: David Fishlock, "How Bell Labs Cultivates Its Links with the Universities," *Financial Times*, February 13, 1987, p. 13.

2. Wayne Biddle, "Corporations on Campus," *Science*, July 24, 1987, p. 353.

3. Research and engineering centers: Robert M. Colton, "University/Industry Cooperative Research Centers Are Proving Themselves," *Research Management*, March–April, 1987, p. 34.

   Research center governance: "A Brief Description of the Engineering Research Centers," National Science Foundation, 1987.

4. Jennifer Stoffel, "Producers Share Research to Whip the Competition," *New York Times*, March 5, 1989, p. 13.

5. UCB: Tim Dickson, "Belgians Close Microchip Gap," *Financial Times*, September 26, 1986, p. 10.

   Norelco: Calvin Sims, "Business–Campus Ventures Grow," *New York Times*, December 14, 1987, p. D1.

   Monsanto: Schneiderman, "Research Universities."

   Rolls-Royce: at Warwick University: "Rolls-Royce Sets Up Ceramics Unit," *Financial Times*, November 10, 1988, p. 25.

6. Schneiderman, "Research Universities."

7. Ciba-Geigy and Sandoz: Lisa K. Winkler, "The New Collaboration Between Business and Academia," *International Management*, November 1986, p. 63.

   Swedish companies: Sara Webb, "Why Bioscience Trail Led Swedes to India," *Financial Times*, February 5, 1987, p. 10.

8. Leo Hanifin quote: Sims, "Business-Campus Ventures Grow."

   Monsanto: Schneiderman, "Research Universities."

9. University–industry priority conflicts: Barbara J. Culliton, "Pajaro Dunes: The Search for Consensus," *Science*, April 9, 1982, p. 155.

   Company sponsorship affecting research agendas: David Blumenthal, Michael Gluck, Karen Seashore Louis, Michael A. Stoto, and David Wise, "University–Industry Relations In Biotechnology: Implications for the University," *Science*, June 13, 1986, p. 1361.

   Carnegie-Mellon withdrawal from project: Sims, "Business Campus Ventures Grow."

10. Bell Labs' university relations: Fishlock, "How Bell Labs Cultivates Links."

    Liaison people: Biddle, "Corporations on Campus."

    Japanese firms' liaison: Stuart Gannes, "The Good News About U.S. R&D," *Fortune*, February 1, 1988, p. 48.

Value MIT gets: Mark Crawford, "MIT-Industry Links Draw Congressional Attention," *Science*, June 9, 1989, p. 1136.

11. Bell Labs' choice of universities: Fishlock, "How Bell Labs Cultivates Links."

ICL's choice of universities: Winkler, "New Collaboration."
IBM and universities: Biddle, "Corporations on Campus."

Chapter 14
Scanning for Opportunities

1. Minnetonka quote: Ronald Alsop, "U.S. Concerns Seek Inspiration for Products from Overseas," *Wall Street Journal*, January 3, 1985, p. 13. In addition to pump toothpastes, Alsop reports, U.S. firms have found aseptic beverage cartons, hairstyle mousses, and body fragrance sprays in Europe.

    Scanning at Bell Labs: Nancy Rica Schiff, "The Big D," *Bell Telephone Magazine*, no. 3–4, 1982, p. 46.

2. New products from early users: David C. Mowery and Nathan Rosenberg, "Technical Change in the Commercial Aircraft Industry," in Nathan Rosenberg, ed., *Inside the Black Box: Technology and Economics* (Cambridge, England: Cambridge University Press, 1982), p. 163; Eric von Hippel, "Get New Products from Customers," *Harvard Business Review*, March–April 1982, p. 117; von Hippel, "The Dominant Role of Users in the Scientific Instrument Innovation Process," *Research Policy*, July 1976, p. 212; von Hippel, "The Dominant Role of the User in Semiconductor and Electronic Subassembly Process Innovation," *IEEE Transactions in Engineering Management*, May 1977, pp. 60–71.

    Black & Decker: Christoper S. Eklund, "How Black & Decker Got Back in the Black," *Business Week*, July 13, 1987, p. 86.

3. Jacquie McNish, "Northern Telecom and Apple Computer Join Forces in Office Automation Field," *Wall Street Journal*, September 15, 1986, p. 4.

4. Ronald Henkoff, "What Motorola Learns from Japan," *Fortune*, April 24, 1989, p. 157.

5. Campbell Soup: Richard Koenig, "As Fashions in Dining Evolve, It Takes Savvy to Keep Folks Amused," *Wall Street Journal*, December 31, 1984, p. 1.

    Genentech: "The New Entrepreneurs," *The Economist*, December 24, 1983, p. 61.

    Kodak's disk camera: "A Missed Opportunity?," *Forbes*, September 13, 1982, p. 206.

6. Vladimir Babkin, "Rotor Forges Solid International Ties," *Wall Street Journal*. December 1, 1988, p. B14.

    Soviet welding technology, seat belts: Paul Ingrassia, "Industry Is Shopping Abroad for Good Ideas to Apply to Products." *Wall Street Journal*, April 29, 1985, p. 1.

Southern California auto buyers: Michael Cieply and Kathleen K. Wiegner, "California Dreaming," *Forbes*, April 23, 1984; Stewart Toy, "Carmakers Are Doing Their Dreaming in California." *Business Week*, March 30, 1987, p. 50.

Procter & Gamble's Liquid Tide: Ingrassia, "Industry Shopping Abroad."

7. Azusa Tomiura, "How Nippon Steel Conducts Joint Research," *Research Management*, January–February 1985, p. 22.

8. Superconductivity discovery: James Gleick, "Electricity Rushes into a New Era of Discovery," *New York Times*, March 10, 1987, p. C1.

Acceptance of scanners: Intelligence experts are often seen as outsiders who do not understand the business; see Sumantra Ghoshal and Seok Ki Kim, "Building Effective Intelligence Systems for Competitive Advantage," *Sloan Management Review*, Fall 1986, p. 49.

9. W. Hagstrom, *The Scientific Community* (New York: Basic Books, 1965); T. J. Allen and S. I. Cohen, "Information Flow in Research and Development Laboratories," *Administrative Science Quarterly*, 14 (1969): 12; T. J. Allen, *Managing the Flow of Technology* (Cambridge, Mass.: MIT Press, 1977); Thomas J. Allen, Michael L. Tushman, and Denis M. Lef, "Technology Transfer as a Function of the Position in the Spectrum from Research Through Development to Technical Services," *Academy of Management Journal*, December 1979, p. 694; Ralph Katz and Michael Tushman, "An Investigation into the Managerial Roles and Career Paths of Gatekeepers and Project Supervisors in a Major R&D Facility," *R&D Management*, 11 (1981): 103; Robert L. Taylor, "The Impact of Organizational Change on the Technological Gatekeeper Role," *IEEE Transactions on Engineering Management*, February 1986, p. 12.

10. For research on the importance of culturally close contacts in scanning, see Thomas J. Allen, James M. Piepmeier, and S. Cooney, "The International Technological Gatekeeper," *Technology Review*, March 1971, p. 37.

11. Special scanning units: Lenz and Engeldow have reported on the effectiveness of environmental scanning units placed in different corporate locations—at the corporate policy level, tied into strategic planning, and functionally oriented. They found that (1) access to decision-makers was limited as scanning became organizationally remote from them, and (2) sponsorship by at least one top-level officer was necessary to assure the scan units' survival. See R. T. Lenz and Jack L. Engeldow, "Environmental Analysis Units and Strategic Decision-making: A Field Study of Selected 'Leading-edge' Corporations," *Strategic Management Journal*, 7 (1986): 69.

GEVENCO: G. Felda Hardymon, Mark J. DeNino, and Malcolm S. Salter, "When Corporate Venture Capital Doesn't Work," *Harvard Business Review*, May–June 1983, p. 114.

IBM software unit: Von Hippel, "Get New Products from Customers," p. 117.

12. Christopher Power, Joseph Weber, Joan O'C. Hamilton and Jeffrey Ryser, "At Johnson & Johnson, a Mistake Can Be a Badge of Honor," *Business Week*, September 26, 1988, p. 126.

13. The value of informal internal networking is discussed further in Warren J. Keegan, "Multinational Scanning: A Study of the Information Sources Utilized by Headquarters Executives in Multinational Companies," *Administrative Science Quarterly*, September 1974, p. 411.

    Informal networking at Minnetonka: Steven Greenhouse, "Minnetonka's Struggle to Stay One Step Ahead," *New York Times*, December 28, 1986, p. F8.

Chapter 15
Choosing Partners and Building Alliances

1. Milt Freudenheim, "Drug Makers Try Biotech Partners," *New York Times*, September 30, 1988, p. D1.

2. Yves L. Doz, "Technology Partnerships Between Larger and Smaller Firms: Some Critical Issues," in Farok J. Contractor and Peter Lorange, eds. *Cooperative Strategies in International Business* (Lexington, Mass.: Lexington Books, 1988), p. 317.

3. A. Craig Copetas, "Perestroika's Yankee Partner," *New York Times Business World*, June 11, 1989, p. 20.

4. Survey evidence from managers involved in joint ventures suggests that negotiations place too much emphasis on technical and financial issues and too little on how relations between potential partners and with the venture would be managed. Katheryn Rudie Harrigan, *Managing for Joint Venture Success* (Lexington Mass.: Lexington Books, 1986), p. 168.

5. Roger Fisher and Scott Brown, *Getting Together* (Boston: Houghton-Mifflin, 1988).

6. Two other kinds of alliances—franchises and cooperatives—have not been described earlier but are worth placing in context.

    A well-managed franchise is by all accounts a strategic alliance: Franchisor and franchisee have a common objective, mutual need, and shared risks. Franchising combines aspects of contractual alliances and joint ventures, in that franchisor and franchisee control separate aspects of the business, and some decisions are shared.

    Business cooperatives or consortia are many-parent joint ventures. Their strength comes from scale economies, which argues for a large membership. Yet with more participants each firm's influence in control is reduced. Also, increased numbers tend to push cooperatives toward lowest common denominator activities. Thus cooperatives must balance the need for scale, on the one hand, with less effectiveness, on the other.

Chapter 16
Developing Effective Relationships

1. James A. Narus and James C. Anderson, "Turn Your Industrial Distributors into Partners," *Harvard Business Review*, March–April 1986, p. 66.

2. Elizabeth Corcoran, "Cooperating to Compete," *IEEE Spectrum*, October 1987, p. 53.

3. Azusa Tomiura, "How Nippon Steel Conducts Joint Research," *Research Management*, January–February 1985, p. 22.

4. Roger Fisher and Scott Brown, *Getting Together* (Boston: Houghton-Mifflin, 1986).

5. Narus and Anderson, "Turn Distributors into Partners," p. 66.

6. *Ibid.*

7. For a seminal early discussion of the importance of equality in relationships, see Gordon W. Allport, *The Nature of Prejudice* (Reading, Mass.: Addison-Wesley, 1954). It is also worth looking at Muzafer Sherif, *In Common Predicament: Social Psychology of Intergroup Conflict and Cooperation* (Boston: Houghton-Mifflin, 1966).

8. Narus and Anderson, "Turn Distributors into Partners," p. 66.

9. Michael Gerlach, "Business Alliances and the Strategy of the Japanese Firm," *California Management Review*, Fall 1987, p. 126.

Chapter 17
Working with Other Cultures

1. When we solve a new problem together, we try various approaches until we find something that works. If the same problem comes up again, we will try the solution we found the first time. If it continues to work each time we try it, the solution eventually becomes part of our routine behavior.

   Over time, the patterns we develop this way foster shared values or beliefs about how things get done. Some tasks can become so taken for granted that we stop thinking about them. When this happens, we accept our behavior implicitly. Often we cannot identify the reasons for such actions. We refer to the collection of beliefs, values, norms, or assumptions shared by a group which support these patterns as its *culture*.

   The strong role culture plays in people's behavior is consistent with growing evidence on the importance of the individual subconscious. In spite of our subjective belief that we are in conscious control of our thoughts and actions, we appear to be guided by subconscious habits far more than we are aware. For a review of research on the subject, see Daniel Goleman, "New View of Unconscious Gives It Expanded Role," *New York Times*, February 7, 1984, p. C1.

2. These observations appear to clash with the belief that group heterogeneity
   spurs innovation. To see why they don't conflict, take a closer look. First,
   heterogeneity *is* important for creativity—people seeing things from the
   perspective of different backgrounds more readily conceive novel approaches. But to *implement* new ideas, a group must have shared understandings about its objectives, its priorities, and how it will do things. In fact,
   groups that are unable to assimilate creative members perform poorly when
   it comes to implementation.

   Thus groups that innovate successfully tolerate some discord on the
   way to developing new ideas, but share overarching values about how
   new concepts will be introduced.

   Here is a brief summary of the research on culture and group behavior.

   For the performance of homogeneous versus heterogeneous groups, see
   W. Clay Hamner and Dennis W. Organ, *Organizational Behavior* (Dallas:
   Business Publications, 1978), p. 308.

   Regardless of the idea or setting, new ideas spread more slowly among
   individuals having different beliefs, values, education, and social status—
   based on a review of more than a thousand case studies of new ideas
   introduced into a wide variety of contexts, including Third World peasant
   villages, American high schools, and business enterprises. Everett M. Rogers, *Communication of Innovations* (New York: Macmillan, 1971).

   People prefer to conduct their business with others who are familiar to
   them, which helps build trust. Jeffrey Pfeffer and Gerald R. Salancik,
   The External Control of Organizations (New York: Harper & Row, 1978),
   pp. 143–150.

   Groups whose members are socially heterogeneous experience greater
   social stress than homogeneous groups and are also less creative. When
   the stress is reduced through improvements in communications and mutual
   trust, creativity increases, as shown by experiments with pairs of selected
   subjects. Harry C. Triandis, Eleanor R. Hall, and Robert B. Ewen, "Member
   Heterogeneity and Dyadic Creativity," *Human Relations*, 18 (February
   1965): 33.

   When individuals do not share values and technical language, their
   work-related communications are less efficient, often resulting in severe
   misperceptions and misinterpretations. R. Dearborn and H. Simon, "Selec-
   tive Perceptions in Executives," *Sociometry*, 21 (1958): 140.

   People are less creative when they work with others they dislike. L. D.
   Zeleny, "Validity of a Sociometric Hypothesis: The Function of Creativity
   in Interpersonal and Group Relations," *Sociometry*, 18 (1955): 439.

   The innovation process is significantly hindered by the presence of psychological blocks to interpersonal communication and problem-solving. Chris
   Argyris, *Organization and Innovation* (Homewood, Ill.: Irwin-Dorsey, 1965).

   A study conducted for the Financial Executives Institute found the implicit social and psychological constraints corporations impose on profit

center managers to be at least as important as explicit financial and economic controls. The effectiveness of a profit center manager depends upon his or her knowing the right action to take in a given situation. Formal controls can convey only a fraction of this message without becoming unwieldy. Much of a manager's understanding of acceptable conduct comes from the numerous cues and informal rules that pervade every organization. The longer a manager has worked in an organization, the easier it becomes for him or her to "read" these signals. Richard F. Vancil, *Decentralization: Managerial Ambiguity by Design* (Homewood, Ill.: Dow Jones–Irwin, 1978), p. 64.

3. Young & Rubicam and PaineWebber: Joanne Lipman, "PaineWebber May End Venture It Has with Young & Rubicam," *Wall Street Journal,* April 3, 1989, p. B4. Caterpillar: John W. Wilson and Judith H. Dobrzynski, "The Hollow Corporation," *Business Week,* March 3, 1986, p. 57.

    DuPont and RPI: Seth H. Lubove, "The Old College Tie," *Wall Street Journal,* November 10, 1986, p. 10D.

4. A useful discussion of these concepts may be found in Vern Terpstra and Kenneth David, *The Cultural Environment of International Business* (Dallas: South-Western Publishing, 1985), and in Geert Hofstede, *Culture's Consequences* (Beverly Hills, Calif.: Sage Publications, 1980).

    A brief comparison of Japanese and American patterns is instructive. Japanese' emphasis on relationships is nurtured from early childhood and depends on social homogeneity for later reinforcement. Japanese children receive little discipline until they are about five years old. By then they have developed particularly close bonds with their mothers. Japanese psychiatrists believe that because of this there is a strong dependency at the core of the Japanese character and social structure. Beginning in the Japanese family the child's identity is absorbed into a group self, so that one's fate is identical with that of one's group, be it a corporation or Japan itself. The bond between a dependent child and an indulgent mother is duplicated in the main social relationships throughout Japanese society: boss–employee, teacher–student, and so on. Daniel Goleman, "In Japan, Gratitude to Others is Stressed in Psychotherapy," *New York Times,* June 3, 1986, p. C1.

    Americans' emphasis on individuality is also introduced in childhood and reinforced by family and social context—which, being heterogeneous, places more emphasis on each person as an individual and far less on collective belonging, compared with Japan.

5. Geert Hofstede, "The Interaction Between National and Organizational Value Systems," *Journal of Management Studies,* July 1985, p. 347; also, Hofstede, *Culture's Consequences.*

6. Texaco–Pennzoil–Getty: Thomas Petzinger Jr., *Oil & Honor: The Texaco–Pennzoil Wars* (New York: Putnam, 1987).

Relative emphasis on rules and structure: Hofstede, *Culture's Consequences.*

Silicon Valley: Compare Silicon Valley with the Route 128 area outside Boston. Route 128 workers are conditioned by a longer history of industrial enterprise. They are more homogeneous, more conservative, and have a longer-term orientation. People in the Northeast are less eager to take business risks or change jobs. Along Route 128, employees prefer merit raises and pensions; in Silicon Valley, they want stock options. In the Boston area "long-term" often means at least five years; out West it can mean two or three years. "Culture Counts," *IEEE Spectrum,* September 1986, p. 28.

7. Cultural differences in science appear in the way scientists work in groups. In Japan, for instance, there is a stronger sense of hierarchy and follow-the-leader style in laboratories than in the United States, where individuals are free to take more initiative.

8. Firms begin with a founder's business idea and a concept of the kind of place he or she wants to build. The founder imposes this belief by setting initial goals and strategies, by recruiting people who accept his or her vision, and by installing incentives and controls that reinforce important patterns. See Edgar H. Schein, "The Role of the Founder in Creating Organizational Culture," *Organizational Dynamics,* Summer 1983, p. 13.

As examples, take Honda's Soichiro Honda, IBM's Thomas J. Watson, Sr., and General Motors' Alfred P. Sloan, Jr. At Honda, Mr. Honda's own individualism gave the company a management style rare in Japan. The firm discourages hierarchy, grants substantial responsibility to young employees, and involves workers from many divisions and levels in new product development. Tetsuo Sakiya, *Honda Motor* (New York and Tokyo: Kodansha International, 1982).

IBM's emphasis on customer service was not a mainstream U.S. trait when the company introduced it. The idea was imposed by Thomas J. Watson, Sr., IBM's founder, and was rooted in his Quaker past. T. G. Belden and M. R. Belden, *The Lengthening Shadow: The Life of Thomas J. Watson* (Boston: Little, Brown, 1962).

Alfred P. Sloan, Jr., who shaped General Motors, believed in planning big. He created a mindset at GM that emphasized capacity expansion far more than at any other car maker. This practice persisted even after a fixation with sheer size had become a liability. John Holusha, "G.M.'s Obsession with Size," *New York Times,* November 8, 1986, p. 37; Alfred P. Sloan, Jr., *My Years with General Motors* (Garden City, N.Y.: Doubleday, 1972).

9. Jane Rippeteau, "The Symbiotic Search for Anti-Cancer Drugs," *Financial Times,* April 23, 1987, p. 13.

10. Robert J. Brown, "Swatch vs. the Sundial: A Study In Different Attitudes Toward Time," *International Management,* December 1987, p. 80.

11. See Richard W. Brislin, *Cross-Cultural Encounters* (New York, Pergamon Press, 1984). p. 155. For a discussion of the relationship of uncertainty, anxiety, and performance, see George Mandler, "Stress and Thought Processes," in Leo Goldberger and Shlomo Breznitz, eds., *Handbook of Stress* (New York: Free Press, 1982), pp. 91–93; Vernon Hamilton, "Cognition and Stress: An Information Processing Model," *ibid.*, pp. 113–16; and Leonard I. Pearlin, "The Social Contexts of Stress," *ibid.*, pp. 376–77.

12. Koreans and Japanese: Bernard Wysocki, Jr., "Weak in Technology, South Korea Seeks Help from Overseas," *Wall Street Journal*, January 7, 1986, p. 1.

    British investments in United States: *Statistical Abstracts of the United States,* 1989 edition (Washington, D.C.: U.S. Government Printing Office, 1989).

13. Emily T. Smith and Evert Clark, "Now, R&D Is Corporate America's Answer to Japan Inc.," *Business Week*, June 23, 1986, p. 134.

14. Acme-Cleveland: Bruce G. Posner, "Strategic Alliances," *INC.*, June 1985, p. 74.

    Racal in China: Nigel Campbell, *China Strategies: The Inside Story* (University of Manchester/University of Hong Kong, 1986), p. 57.

15. John Hoerr, Michael A. Pollock, and David E. Whiteside, "Management Discovers the Human Side of Automation," *Business Week*, September 29, 1986, p. 70. The control which habits have on perceptions is illustrated by an experiment with a group of Mexican and American children. They were shown stereograms in which one eye was exposed to a bullfight, and the other eye viewed a baseball game. When they were asked what they saw, the Mexican kids most often reported the bullfight; the Americans tended to see the ball game. Robert T. Moran and Philip R. Harris, *Managing Cultural Synergy* (Houston: Gulf Publishing, 1982), p. 65.

16. Transfers to a foreign culture: International personnel who go abroad without cross-cultural preparation have a failure rate ranging from 33 to 66 percent, in contrast to less than 2 percent of those who have had such training. Philip R. Harris and Robert T. Moran, *Managing Cultural Differences* (Houston: Gulf Publishing, 1987), p. 3.

    Training at NEC: Bernard Wysocki, Jr., "Japanese Executives Going Overseas Take Anti-Shock Courses," *Wall Street Journal*, January 12, 1987, p. 1.

17. John Koten and Lawrence Ingrassia, "British Car Maker's Tie to Honda Shows Why Auto Linkups Increase," *Wall Street Journal*, December 12, 1983, p. 1.

18. Carol Hymowitz, "A Survival Guide to the Office Meeting," *Wall Street Journal*, June 21, 1988, p. 41.

19. Brown, "Swatch vs. Sundial," p. 80.

20. Autolatina has tried to address the Argentine–Brazilian cultural issue by

basing its bonus system on total profits of Autolatina regardless of source. This resulted in a bonus paid in Argentina in 1988, even though profits there had not earned it. Efforts are also being made to integrate people from Argentine units into Autolatina. But this is necessarily limited to culturally adaptable people and is an inherently slow process.

Chapter 18
People and Practices: Getting More Value from Alliances

1. Christopher Lorenz, "Why Strategy Has Been Put in the Hands of Line Managers," *Financial Times*, May 18, 1988, p. 12.

2. Rosabeth Moss Kanter, *The Change Masters* (New York: Simon & Schuster, 1983).

3. Considerable evidence exists to the effect that outward-looking cultures adopt innovations more quickly than inward-focused cultures. Everett M. Rogers and F. Floyd Shoemaker, *Communication of Innovations* (New York: Free Press, 1971).

    For evidence that innovative firms scan more than less innovative firms, see Donald C. Hambrick, "Environmental Scanning and Organizational Strategy," *Strategic Management Journal*, 3 (1982): 159.

4. Carol Hymowitz, "One Firm's Bid to Keep Blacks," *Wall Street Journal*, February 16, 1989, p. B1.

5. Michael Skapinker, "Ford's Cosmopolitan Carousel," *Financial Times*, May 12, 1989, p. 9.

6. Lucy speculates that one reason for Corning's openness to outside ideas may be its leadership, which has always been cosmopolitan and focused on collective performance. Another may be its location. Corning is away from the dog-eat-dog mainstream, say, of a large urban setting. Thus Corning people are less subject to the competitive forces that push individuals to look out for themselves at the expense of their firms.

7. Japanese financial institutions: Michael W. Miller, "Foreign Exchange Students," *Wall Street Journal*, September 23, 1988, p. 14R. Japanese financial institutions that have invested to learn seem to have a better chance than those that entered the U.S. market directly on their own. See James Sterngold, "Japan's Washout On Wall Street," *New York Times*, June 11, 1989, p. 1. For a discussion of the effect of entrepreneurial departures on the U.S. semiconductor industry, see Charles H. Ferguson, "From the People Who Brought You Voodoo Economics," *Harvard Business Review*, May–June 1988, p. 55.

A Note of Thanks

THIS book exists because many people chose to make it possible. First and foremost, *Partnerships for Profit* reports the experiences of many firms, as described by more than a hundred of their executives and interpreted by me. My debt to these men and women is tremendous: Their insights and understandings compose much of the text. Yet listing them in a long record of names would dilute the role each played. The best way I know to thank them is to acknowledge their contributions first.

Within this larger group five individuals stand out: Chuck Lucy and Bob Turissini at Corning, Frank Whitley at Dow, Paul Drenkow at Ford, and Brien Hope at General Electric.

Chuck Lucy was an early champion of alliances at Corning and rose to become vice president and director of international operations, telecommunications products. Bob Turissini was also one of Corning's first international managers; his credits include the formation of Samsung Corning. Bob became Corning's senior vice president, international. Frank Whitley, Dow's director of licensing and acquisitions, has played a key role in a number of his firm's alliances. Paul Drenkow heads Ford's Northern Pacific Business Development office, which places him at a key crossroad between Ford and its Asian partners. Brien Hope is the longest-tenured executive at CFM International, and has gained a wealth of knowledge about strategic alliances.

I am especially grateful to these five people. They made themselves constantly available through the course of my research and writing,

325

and tolerated my incessant questions. Their patient help greatly expanded my understanding of alliances.

My work on *Partnerships for Profit* began when I was teaching at the Wharton School, University of Pennsylvania. After many months of research it was obvious the topic was more complex than I had imagined. It also was clear I could not continue to juggle teaching and consulting, and still make progress on the book. My thanks to Professors Bill Hamilton and Peter Lorange for their encouragement to take time off and get the job done.

In the course of my research two excellent books were especially valuable for me. Both are acknowledged in the text, yet more credit is due. Roger Fisher's and Scott Brown's *Getting Together* contributed greatly to my appreciation of relationships. Their ideas enrich my work. Rosabeth Moss Kanter's *The Change Masters* is a key building block in my understanding of how organizations function.

Several people took time to read the manuscript and comment on it in detail. Thanks to them, the quality of this book is vastly better than the manuscript they saw. They include Corning vice chairman Van Campbell, group president Dick Dulude, Chuck Lucy, and Bob Turissini; Dow Chemical executive vice president Bob Keil; Ford's Lynn Halstead, now chairman of Ford of Europe, and Paul Drenkow, and Dick Place, now technical director, product and manufacturing engineering; Bob McNinch, manager of strategic alliances at Apple Computer; Mark Maremont, *Business Week*'s correspondent in London; and Bob Wallace, my editor at The Free Press.

Partnerships for Profit would not have begun without the prompting and vision of my literary agent, Leona Schecter, whose ongoing encouragement was indispensable. Thanks are also due to my friend and former client Howard Philipp, who arranged early support.

Writing a book is sometimes exciting and sometimes discouraging. But at least an author knows what he wants to achieve. No matter what others say, he believes the final result will prove him right. It is different for the author's family. Even families like mine who are truly interested and supportive cannot have the same vision. They are more distant from the intended market and less informed about the projected product. They mainly have hope and faith to lean on.

In a fundamental sense then, an author's ability to persist and to produce his best work depends on his family's hope and faith. That is how it was for me during those challenging six years. I will always treasure the constant support my children, Katherine and Matthew, and my mother, Ruth Lewis, gave me.

Most significantly, this book is a product of a very special alliance I have long enjoyed with my wife, Lynn Lopata Lewis, an accomplished professional writer and editor. Without her tolerance of my many absences from other activities, the work could not have been done. Without her expert and detailed attention to my writing, the book's clarity and flow would not exist. Without her encouragement and willingness to share the risks as we reached for the same objective, there would be no book.

Washington, D.C.
September 20, 1989

Index